ECOTONE

SUNY Series, Feminist Theory in Education
Madeleine Grumet, Editor

⚘ ECOTONE ⚘

wayfaring on the margins

Florence R. Krall

State University of New York Press

Published by
State University of New York Press, Albany

©1994 State University of New York

For information, address the State University of New York Press,
State University Plaza, Albany, NY 12246

Production by Bernadine Dawes
Marketing by Theresa Abad Swierzowski

Library of Congress Cataloging-in-Publication Data

Krall, Florence R., 1926–
        Ecotone : wayfaring on the margins / Florence R. Krall.
            p.   cm. — (SUNY series, feminist theory in education)
        Includes bibliographical references.
        ISBN 0-7914-1961-4. — ISBN 0-7914-1962-2 (pbk.)
        1. Krall, Florence R., 1926—   . 2. Naturalists—United States—
        Biography. 3. Natural History. 4. Feminists—United States—
        Biography. 5. College teachers—United States—Biography.
        6. Ecofeminism—Philosophy. 7. Feminism—Philosophy. I. Title.
        II. Series.
        QH31.K72A3 1994
        508.73'092—dc20
        [B]   93-40143
                                                                           CIP

1 2 3 4 5 6 7 8 9 10

CONTENTS

PREFACE

Academics talk theory more often than we live it. Theory functions to challenge our categories. When we stay within a set of assumptions, our findings are domesticated, but when we undermine the divisions that separate public from private, individual from collective, and nature from culture, our work grows wild. As this writer, Florence Krall, moves from classroom to desert, from office to museum to tundra, she walks theory. Literally grounded, her explorations cling to the shape of things, catching light from the sunset in the red eye of a grebe, caught in Florence's eye as she travels home to Wyoming.

Krall walks on the wild side, Anasazi ruins, Alaska, the Arctic, only to discover the drama of dominance in campus politics and the inexorable struggle for power in herself. Her candor and ruminations challenge the reassuring homilies of the women's movement as she, who cherishes reciprocity and interdependence in nature, fails to find it in her colleagues or in herself.

For many women, separated in space and time from the lives of our mothers and grandmothers, feminist consciousness—for all its talk of sisterhood, reciprocity and context—is isolating. As she walks in deserts and tundras scoured and carved by time, Krall reminds us that our questions about existence are ancient and continuous. She brings back the material, sensuous stuff that appeared for awhile in *Our Bodies, Our Selves,* in Mary Daly's puns and etymologies, in Adrienne Rich's poems, and in novels like Atwood's *Surfacing* and Robinson's *Housekeeping*. But Krall does not get lost in lyricism. Krall portrays the vivid conviction that the world is just as rich and challenging as our minds. She makes us at home in a world where we must constantly work to determine how to live.

During our correspondence concerning the development of this book, Florence sent me a photograph of the house that she and her husband, Paul Shepard, were building in Wyoming. Although just the frame of the house was up, the entire line of the building was complete, standing out against the mountains behind it. Looking clear through the house to the world around it, I think I saw the world as Florence sees it in this book. Her house has walls, now, its transparency sacrificed for warmth and shelter. But the spine and covers of this book can not close up the questions and possibilities that Florence Krall has gathered together and returned to our feminist imagination.

Madeleine Grumet

ACKNOWLEDGMENTS

At the same time I recognize those who have helped me bring forth this book, I apologize to those whose names I have forgotten or whose words I have borrowed unknowingly. I am humbled by the whole process of writing, I realize all the more, as Catherine Clement reminds us, that we "never think alone," nor does a "mind give birth to itself."

I am deeply indebted to the editors and staff at SUNY Press. Madeleine Grumet, editor of the Feminist Theory in Education Series, worked with me over several years and encouraged me to open my mind to the themes hidden in my language. She generously housed and counseled me and then sent me back to rewrite, insisting that I was doing theory. Lois Patton, Associate Director and Editor-in-Chief at SUNY Press, has been a blessing. Extremely supportive and considerate, she has guided this novice author and her book tenderly through the publication process and toward others who have been equally sensitive and helpful, in particular, Bernadine Dawes, production editor, and Wendy Nelson, copyeditor.

Although I have not written my children directly into this book, Bob Krall, Lisi Krall, Matt Krall and Kathryn Ann Morton have been the most influential and fulfilling aspects of my life. Now adults with children of their own, they have been, since the time they were young and joined me on my journeys, entirely supportive of my wayfaring. I thank them for their abiding interest and faith in me.

I owe much to my husband, Paul Shepard. Long before I met him I was profoundly influenced by his books, which helped shape my ecological consciousness. The first time he read one of my essays, he insisted I had a book in hand. He has encouraged me to write, and his wit, incisive criticism, prodding, astute editorial comments, and love have been major factors in the writing of this book.

In part this book is about friends and their impact on my understanding of place and self. Some have passed from this Earth, but their influence lingers on. I will never forget Edward Abbey, Carolyn Frerichs Benne, Aaron Boswell, Rae Roberson Cosgrove, Ladd Holt, Ronald Padgham, and Dottie Tupper.

Diane Brennis, Linda Fillippi and Sharon LaSalle gave me valuable feedback on a first draft of this book. Bill Baker helped me through the dark chapter of my life related in "Minerva's Owl," as did Mary Buchanan, Kaye Coleman, Amy Howard and Margo Sorgman. Frank Caccamise provided helpful critique of a first draft of that chapter. Noreen Garman, Meredith Reiniger, and other friends at the JCT Bergamo Conferences on Curriculum Theory and Classroom Practice encouraged me to get on with a book. Terry Tempest Williams has been an inspirational companion on many of my journeys into place and being. I would not have seen "The Shape of Things" if Jeff Soder had not introduced me to Henry Moore and if Walt Prothero had not generously guided me into the dazzling Alaska wilderness. Velma Ward and other schoolmates helped me remember those formative years in "Flesh of the Earth." I am indebted to the family of Carolyn Frerichs Benne for allowing me to draw from her journals for the chapter, "Indwellings" and to Ruth Holt for her feedback and permission to include the paragraphs on Ladd Holt in "Equinox."

I owe a great debt of gratitude to the American Indians I have listened to and learned from along the way. I especially thank Nola Lodge (Oneida), and Donna House (Navajo) for their affection and trust. Navajos Sam Alonzo, Helena Rosa, Roger Tsotsie, and Jim Tutt were especially helpful in the weaving of "Navajo Tapestry." Navajo medicine woman, Annie Kahn, made a deep and lasting impression on me; as did Joe Aragon (Acoma), and Bernita Humeyestewa (Hopi), and the other American Indian participants of the AISES (American Indian Science and Engineering Society) workshop in Durango, Colorado, during the summer of 1992. They helped me bring closure to this book.

By sharing their unique vision and energy, students have been some of my most inspiring teachers. In addition to those mentioned in the text, I wish to acknowledge Ligia Albuquerque, Lois Baldwin, Desiree Beaudry, Ed Brady, Tom Cammermeyer, Bob Chance, Lance Cole, Dan Cortsen, Cal Evans, Doug Gregory, Ken Guest, Shirley Hager, Elizabeth Haslam, Kim Heimsmith, Dave Holmes, Tom Kemp, Louie Landgren, Gary Lewers, Diane Livermore, Marie Magelby, Jeff Metcalf, Debra Musso, Edwin Napia, Diane Nofs, Danielle Patterson, Bruce Plenk, Jay Reed, Terry Deal Reynolds, Peter Twichell, Hsu Ying, and Greg Zeigler.

I thank colleagues and writers who have influenced my thinking and career. William F. Pinar has supported my writing since the first time we met in the late 1970s. During seminars around my dining room table, Dolores LaChapelle taught me much about deep ecology and biregionalism. Max Oelschlaeger has shown continuing support for my work. Cecil Miskel was a knowledgeable advisor in my adventures into university administration. Ted Aoki, Maxine Greene, and James Macdonald influenced me with their friendship and writing. Robert V. Bullough, during the years of earning his doctorate at Ohio State University, sent me "good news" that changed my life and mind. Earl Harmer was instrumental in my getting my first university appointment—which made it possible for all of this to happen.

As time passes, I am evermore grateful to my mother and father, Matilda and Batt Bertagnolli, now both deceased. They gave me life and their unconditional love and support. Finally, I acknowledge the importance to me of my Aunt Jennie Creer and Uncle Jim Coletti, the remaining elders who embody our family traditions.

1 ✤ Introduction

I have known her all my life, yet she reveals stories to me, and these stories are revelations and I am transformed.

—Susan Griffin[1]

I came to academia in mid-life and began writing autobiographical essays grounded in the natural sciences even later. I remember clearly the day I took the turn toward writing. It was a time when, as a mature but younger woman who preferred to hike a trail rather than to sit still, I forced myself to remain on a hillside throughout one afternoon recording all that I saw. Amazing creatures and events from that afternoon still visit me and humble me to the incredible complexity of life within eye's reach.

Although I could not sit still for long, I began keeping in-depth journals of my travels. Once or twice a year I would sequester myself with them and translate the most memorable experiences, those that would not let me be, into essays. I soon learned, as others have observed, that writing is always on the margins. We keep having second thoughts that expand into greater complexities. As I abandoned the prescription of "meaning" that I was taught and had accepted through most of my life, I began discovering the pleasure and understanding that evocative discourse brings. Remembering past significant events, striving to describe them authentically and clearly; invoking, reflecting on, and questioning them; and inviting other voices to enter, was how I chose to participate in the intellectual life. My travels and writing soon began crisscrossing natural and cultural boundaries.

I think back on these journeys. A collage of images erupts and spirals outward, vibrating and expanding at the outermost edges. The spiral is not symmetrical: Opaque, dense areas alternate with transparent, transitional zones filled with turbulence and energy. Ephemeral images emerge that match my dreams and leave me uneasy: Earth and mother, archetypal animal and human forms. Brilliant colors burst forth and send spasms through my viscera, like sunshine through the cobalt blue of stained-glass windows or iridescent reflections from the feathers of a bird. Translations of human ambivalence, these images breach rational barriers and allow me to pour into the world.

Taos Pueblo, New Mexico. Winter solstice/Christmas celebrations. A time when darkness turns toward light and new life:

There is no making sense of it: the words of priest and acolytes, the Indian women standing reverently together, the sounds of the seesaw organ and simple hymns honoring the dark Madonna dressed as a bride. Linda and I are in the church crowded with people from all parts of the Earth. The light changes, and I turn, expecting to see a procession with lighted candles entering the open door of the church. Instead, beyond the intent faces of worshipers standing at the back, the immaculate white courtyard gate rises into a lapis sky with coral spirals of smoke reflecting dancing firelight from all sides. Vespers ends; the drums begin. A procession bearing the Madonna exits from the church, accompanied by women. One of them reaches over and touches Linda's hand. We follow through the open door of the church into the chill night air. People in regional dress warm themselves by bonfires that surround the courtyard. A dog leaps into the air, snapping at sparks as they descend. Drum, flame, adobe, night sky, and humans mingle.

On the threshold of that chapel, held for a moment in transition, viewing the incongruent scene—the night sky above, the incredible mix of people, the diverse views of the sacred—I was keenly aware of differences and at the same time embraced by the merging ecological, social, and spiritual aspects of our lives.

Time passes. At this moment, in this holding place, we pause to take a bearing. Past and present mingle; we can see where we have been and imagine what lies beyond. We may rest briefly, contemplating our journey, cataloging our accomplishments and failings. We may cross over with greater maturity and understanding, or go back, retrace our steps and begin again. We also have the choice to remain where we are, fearful to welcome what comes next. Depending on our ken, we may grow wiser or more skeptical and embittered. But if we open ourselves to life in its fullest, we will accept the inevitable ambivalence, our doubts as well as our hopes, and through reflection achieve more realism— and patience with our flawed humanity.

The realization that came over us during the past two decades that the majority of the humans on this Earth[2] are marginalized should not have been news to any of us, no matter what our race or gender. Although I do not mean to dismiss the vast separation from mainstream culture of oppressed people throughout the world, in a sense we humans are all marginal creatures. On the edge or crossing over, we are held tenderly and tenuously in transition. We know we are separate beings, kept apart from the Earth and from each other. We are repeatedly told that our very selves are split inside from outside. As we grow older or encounter the unforeseen, we find ourselves inevitably on strange edges where the familiar mixes with the uncommon. And ultimately we are faced with the most profound mystery, that fine line that separates life and death. Throughout our lives, we encounter cultural circumstances, changing relationships, and our own growth in these zones of interdigitation of the known and unknown.

3

In the natural world, edges where differences come together are the richest of habitats. Animals often choose these ecotones, where contrasting plant communities meet, to raise their young where the greatest variety of cover and food can be found. A doe will give birth to the fawn on the edge of a forest, where she can find shelter as well as food in the open area beyond the trees. Transitional species, plants and animals such as those found in tidal zones, have become highly adapted for life "on the edge." Marshes where fresh- and saltwater habitats meet are some of the most productive places on Earth in terms of fecundity and diversity of species. Change is a fundamental part of all natural communities, even those that seem stable, as the cycles of life and death set into play a succession of regenerating events. But at the ecotone change is most evident and inevitable. To an ecologist, the "edge effect" carries the connotation of the complex interplay of life forces where plant communities, and the creatures they support, intermingle in mosaics or change abruptly.

Likewise, margins in social and cultural contexts are not necessarily areas of isolation where we balance between two worlds, looking out or looking in, without legitimacy or equality. Although they can become boundaries that separate—chasms that block our movement toward fulfillment and joy in living, or frontiers where we wage power battles—they may also be dwelling places that connect rather than separate. Much like the ecotones in biotic communities, they may be rich and dynamic transitional zones and may provide great learning as well as suffering. The margin as a cultural metaphor for this edge experience has given us much more than a viewing area from which, oppressed and alienated, we watch mainstream society pass us by or a staging area from which we launch a new course. We have begun to understand with Julia Kristeva that this edge is, in fact, an abode. We "live on the border." We are "crossroads beings."[3] Cultural ecotones are the pluralistic contexts out of which conflict and change emerge; they are the places where society smooths the wrinkles in her skirts.

When I claim my place on the margins, I am not unsympathetic to or unaware of the great inequalities and oppression suffered by minorities, people of color, and women in particular. Many women, unaccounted for and unacknowledged, live entirely outside of the economics and politics of mainstream society. The ecotone, which, in the natural world provides a dynamic interchange, becomes exceedingly complex as a cultural metaphor and may represent a barrier that blocks some people from their rightful place in the scheme of things.

The blue planet as seen from space gives us a clear picture of the place that is home to all, but it is an icon that misleads. It implies that we are all one, when in fact we are separated by vast differences of circumstance and privilege. We have been reminded repeatedly that global problems must be resolved locally, yet localities are inhabited by uninfluential individuals whose inequalities cannot be explained away by planetary discourses or international rhetoric. On the other hand, emphasis on differences and distinctions erases the commonality that we seek. However trite it may ring, we are all children of the Earth. Our continuation, no matter where our particular home, what our ideology, or how we make a life, relies fundamentally and inextricably on the health of this planet. No technological fix or redistribution of wealth can alter this fundamental premise.

The margin as a metaphor is indeed subject to antithetical interpretations. Yet it serves me well as I examine my own condition and particularly that fuzzy line that separates my selfhood from other creatures and the Earth's environment, that emotional ground and psychic space where existential questions of purpose and self-worth appear. This place of soul-making borders on private, virginal territory, "uncontaminated by man's misconceptions," that I explore "solo," a difficult undertaking in itself that carries the added danger of my becoming "moonstruck," too isolated, self-sufficient, and self-absorbed.[4] On the other hand, this "staying place" between my own particularity and inner nature and the demands and rules of civilization leads me to a recovery of the psycho-physical self and to psychic transformation—a word that denotes a change of mind and heart but does not carry the great imprecision of feelings that accompanies such a metamorphosis.

Undefiled land is sought by pilgrims and exploiters alike as well as naturalists who seek wilderness, where Nature is untouched by the effects of civilization. Such areas hold great fascination for "nature lovers" for here they can explore the fecundity of wildness, uncontrolled, chaotic, and pure. It may very well be that wilderness "trips," in fact, are of the same character as, and an extension of, withdrawals into inner psychic territory, a place where we seek unimagined and fantastic landscapes.

I have chosen the concept of ecotone, then, to represent that place of meeting and tension between diverse and sometimes conflicting aspects of our lives. Underlying the familiar culture/Nature dichotomy is instead a webbing of gender, race, politics, economics, and spirituality that preoccupies wayfaring humans on this planet. Ecotone, that place of crossing over, provides sanctuary, solitude and peace, growth and transformation, as well as isolation and inner or outer conflict. It is all of these as well as a psychological space of natural tension where we transcend our present limitations and move to new possibilities, a time when individuation brings with it a deeper sense of interrelatedness, or a region where we "escape role and status, a crossing of boundaries or margins into an opposite role or perhaps into rolelessness."[5]

I have spent most of my life on margins, imposed as well as self-selected. I am the daughter of Italian parents who fashioned a viable sheep ranch on arid Wyoming rangeland. As a child I was embedded in a nonelitist adult world where every action represented a survival game played with the seasons—a world set apart from mainstream American life. As a middle child, I was separated from my two sisters by age as well as temperament. In the evenings I warmed myself and dozed by the wood-burning stove as I listened to parents and hired men speaking in Italian about the "Old Country" and world events far removed from our lives.

The terrain beyond beckoned as my mother in proper fashion increasingly failed to meet my needs and allowed me to wander in other realms of sky and birds, desert scrub and lizard, a swamp filled with frogs in the summer and colossal snowdrifts in the winter. Nature, calling to me, led me down game trails: some of these disappeared into thickets, others circled back, and still others carried me to unheard-of places.

School provided glimpses of the "American way." Best friends, learning, and play were my main concerns. I liked school; it was that meeting place of the public and private domains where a shy outsider could legitimately mingle with others. I sat at my own desk in the company of others whom I could observe unabated. My early school pictures show a serious child standing to the side of the group looking at the world with what I now recall as a mixture of skepticism and interest. I recognize that look in a recent photo; it still carries those emotions I have felt consistently since those early years.

As a youth I worked at the side of my father and mother on seasonal subsistence and later returned each summer from college to help on the ranch. Following college, where I studied zoology and chemistry, I returned to the place of my birth as a young wife, mother, and teacher. Teaching high school biology provided a sanctuary and personal territory where I struggled

with the complications of my life as students began discovering
the meaning in theirs. Countering the bureaucracy of public
schooling, I retreated to my classroom, where I fashioned my
niche, as animals do in Nature, as I interacted with students
through a personally designed curriculum and where I performed a self-fulfilling function in the day-to-day world.

With the ecology movement seen as a fringe activity by the
local community as well as the school administration, we moved
outdoors to a "laboratory" fashioned from an overgrazed bull
pasture that ran from the school down a swale where a permanent spring trickled into a tiny pond.[6] There we studied "life."
The outdoor lab provided materials and impetus for most of the
year's curriculum, fashioned by student interpretation from the
natural materials at hand, a "poor curriculum" as portrayed by
William F. Pinar and Madeleine R. Grumet.[7] During the cold
winter months we studied pond water, and in the spring at the
end of the school year we returned it ceremonially to its source.
The students' naive point of view diminished steadily as the year
progressed, and they learned to trust their perceptions and abili-
ties to inquire and to wonder. They were expected to verify their
findings, but the fundamental purpose of the course was to show
faith in their own experiences, in their powers of observation,
and in their records and interpretations of what they had learned.
I believed that the natural world offered possibilities for unbridled learning. My plans were constantly revised by the understanding that students brought to my teaching. I learned much,
but it would be years before I fully appreciated how that decade
of teaching biology molded my pedagogical philosophy, a heuristic search for the untried curriculum transacted between place,
students, and teacher outside of traditional settings.

Leaving marriage and classroom, I moved on to a doctorate
in education and ecology, the template for much of what I now
see, and a university position. The classroom as haven was

replaced by the intellectual space shared with university students. Under the umbrella of "environmental education," we inquired into natural history of place, ethical action and patterns for change, and reverence for life, topics that fit poorly the subject matter of mandated teacher education. With courageous public school administrators and student teachers, I chose to work on the educational fringe in alternative education programs for disaffected youth. Offered apart from traditional requirements and settings, the "experimental" programs were barely tolerated by the university and public schools. We strained the limits of institutional tolerance as we fashioned master's programs out of the stuff of deserts and mountains and disenchanted youth. Personal narrative became our form of interpretation long before it reached present acceptance.[8]

Constantly challenged by alternative teachers' spontaneity, resistance to traditional subject-oriented methods of teaching, exuberance for life, and disdain for conventional science, I was forced to recognize the uniqueness of each person's relationship to the environment and to consider Richard Rorty's thesis that Nature mirrors our own psychology.[9] Yet I was unwilling to admit that Nature was merely a social construct and to give up natural-history study for its own sake. From where I stood, the nonhuman world was not simply a sentimental extension of our inner landscapes, not just there for pleasure and edification and utility, not merely an escape from the frustrations of human interactions, certainly not just scenery.[10] She was constant, complex, mysterious, unpredictable, destructive, beautiful, magical, and uncontrolled.

I became increasingly attentive to social implications of my educational encounters and skeptical of theories that did not ring true to my experiences. Insightful analyses by feminists such as Madeleine Grumet helped me to face the keenly felt oppression that went unnamed as I "sentimentalized the powers" I had "already surrendered."[11] Only recently have I been able to recognize the patriline, as shown by Donna Haraway, that slanted my study of the "objective" domain of science.[12] Yet none of these analyses, helpful as they have been, articulate fully the richness and depth of my life as woman, teacher, and naturalist. They do not uncover the inner motives that have driven my preference for margins.

Travel, on the other hand, foregrounded this predilection. I finally ventured abroad, on my first sabbatical to Mexico and Central America and later with my mother to the homeland of my ancestors in the Italian Alps. I felt completely at home in the small villages, especially with relatives, where to my surprise I discovered my forebears had lived for centuries on Italian alpine borderlands where language and custom changed abruptly.[13] Understanding the historical antecedents of my separation from mainstream culture, I was able to view my childhood, living as I had in the "Little Italy" my parents had created, with more empathy and understanding. With a deepened sense of family, I determined upon returning home to explore the *genius loci,* the spirit of place, in my own life and in the context of my American homeland. I needed to remember my preference for dwelling on ecotones.

As a young mother and teacher I had been socialized thoroughly to woman's role, and later I was too busy supporting and raising my children and establishing a career to become involved in what I considered the frills of assertiveness or awareness training. After years of surviving blatant discrimination, I felt attuned to the plight of women and our survival in a man's world. Traveling and watching other women was more helpful to me than any training I could have received. The images of women revealed my denial and repression. I began seeing in them what I could not admit to in my own life: Pushed to the side and devalued, women the world over accepted roles that diminished their capacities.

Travel is a great teacher, but it invites self-indulgence. Even as ethnographers we may become colonizers, sacking the villages and countryside for good buys and perfect photos, savoring the food, indulging in differences, coming to conclusions when none are possible. At its best, travel itself provides an "edge effect." With our feet planted in our own culture, we can legitimately venture into another. We may also, as the Dalai Lama has suggested, go forth as pilgrims, humbly, with openness and with questions about our own existence and our relatedness and responsibility to others.[14] Whatever our approach, travel gives us time to think, takes us out of the security of familiar surroundings, and forces us to reconsider differences and commonalities as it awakens memories of home.

Travel gave me courage and pushed me toward maturity. Returning home, I was determined to let my teaching carry me where it would, to the depths of my subjectivity where I could tap the springs of personal experience yet remain firmly grounded in place. I offered graduate seminars where we explored social ecology and new paths of living together and interdependence based on direct engagement with Nature and ecological truths. The crone in me emerged, wagging her finger and offering suggestions for right living. The Original People beckoned as I gleaned from their vision truths that helped clarify my immediate concerns.

Ecotone has unfolded from these explorations on natural and cultural margins that began two decades ago when I divorced, left the church, became a grandmother, and entered academic life. It is the chronicle of a woman with a bent toward wayfaring. In a reflexive mode, I have considered the context of my lived experiences. Each of the chapters reconsiders an edge experience and the tension and ambivalence, as well as deep learning, that accompanied it.

With chapter 2, "Flesh of the Earth," the book takes up a class reunion in my home town. Much more than a foray into the nostalgia of rural America, the reunion provided a temporal boundary between past and present where we could remember our formative years, take stock of where we had been, and contemplate where we were going. It led us to the brink of our present existence, forcing us to deal with our own aging and mortality. Although I rejoiced in revisiting my childhood, reflection during the weeks that followed led to some tension as I considered how far I had wandered from the conservativism of my formative years.

In chapter 3, "Navajo Tapestry," I reconstruct a field seminar with students in which we explored a zone of difference, the cultural boundary between mainstream American and contemporary American Indian life. To out untrained eyes, Navajoland at first provided a textured, harmonious landscape. We achieved more realism in the border towns, where the impact of cultural disruption was laid bare as indigenous values and the appeal of mainstream materialism clashed. Likewise, the incongruence in stories of The People at times revealed the tension between traditional and nontraditional ways. Out of this curriculum journey, an ethno-ecological view began to emerge, one in which culture and ecosystem interacted as place. Our experiences accentuated not only the inadequacy of the maps and books we had been using to educate ourselves for the journey, but the diversity of views within our group. I emerged from the experience profoundly changed: Henceforth I would be preoccupied with the application of First People's cosmology and ecology to modern life.

Abiding interest in indigenous peoples and their interaction with place drew me to Alaska, where land and culture were relatively less disturbed than in the "lower forty-eight." Two graduate students, Carolyn Frerichs Benne and Fred Edwards, joined me. Carolyn and I carried what we needed in backpacks. We intended in six weeks to see all that we could, to write extensive field and journal entries, to interview people along the way, and to eventually collaborate on a paper. Fred joined us part of the way and then continued on his own.

What began as a joyous unfolding ended in tragedy. Shortly after returning home, Carolyn died suddenly. Desolation and sadness entered my life as it had not before. A reconstruction of our journals and journey, chapter 4, "Indwellings," explores the mystery of life as it unfolds at the interface of place, relationship, and death. I gained a new appreciation for friendship, that realm where, in the company of a trusted companion, we explore new ground.

As I traveled and taught and reflected and wrote, my mental map was crisscrossed with other places and different cultures. I had moved slightly toward an Earth-centered ethic, but life would not stand still for me. New tensions arose at the university as I began assuming administrative duties. At first I was filled with idealism and visions of a social ecology that could transform our department into a nurturing community. But I became progressively more disappointed with the results of my hard work. There was always more to be done, another problem to solve, something to change. The constant round of necessity seductively intensified my need to achieve. A tremendous expenditure of energy led me further from common understanding with the faculty as I retreated into efficient management, isolated myself behind administrative protocol, and increasingly pitted my power against theirs.

Little of what I had learned as teacher and mentor, environmental activist and naturalist, householder and mother seemed to apply to the subtle struggles for power that drive academic lives. The irony of this episode in my participation story poses an interesting question for all women: How can we, as we move between dissimilar social and political contexts that elicit differing responses, maintain integrity in our sense of person and of place?

"You'd better get out before it kills you," advised my good friend, Dolores LaChapelle.[15] Getting out of administration did not heal the anguish that persisted, as I was unable to forgive myself for failing and unable to understand why knowledge of self, relationship, and place did not transfer to administrative life. As portrayed in chapter 5, "The Shape of Things," it took a change of perspective, a shift in attention and a new way of seeing, to save my life. This new vision came unannounced as one day I gazed upon a primal form sculpted by Henry Moore. No longer able to face abstractions, I was drawn to pure forms and the spaces that lay between them. I returned to Alaska, to the edge of civilization. There, in the presence of wildness and the healing power of the bear, I began a regenerative process. A new partner entered my life, and new interests emerged from archetypal images of woman. Henceforth, wherever I looked, in Nature, art, or the social milieu, I would see Her.

After an extended leave, I returned to the university with new interests in women's studies, but much to my chagrin I discovered that I had not yet dispelled the nagging guilt of failure. James Hillman explains our need to return repeatedly to "deep hurts." "[T]he soul," he says, "has a drive to remember."[16] I was determined to interview faculty members concerning my "failed leadership." Chapter 6, "Minerva's Owl," grew out of those interviews and my attempt to uncover the subtle, strangling hold that patriarchal society has on us all, women and men alike. More importantly, the writing of this chapter of my life cracked my defensiveness and bitterness and brought me insight as to my

14

part in the affair. Rather than an open sore, I now have a scar to remind me of the self-defeating behavior that I reverted to in the face of political situations when I was unable to call up skills of persuasion and negotiation.

Ecotone ends with chapter 7, "Equinox," the autumnal equinox, that time of year when daylight and darkness are in balance and the Earth glows in mellow light. In the ambience of changing seasons and the Wyoming landscape, I consider my return to my homeland as I pose the question: What does it mean to be a woman living in relation to the Earth and to others? In this final chapter I speculate about biocentric communities founded on Western interpretations of American Indian mythology and cosmology and Goddess literature.

Facing the problem of being human, I end on a tentative note. Social and psychological theories, political philosophies, and "five-year plans" won't suffice. Although we may never get things just right, we must continue trying. We have arrived at a new frontier, where we acknowledge the ecological, social, and spiritual basis of our lives. The polytheistic Taos Pueblo ceremonies, as celebrations of ambiguity and hope, come to mind. Our greatest challenge will be to replace bureaucratic, institutional, rational, and arbitrary worldviews with those grounded in ecological wisdom and responsibility where difference is played out in healthy social contexts that are dynamic and pluralistic.

2 ❧ Flesh of the Earth

> What is given is not a massive and opaque world, or a universe
> of adequate thought; it is a reflection which turns back over the
> density of the world in order to clarify it, but which, coming
> second, reflects back to it only its own light.
>
> —Maurice Merleau-Ponty[1]

Sunset. Once more, at this magical conjunction, I found myself
turning toward reflections rather than the source of light. Long
shadows, stretching across my path, intensifying the gray-green
of desert shrub, assured me that I would arrive about on time.

When the announcement of the reunion arrived in the
spring, I knew I would make an appearance. Having avoided the
twenty-fifth reunion, I felt this time a need to attend out of a
sense of obligation to classmates who had organized the affair
and also, more importantly, out of some inexplicable desire to be
there. I needed to tie down some loose ends. It was about time
that I, a professor of education, resurrected my own public-edu-
cation-laid-to-rest some forty years before, an education shared
with classmates in the high, rugged terrain of southwestern
Wyoming. Furthermore, I needed to make that reflection question my relationship to the world, as the philosopher Maurice
Merleau-Ponty had once suggested, to "make it say, finally what
in its silence it meant to say."[2]

As the time approached for the reunion, in spite of my logi-
cal reasons for being there, I became a disjointed triad. One part
of me was a skeptic, being dragged reluctantly along, dreading the

17

event, refusing to get caught up in the moment, waiting to see. Another part of me circled the dates on the calendar, returned the questionnaire and deposit, set out clothes, and had the car serviced. A third part stood to the side, waiting, eyes cast skyward, eyeing reflections, "ears pricked,"[3] listening for deep rhythms.

As the weekend approached, I became busier and busier at my desk at the University of Utah. Everything planned down to the last minute. No time for thinking—or backing out. At the same time, the unusual clarity of the air made the natural surround, the horizon where the contours of mountain and sky joined and the tiny bit of lake showing through the drooping branches of paper birch, more accessible and palpable.

The day before was a good example. Shadows, showers and sunshine intermittently raced across the plaza outside my office window, the aftermath of a summer storm that had exploded over the valley the previous night, shaking me to wakefulness with crashes of thunder and flooding my bedroom with flashes of light. All day the storm reconsidered. In the evening I left my office anticipating the sky.

A dense, gray, disc-shaped cloud hovered above the campus, blocking the sun. In sharp contrast, cumulus clouds billowed on the horizon, forming an immaculate backdrop to the mauve mountains silhouetted without relief. Between the white and gray clouds ran a strip of azure sky. The contrast was breathtaking; the beauty, relentless.

I drove to a friend's home for dinner and two hours later walked into a new valley flanked with different mountains. After releasing its load, the rain cloud had moved eastward forming a purple curtain behind mountains etched precisely in golden light. As I watched, the golden lines faded and the rocks and the bare soil of the mountains began radiating red tones. It wasn't until the tones turned to deep magenta that I looked west to see the sun setting in a blaze of colors.

Despite the need to get home, I drove my car to the Eleventh Avenue Park, high above the city, where I could look out to the lake and beyond, westward. I parked the car and ran along the jogging trail, racing the setting sun.

"Did you get some good shots?" I asked a photographer on his way back to his car.

"Yes, a magnificent sunset with kites in the foreground."

"But did you happen to take any pictures of the mountains to the east? The light was unbelievable."

His puzzled expression told me he had not thought to photograph the reflections of a sunset. He walked to his car, eyes fixed on the eastern mountains as I headed westward into his tangerine sunset, kites still floating in the foreground. Just as I could not see exactly what he had seen, my experience was inaccessible to him. In Merleau-Ponty's words, "This is as it must be if the other is really the other . . . . His views and my own are inserted into a system of partial perspectives, referred to one same world in which we coexist and where our views intersect . . . two entities into the same being."[4] Nevertheless this chance meeting of strangers and their exchange in passing opened a window to each other's view of that "one same world."

The next day's sunset in a totally different setting drew me in the same way into the landscape and into reflections. Since turning off the interstate and heading north, like a bird locked into some incomprehensible migratory pattern, I had been driving over a broad valley flanked on either side by high ridges. It was named the "Cumberland Flats" by Scottish miners who first came into the area and saw in it similarities to their homeland. The valley floor was composed of softer sediments that had been eroded between more resistant layers of upturned, tilted strata buckled eons ago by compressional forces of the Earth. The prominent ridges on either side contained seams of cold, black coal, the lifeblood that brought immigrants to the area at the end of the nineteenth century.

Junipers grow on the ridges, and in protected sandy areas one can find fire rings and obsidian chips, manos and matates, and, on a good day, a perfect arrowhead. Shoshone Indians migrated north and south along this route with the season. And eight thousand to ten thousand years before these "modern" Indian Americans, ancient tribes dwelled here.

Less than a century ago, mining camps sprang up along the foothills of the two ridges running northward. A barren knoll off to the east marks the halfway point as I drive homeward over this vast expanse. My mother was born there in 1903 in Cumberland Number Two. It, Conroy, Glencoe, Blazon, and Elkol are now ghost towns, remnants of tent camps that grew into company towns with frame houses through which the winter wind howled. The remains of these communities are presently distinguished only by middens where local folk sort through old Prince Albert Tobacco, Calumet Baking Powder and Red Star Lard cans, and rusted parts of kerosene lamps, to find purple bottles that once held patent medicines and vanilla, and small vials for perfume and opium.

In the winter the road is hellish. One loses all perspective during "ground blizzards," which send a sea of wind-driven snow streaming across the highway, erasing its boundaries and leaving drifts and black ice. Like a bush pilot flying through a cloud bank, on such drives one must give full attention to remaining on course.

But during nonwinter months (of which there are about seven in a "good year," if you disregard an occasional snowstorm) I can abandon myself to the horizon and remain open to expected encounters: deer and antelope herds, and occasionally an elk, sandhill cranes in their spring or fall migrations, and golden eagles who make this their home range. In the spring, small bands of sheep, called "drop herds," composed of ewes heavy with lambs are scattered across the flats. Their lambs will be birthed onto this desert soil and, bleating, will pick themselves up and follow their mothers to summer ranges in the high mountains to the north. Along the way, the ewes will be sheared and the lambs "docked" of tail, testicles, and parts of their ears for marking ownership. The bands will coalesce into larger herds tended by herders on horseback, trailed by trusty sheepdogs and "camp jacks" with sheep camps, their "homes on the range."

I was raised on a sheep ranch ten miles east as the crow flies. As a child, I was bonded to the look, sound, and smell of sheep, and, unlike most environmentalists, I like them. My father lambed his sheep around the old Conroy mine. An opportunist, he once drove his herd into the mine shaft and houses at the abandoned mining camp to save them from a devastating May snowstorm.

But that was another time and another place. I put thoughts of the past aside as my eyes, ignoring fences, railroad spurs, and the maze of roads that had sprung up in response to the discovery of gas and oil and subsequent "progress" and "development," sought the horizons. Off to the west, the mountain, stripped of its natural contours by the insatiable power plant at its base, came into view. Keeping the strip mine at the periphery of my vision and slightly out of focus, I vowed that I would not take part in the field trip planned there the next day. After making a showing that evening, I would slip out and head home.

As I started up a slight grade, the puffing smokestacks faded in the rearview mirror, and within minutes I was driving through a small community sprawled in abandonment across foothills flanking a river. For better or for worse, and for whatever reasons, I was home.

$\mathcal{O}$

I had butterflies in my stomach as I opened the door to the Friendship Center. It felt like the first day of school. Members of "the Class of '44" had clustered in small groups and were talking with great animation. Like a faded corsage at the bottom of a trunk, the scene released waves of remembrance. Faces, reflecting my own estrangement, turned toward me.

"There she is now."

"Floss, is it really you? I would never have recognized you."

"Did you always wear glasses?"

"I won't tell her who I am. She has to guess."

"Tell me the truth. You don't remember me, do you? You never did know I existed."

"I've waited for that kiss since the seventh grade."

Hugs, tears, kisses, self-conscious giggles. We picked up the pieces, like purple glass in a ghost town, and fitted them together—gently. The story, interrupted by graduation forty years before, began again where it left off. The beat commenced, picked up the rhythm that was there before, had always been there, is there at this moment even though we are parted once more. Bonded in common to sagebrush, strong winds, and open sky, we needed no time to learn to relate. We had come to help each other understand where we were and how we got there.

Originally we numbered forty-five. Five were dead. Fifteen did not return. Twenty-five of us had come together to justify the ambiguity of our lives. In an incredulous moment of recognition, we were brutally confronted with our aging and with the path to death that began when, like lambs, we were "dropped" onto Wyoming soil.

After dinner "the Class of '44," separated and coalesced like some super-amoeba as each of us moved from one classmate to the next. Conversations were interrupted or left dangling to be taken up with someone else:

"You always . . . "

"Do you remember . . . ?"

"I'll never forget . . . "

"Remember the time . . . ?"

"I've always wondered . . . "

"Whatever happened to . . . ?"

"Kids nowadays . . . "

Under the talk another voice articulated the expansive reality unfolding between us. Clustered together, shoulders touching, feeling the proximity of others and yet aware of their strangeness, we peered at photos passed around. The faces were so tiny and blurred! We adjusted our glasses, took them off, put them on—laughed in frustration at our inability to see or remember. Who was that person fourth from the left in the back row in the '38 class picture? And what about the little one in '35 sitting on the school steps, chin in hands, looking out at a world long since dimmed? The old photo taken from a dusty box on a closet shelf or from an old album drew us toward it. It became the lover's gaze reflecting back caring that began building in each of us. Like a giant fly with a many-faceted eye, we viewed the photos from different dimensions.

We were, in fact, very different. We had come together from Alabama, Texas, California, and places in between. The pictures joined us, fixed our attention, provided inroads into our separate beings. We went over and over the photos, named the faces, delighted in our childlikeness. Still uneasy about looking into each other's eyes, we looked and looked at the pictures.

The looking was important. It drew us to each other and to a shared perception that removed us from our private worlds and placed us in the context of a larger territory. We could not discount a single face, could not abandon a single waif unnamed and uncared for on the school steps. To do so would have been to annihilate ourselves. And so we looked and looked and worked at remembering.

As our caring revivified the faces in the pictures, the persons standing at our sides became more familiar. Our separate perceptions drew us together and in the process transformed us. It was the looking that was important as well as the wanting to see. Our private, isolated lives were joined in this commonplace experience of the world.

Velma Ward. Unable to meet her gaze until then, I had treated her politely, yet distantly. Now I sensed our sisterhood. Although not the closest of friends, we had lived through the hard years of our early, unsuccessful marriages in this small town. Our children grew up together. I had been their teacher. Now I felt drawn to her. We stopped in passing, looked at each other with unarticulated understanding, and embraced. Merleau-Ponty beautifully describes such an experience:

> And suddenly there breaks forth the evidence that yonder also, minute by minute, life is being lived: somewhere behind those eyes, behind those gestures, or rather before them, or again about them, coming from I know not what doubleground of space, another private world shows through, through the fabric of my own, and for the moment I live in it. I am no more than the respondent for the interpellation that is made to me . . . . But at least my private world has ceased to be mine only; it is now the instrument which another plays, the dimension of a generalized life which is grafted onto my own.[5]

On a rack holding old yearbooks donated by senior citizens, I found a copy of The Leader published in 1926, the year of my birth. In it was a picture of Mr. Burgoon, my principal during those elementary school years. At assemblies, he would stand before the canvas curtain painted with romantic landscapes (I can still hear the thud of the roller when the curtain came down) to deliver little lectures to the student body. We marveled at his potbelly and his round face that flushed when he talked. His "Message to the Boys and Girls of School District Number Two" recalled the tone of those talks.

It is no disgrace to be poor; it is sometimes a disgrace to be rich; it is always a disgrace to be ignorant. Ignorance implies not lack of opportunity but lack of ambition. A good education is a guarantee of a man's willingness to work, and his ability to accomplish. There is no royal road to learning; every step of the way must be won by hard, sweaty labor. But an education is worth every effort that it takes—not for the mere dollars and cents that it will bring, but for the power that it gives a man to get and enjoy the best things in life.[6]

That night, tossing sleeplessly, I found my life joyfully yet painfully suspended somewhere between the child in the photos and the woman who followed sunsets. The best things in life. Enjoyment. Was that what led us here? Was that what we still desired? Toward what end were we all working our way through this life? I had come full circle and found myself tumbling in space.

The morning was overcast and threatening rain when we boarded the yellow school bus at the high school in preparation for the tour of the strip mine. I had abandoned all thoughts of heading home early. A team of horses could not have dragged me away from these experiences that were drawing up memories long buried.

The jubilation of our first encounter was replaced by deep introspection. We boarded the bus quietly, admitting to each other that we "hadn't slept a wink." The previous night we had joyfully taken up our cohort once more. Our isolated, individual horizons had been fused in remembrance. On the bus, moving together and listening together to the guide, we were united by a deeper voice that resonated within us. The previous day we had abandoned ourselves to the joy of reunion. On this overcast morning, we sat in the company of others, wondering what it all meant.

Our guide had been well indoctrinated through years of work primarily with the original coal company that began operations in this area but had recently sold out to a large national corporation. He spoke with some nostalgia of the good old days when the coal company owned the stores and the homes—and, I added silently, the souls—of the miners. His loyalty to the company was understandable. Although presently a supervisor, he had always been a miner. Looking at him with tenderness, I remembered that after a hard day in the mines he brought me roses and candy. I stared at the rain that had started to fall in a fine drizzle and wondered how long ago that was.

We headed out toward the flats and the strip mine. Most of the passengers were children of immigrants, and many had lived in one of the mining camps that had been reduced to rubble by time and were mentioned by our guide in passing. He explained how old company houses were transported into the present community and used to build new homes for a population that has waxed and waned with energy development since the camps closed and the strip mine and power plant opened.

The yellow bus lumbered along through a fine drizzle that turned the coal dust into black muck. The guide's monologue on sulfurfree BTUs, the EPA, and reclamation faded in my thoughts as the swaying of the bus drew me back to other days—the one, for example, when our schoolyard collapsed into an old mine tunnel. As we left the bus on that long-ago morning, our rotund principle had greeted us as always, but this time his Santa Claus face was serious as he warned us not to go near the gaping hole in the middle of our playing field. Other than cautioning us to stay away, our teachers paid little attention to this unnatural disaster. I was fascinated with the chasm and for days entertained fantasies of the schoolhouse, children included, sinking into the ground. They built a fence around the hole and eventually filled it with truckloads of coal slack, the ubiquitous material used in the town the way concrete, asphalt, and sod are used today.

Now riding along with my former classmates, I could see us filing into that frame schoolhouse, a fire marshal's nightmare, with its oiled wood floors and its schoolyard covered with coal slack. What a sight we must have been when we returned home each evening to mothers without automatic washers. And what a contrast we would make with the brightly clad children of today. The boys wore overalls. I wore cotton dresses, purchased at $1.98 through the fall Montgomery Ward catalog, and felt elegantly clad compared to some of my classmates in sack dresses whose fathers were "on relief."[7] We were children of the Great Depression. No one told us we were dirty; no one told us we were poor; yet we must have been both. Our proud parents, most of whom were illiterate, wanted us to be educated and freed of the labors they had known. Like our principal, they believed in the American dream: that anyone could choose to be successful, and that education would lead to the good life.

The bus stopped next to a huge truck. There was a lot of talk about horsepower and tons as the men disembarked to take pictures next to tires that dwarfed them. Removed from this great interest and faith in power and machines, I peered skeptically through the rain-streaked window.

Once more loaded, the bus continued between huge pits and past revegetation projects that in three years had produced amazing growth from topsoil that had been carefully set aside and, when returned, provided a good seedbed as well as a base for many uprooted plants that began growing again. Yet the guide explained, somewhat resentfully, how government regulations for stockpiling topsoil and for reclamation increased costs and thus decreased profits.

The bus pulled to a stop next to the main pit. I sat inert, not wanting to acknowledge the gaping chasm, the high wall that might collapse, the black hole into which we could tumble. I forced myself to join the others at the edge that fell away below us, its depth accentuated by striations of coal seams distorted by distance. At the bottom of the pit was a tremendous "steam shovel" used to load enormous trucks that hauled tons of coal. How many thousands per day did he say? Our guide explained the problem of subsidence, the caving in of the bottom or sides of the pit into old mine tunnels. His description drew me down, down under the pit, down to where subterranean tunnels weave through and interconnect the thick, black seams.

Our grandfathers and fathers, hunched over, their faces streaked with sweat, follow the light of kerosene lamps, listening fearfully for the creaking sounds that warn that the earth is pushing up, moving to fill the gap they have created. They are accompanied by young boys, our fathers and uncles, who help them load cars of coal paid for by the ton. At nightfall, they emerge to justify their existence over homemade wine to brighten the darkness of the days in this cold, gray land, or beer served in bars where "maids" work as white slaves to pay their "mentor" for transportation to the United States.

Compared to the giant machines biting hungrily into the pit, the picks and shovels of our ancestors were nothing. Yet it is with the same movement that the pit is dug and filled today. The difference is only in magnitude, time, and space. The striations of the pit drew our history into the present in bold strokes, releasing memories from the forgotten past into reflection. Conceived in this high, cold, sagebrush desert, we were the flesh of this Earth. Children of immigrants, unaware of class and poverty, we were joined in cultural diversity and in strife.

On the ride back to town my thoughts soared above the landscape, tracing the contours of a new reality.[8] A "natal bond"[9] had been reestablished, and it ran deeper within this cohort than group consciousness. Our continuity resided in the common substance out of which we were formed. Coal dust, Eocene sediments, and snowmelt coursed through our veins. The tunnels dug and the faces on the back row demanded to be acknowledged for the same reason. Our existence depended upon it. We all counted the same.

We celebrated that evening with youthful abandonment. Interspersed with prayers, jokes, and eating, awards were given for looking young or having the most children. Motherhood and apple pie were still alive and thriving in good, solid American conservatism.

The class picture was a phenomenon in its own right. Amid joking and laughter we rearranged ourselves repeatedly by size and shape so that every smiling face was totally visible. I finally came to rest next to him. He took my hand, reminding me that at our graduation ceremony we had stood next to each other, just so.

Later, on a tiny dance floor circled by tables of youth staring in amusement, we danced to a western band. At first shy, I gained confidence through the expert hand of my partner. Only a moment had passed since we were jitterbugging to "Chattanooga Choo-Choo" or dancing cheek to cheek to Glen Miller's Big Band.

At the final meeting of the Class of '44, we were served a delicious luncheon in a circular, windowed mansion and museum on the desert overlooking fossil cliffs from which the owners had fashioned an international fossil-fish enterprise. I left early, keeping my composure throughout the good-byes—with one exception. With eyes closed, we embraced, sobs vibrating silently through our breasts.

As I left, I thanked the host and complimented him on the beauty of their home and the extent of their accomplishments. "Now all I need to do is walk on water," he replied with a grin. "You are walking on water," I mumbled to myself as I got into my car. I drove slowly over the sediments formed millions of years before when an inland sea occupied that space and formed fossil fish and fuel. I took the long way back, over the mountain. At the junction where I should have turned south, I drove west toward the waterfowl refuge across marshlands that, due to excessive rains and runoff, were being inundated by Great Salt Lake. I drove straight on, totally circumscribed by sunset, the gravel road disappearing ahead of me like a vanishing point into the water. I drove until I saw a grebe rise, eye me, and dive again. I needed time and the grebe to prepare me for reentry.

Back in my office, I sat at my desk and stared out the window. The spider plant hung grotesquely to one side. Outside, a cascade of leaves formed a yellow curtain. The brick buildings, trees, and foothills softened in the evening light. Reaffirming the miraculous unfolding of life, where we were all balanced precariously on the edge, the reunion had restored and fine-tuned my senses.

Filled with the season, I could now look forward to winter, when my eye's reach, laced only with a few bare, brown branches, would range unobstructed across the meeting place of sky, lake, and mountain clad in white.

Walking across the parking lot that morning, I frightened a flock of feeding birds from a diminutive tree, its limbs adorned with clusters of tiny crab apples. As I stood for a moment, marveling at their beauty, another crimson tone shimmered at the edge of my vision. I walked past the car in the parking stall, admitting reluctantly to the special quality of the Ford "Thunderbird" redness in the morning sun, when still another scarlet image took form in my mind: It was that grebe again—with its red eye.[10]

The grebe invited me to take up once more that reflective moment that had not yet said what it needed to say. Now at this pause, I returned to the eidetic image, that mysterious engagement between the grebe and myself that continued to shine like a light, a chrysalis with new meaning emerging from and replacing the older form:

> Rays at sunset through long, light years
> collide with the eye of the grebe
> at the precise moment it surfaces,
> golden tufts and sleek head dripping.
>
> Collected secondhand they
> enter my brain and explode in
> a shimmering cascade of consciousness
> that carries me into another's world.

Staring into the red eye of a grebe one evening while I was birding on the marshes, I was overcome by the notion that light rays that had traveled the vast distance from the sun and had stimulated and been reflected from the grebe's eye were now creating images on my brain. The idea that I was seeing something that had "crossed the mind" of another creature was sobering and generated in me a feeling of commonality and reciprocity.

The thoughtful rendering of our human relatedness to each other by Merleau-Ponty brings to light that brief moment when our eyes met. At that instant came the recognition that the grebe and I —as well as my schoolmate, Velma Ward, and I—are made of the same flesh of the Earth and have access to the same Voice.[11] Not only are we composed of the same elements, the matter out of which life-forms came into being, we are also a part of that Nature, our true mother, the "flesh."[12] At that moment and at that place, the grebe and I were in an animal-person-planet relationship, one that was momentary and yet joined us in the stretch of time since this Earth began. Caught in an eternal web of hunger, sunshine, dreams, and storms, we were always and always would be. We were a part of everything that had ever transpired on this planet, including dinosaur, bird song, drum, and "Thunderbird." We were destined to be a part of everything that was to come. We could never leave this planet. We could never die to it. We count in the same world and in the same way.[13] Composed of the same Nature and matter, the grebe and I were "dropped" into the world without volition or consent. In spite of our species differences, we have the same intrinsic worth. Arne Naess, the Norwegian philosopher, interprets this to mean that we have the same right to complete our life cycles in harmony and self-realization; we are a part, he tells us, of a greater mixed community of "humans, bears, sheep, and wolves."[14]

Furthermore, the world belongs to each of us without division or loss, an ideal unity that suffices and untangles every problem.[15] Unlike animals that are more self-limiting, we humans are capable of wanton destruction or compulsive consumption. But we also opt for thoughtful preservation of the Earth's resources and for the protection of other species. What I do to the Earth I do also to the grebe and to myself. Thus, waste and pollution are self-destructive acts. Naess points out that self-realization for all creatures is hindered when our own "high" standard of living, dominated by quantification, takes precedence over relatedness, diversification, and integration.[16] The Earth in its most undisturbed state offers us the most solace and wisdom. We must live in balance with its resources in order to live in harmony with its creatures and ourselves.

Finally, returning once more to the wisdom of Merleau-Ponty, our individual perspectives intersect in the same world.[17] Our relationships are reciprocal. We are not isolated entities but rather are parts of a greater whole to which we have limited access. Our actions, like aftershocks, are felt throughout the system. Our landscapes intersect. A coparticipant, the grebe is not the object of my investigation, created because I think it exists, but a subject in its own right that enters my life intersubjectively. Dichotomies fade in a world where the intrinsic value of the other is acknowledged. In such a nonanthropocentric world, "Of what value is a grebe?" becomes a nonquestion.

The reunion was much more than an excursion into nostalgia or the reawakening of puerile experiences. It purged my rationally constructed selfhood and reawakened the particularities of my origins. Recovering the deep connections to classmates and to that place where we shared our childhood years unexplainably reunited me with all of Nature. It lifted me, in celebration of diversity on the one hand, and, on the other, of commonalities, "common" meaning not what we hold together in general but a sense of the particular, an appreciation for our joint participation.

In the weeks that followed, the magic of the moment receded, and I could see more clearly the distance I had traveled. In those school days as a young woman, I was painfully aware even then of the distinctions made each day. We were not all treated the same. Some of us were chosen; others of us were discounted, and in turn we discounted ourselves. As an alternative to taking my human potential seriously, I was "popular." Capable of handling advanced classes, I neither signed up for them nor was advised into them. No one, including myself, expected that I would "make it through" college. My feigned indifference to the importance of classwork kept me from the threat of success. In this effort I was at the head of the class. I slipped unnoticed through school, though not through the halls, never understanding the processes of learning how to study or the satisfaction of studying something in depth.

At sixteen I decided that I neither should nor could expect help with my academic or personal problems.[18] By this I do not wish to imply that my parents were indifferent to my needs; they were convinced that an education was important, but they had no experience to inform them about the process. From a poor peasant family, my father never attended school in Italy, and my mother, living on a homestead in Wyoming, the eldest of nine children from poor Italian immigrants, attended school sporadically and quit in the seventh grade because of family obligations. Instead, it was the school system that was, and to this day remains, indifferent and unsympathetic to children of the poor or toward nonconforming students, who are often ignored or guided toward technical tracks.[19] It is also very possible that I had developed an "attitude" that resisted assistance and attention.

In the high school library I had found a journal article that reduced my situation to a "class" problem. There were three classes, according to the article: lower, middle, and upper. I surmised from the description that I was in the lower class and that I would never be in the upper class, which, the author said, you had to be born into and had more to do with social position than with affluence. I decided that I would never join the middle class, since that would entail, as the article pointed out, rejecting what you were and climbing over others to get to the top, which at best would be the upper middle class even if you were successful and made a lot of money. No class seemed to fit my case or hold promise for me. The solution? I just wouldn't join the mainstream American rat race.

When I first entered college, I found myself at a disadvantage for not having taken advanced courses in high school. I toughened through failure and somehow eventually made my way through to a degree. But I trailed behind my contemporaries. Insights often came to me in a flash long after they had been discovered, written about, or read about by others. I became a major contributor to the lagging status of women.

But not all was lost. As a result of that uninformed but firm decision, I have lived a somewhat classless life on that edge between selfhood and class or status. As a teacher and traveler, my interest has been drawn to the margins, to the natural world and its creatures, and to humans—in particular, to children, school dropouts, women, and minorities, who contextualize their lives outside of the "civilized" world. These fellow travelers have taught me much. I have been drawn in particular to American Indians who are deeply and authentically embedded in a distinctly earthy ethic of survival and pride that remains tangential to mainstream America. I have gone to them repeatedly to affirm the spirit of place and authentic being in the world that first came to a watchful, shy child in that windswept landscape many lifetimes ago.

3 ✺ Navajo Tapestry

> . . . this was not the first time I had been given a map which
> failed to show many things I could see right in front of my eyes.
> All through school and university I had been given maps of life
> and knowledge on which there was hardly a trace of many of the
> things that I most cared about and that seemed to me to be of
> the greatest possible importance to the conduct of my life. I
> remembered that for many years my perplexity had been com-
> plete; and no interpreter had come along to help me. It
> remained complete until I ceased to suspect the sanity of my
> perceptions and began, instead, to suspect the soundness of the
> maps.
>
> —E. F. Schumacher[1]

Seven graduate students and I gathered around the table with the
map before us of the Four Corners area of Utah, Arizona,
Colorado, and New Mexico that included the twenty-three thou-
sand square miles of the Navajo Nation. The students—Fred
Edwards, Rich and Stella Hageman, Jackie Longmore, Susan
Parry-Montgomery, Terry Tempest Williams,[2] and Gordon
Welsh—watched attentively as I traced the path highlighted in
yellow marker that would take us two thousand miles.

In a seminar the previous quarter on American Indian perceptions of place, we had surveyed the literature, compiled
sources, and invited in speakers. Following our studies, we concluded that brief residence on this continent ill-prepared non-
Indians for understanding dwelling here. We decided to go to
some of the original inhabitants of this land, to learn more
about place, its spirit and essence. I began making preparations
for the monthlong summer field study into the Navajo Nation.

Tracings, circles, and checks on the map represented hours of planning and weighing alternatives followed by letters and telephone calls. The itinerary included scheduled and unscheduled time in areas where we could participate in classrooms and/or natural history explorations. We would camp in national parks and monuments. Participation in schools would alternate with free time for personal exploration, writing, and research.

Around that table with the map before us, I clarified expectations and proposed a methodology for research for participants, adapted from Spradley and McCurdy's descriptions of ethnographic semantics. The intent would be not to make the Navajo People the object of our studies, but to make them the subject and to learn from them and attempt to discover and appreciate their views of reality.[3] Instead of asking, "What do I see these people doing?" we would ask, "What do these people see themselves doing?"[4] Hopefully as we learned from them we would become more aware of our own cultural biases.

Additionally, we would be reading the landscape and attempting to integrate the study of culture and environment into our own perspectives. Students would undertake independent studies and contribute knowledge of the region and of The People. We would teach and learn from each other as well as from the Navajo and their homeland. When plans fell through, it would be the responsibility of all to seek and offer alternatives. Students would keep journals and summarize learnings in brief, final papers that they would read to each other on the last day of the journey.

I stated these expectations again during those days of preparation as we consolidated resource files, arranged transportation, assigned cooking groups, and bought supplies. I wanted the students to understand clearly what I expected of them. At the week's end, however, I no longer wanted to talk about what I thought we were going to do. I was as anxious as the students to get on with the experience.

Thus began what was, from my point of view, an ideal teaching situation, one that offered maximum involvement of students and myself in a mutually agreed-upon topic. The warp had been laid with care, but the pattern would emerge from whorls of chance, circumstance, and student imagination. I would provide the batten. Hopefully the Navajo Tapestry, a curriculum journey that began one bright morning in July, would be beautiful.

Monday, July 2   *Arches National Park, Utah*

Bathed in the soft light of evening, I am high on a rock overlooking the Klondike area with sun and wind at my back. White-throated swifts chatter as they glide over frosted red sandstone. We arrived late this afternoon in a heavy rain. The rocks took on a sheen as if glazed. The remnants of the summer storm—the smell of damp sand, lavender clouds, puddles of water, a soft warm wind—washed away the pollution of the city and cleared our minds for the adventure ahead.

Terry sits beneath a juniper writing in her journal. The others are hiking to Delicate Arch to view the sunset. Rather than join them, I reminisce: It was an evening such as this when sixty of us hiked in the rain up the trail to Delicate Arch high on the sandstone dome for our final session of the writing and natural history workshop that Edward Abbey,[5] the guest speaker, had facetiously entitled "On the Rocks." When we arrived at Delicate Arch, the rain clouds cleared and multiple rainbows appeared as the view below opened before us. Our final words were bracketed by singing "Simple Gifts" accompanied by Ed's flute and Lori Diefenbacher's guitar. At that moment, I felt both prostitute and lover locked in a spiritual embrace with the students I had enticed there with credit and Abbey, a folk hero to western environmentalists. After our closing

*remarks, we hiked the two miles down the trail wrapped in silence
and darkness. I decided then that this would be the grand finale to
the short courses and workshops in "environmental education" I had
been offering from river gorge to mountaintop. Henceforth I would
strive for in-depth studies with small groups of graduate students
within the framework of my regular course load. That decision
brought me back to this place and to this field seminar, where we
will attempt to integrate social, cultural, and ecological aspects within a bioregional study.*

Wednesday, July 4   Hovenweep National Monument, Utah

　　*We are in an Anasazi ruin where we have taken shelter from
the glaring sun. A pair of Cooper's hawks is nesting in the lone cottonwood below. Four downy white offspring keep their parents
hunting. The adults perch in juniper snags on the rim of the
canyon and hunt for small birds below. They miss often but don't
give up, returning time and again to their perch and vigil for prey.*
　　*The ruin is typical of the Anasazi architecture in Hovenweep,
the "Deserted Valley," as the southern Utes called it. The dwellings
were small and made to conform to their bedrock foundation:
Pedestals or entire structures were built on tipping planes. Instead of
altering the underlying structure, the Anasazi built from materials
at hand upon what already existed. They lived self-sufficient lives in
this tiny canyon complete with life-giving springs concealed below.*
　　*We hiked the rim trail today, "naturalizing" as we went
along, exchanging knowledge, ideas, and questions. The students
show a good mix of interests and expertise. They have prepared
carefully and bring knowledge from teaching and life experiences.*
　　*For some, however, natural history is new. Their awe and
delight, building awareness and knowledge of the natural world,
recall my similar responses when as a high school biology teacher
one summer I attended a field seminar at the Audubon Camp of*

the West in the Wind River Mountains in Wyoming. In my first association with "environmentalists," I listened attentively to their conversations about "protest," "citizen participation in government," and "degradation of the environment." In the small town in Wyoming where I taught, the homefolk were exterminating coyotes and sagebrush to provide more habitat for domesticated flocks, whereas participants and instructors at the camp talked about all organisms as a necessary part of a "web of life." But most impressive was the passionate love of nature exhibited by militant activists and nature enthusiasts alike. I watched with interest as they knelt before a tiny nodding flower cupped tenderly in their hands or stood transfixed as an eagle soared overhead. During free hours, binoculars in hand, I hiked the trails alone, mimicking their behavior, trying to see what they saw. Slowly the beauty and meaning that had surrounded me unacknowledged since childhood on that sheep ranch, where survival dominated our thoughts, emerged in a flood of recognition.

When I returned to teaching that fall, I placed the BSCS (Biological Science Curriculum Studies) texts, which had previously provided the structure for my biology classes, on the reference shelf. I created an outdoor laboratory and a "living" indoor laboratory where students actively investigated the overgrazed, sagebrush desert that was their home. The stained-glass slides gathered dust in closets as we spent weeks examining the life in pond water collected from the tiny mudhole over the hill.[6]

Witness to my own change of mind, I have continued to believe that encounters with nature that reveal our interdependence with other earthly entities (landforms and creatures) may trigger in individuals a new ethic and active commitment to environmental preservation and restoration. The beautiful desert classroom stretching before me can never be replicated in institutions. In addition to its human residents who can inform us, it is complete with all the resources for teaching: the tiny canyon wren with descending, flute-

41

like song; the collared lizard spectacularly patterned and yet com-
pletely camouflaged in the spider shadows of desert shrub; sacred
datura, mystical "green thing," releasing secrets at night with tenta-
cled petals; rock and bedrock, gully and mountain; and the ubiqui-
tous yucca, prototype for coevolution with humans and insect.

Here at Hovenweep I can imagine those ancient dwellers
involved in the daily activities surrounding yucca, the fibrous
desert plant called, among other things, "Spanish bayonet" because
of its knife-sharp leaf. I have been reading about the use of it by
Tribal People in the past. After gathering, paring ,and heaping the
yucca fruits, the women chewed the fruit (discarding the seeds) and
spit the pulp into a bowl which they placed on the roof overnight.
The saliva converted the starch to sugar, causing the mixture to fer-
ment. The pulp was then cooked, dried, and formed into dehydrat-
ed cakes; during winter months these would be mixed with water
to form a sweet conserve, syrup, or drink.

They didn't stop there. Juniper bark and yucca leaves were
formed into belts, skirts, and sandals and into utilitarian baskets,
mats, bags, fishnets, head cushions for carrying water, cradles,
brushes for painting pottery, fireplace hoods, fire drills, and poiso-
nous arrows that were dipped in a concoction of scorpions, red
ants, centipedes, and jimson weed. The leaves were chewed as an
emetic in the sweathouse, and dead yucca roots were burned to fire
pottery. Saponin, found in the roots, provided hair coloring and
shampoo.

Utilization of the plant was extraordinary, as is the natural
symbiosis of the plant with its surround. The female Pronuba
moth, the ghost of desert nights, gathers a little ball of pollen from
the milky, white flower that opens wide after dark. A vehicle of
cross-fertilization, the moth flies to another blossom, depositing the
ball of pollen on its stigma. With her piercing ovipositor, she then
lays eggs in the fleshy ovary of the plant. When the larvae hatch,
they feed on the seeds, but some seeds are always left and insure

survival of the yucca just as the Ancient Ones left sufficient yucca plants to continue meeting their needs.

"Armed" with this knowledge earlier today, I sliced through a yucca fruit where, just as I had predicted, a fat larva and plump, ripe seeds lay in conjunction in the three-chambered fruit. To appease my conscience for having broken the cycle, I cut the fruit into slices for the students to savor the starch so miraculously manufactured by the plant. But in the end, I was sorry I hadn't left the pod and larva unharmed to complete their cycle. Like most teacher demonstrations, it was absolutely unnecessary.

Yesterday we spent the day at a county curriculum materials center in a strong Mormon school district where the dropout rate among Navajo students is extremely high. The day was filled with multiple perspectives as conversations revealed many sides to the Anglo/Navajo dilemma. A woman talked to several of us as we ate lunch on the lawn. Her father, a Mormon Indian scout, was "called" by the church to quell fighting between the Navajo and whites in this region, which at the time was cut off from the rest of Mormon territory by the gorge of the Colorado River. She reiterated the philosophy of that day, "It's better to feed them than to fight them," and attested to the continued collaboration and friendship between her family and Indians.

Other students met and talked to an Anglo teacher and a Navajo aide who worked in youth sports programs. The teacher felt that the main difference between "them and us" was technology. He described the Navajo as a "stone age culture" and mentioned their adaptability and polytheistic orientation. "If one god doesn't work, they'll try another and many are also practicing the 'old' ceremonies."

At the center, a teacher expressed the pressing need for trained Navajo aides who can speak the language. Another informed us

*that "The Indians do not want to change. Outsiders who cause
trouble are considered Communists. They welcome development."
His words echoed the familiar testimony of residents from small,
rural communities who at public environmental hearings repeatedly advised against "outside" interference as they extolled the benefits
of development. I walked into the next room, leaving students to
continue what I considered a futile conversation.*

*Later the group debated whether to view a "Coyote Tales"
cartoon prepared at the center. These adventures and misadventures
of the trickster coyote are told by traditional Navajos only when
frost is in the ground. The consensus was to view the film, but two
students, who objected on the grounds that we should abide by
Navajo tradition, would not join in. After the film, we drove on to
Hovenweep, as students attempted to sort through the conflicting
perspectives that had bombarded them that day.*

Thursday, July 5   *Shiprock, New Mexico*

*The vista unfolds to the east: desert shrub streaked yellow by
the setting sun, lavender mesas in the distance, navy-blue stratus
clouds topped with pink cumulus puffs. At my back is Winged Rock,
called "Shiprock" by immigrants whose view was more technological
than mythological. Lingering rays penetrate deep crevices, revealing
fissures and flow lines, features confirming the liquid origin of this
massive, fourteen-hundred-foot volcanic neck. High on an igneous
seat silhouetted by crimson clouds, Susan and Terry sit motionless,
looking for raptors. Plumes of smoke that could be seen from the
moon by astronauts trail from the Farmington Power Plant.*

*The serenity soothes the discomforts of the day: sweltering
heat, hundreds of festering and itching "no-see-um" bites acquired
at Hovenweep, and disappointment when, arriving at a BIA*

(Bureau of Indian Affairs) school that had confirmed a two-day visit, we were told school had been dismissed for the entire week. Faced with finding an alternative, we headed for Shiprock.

On our way we stopped at an old trading post. Ignoring the elderly couple who ran the post, students headed for the rug room. Later at a birding stop by some large cottonwoods, I questioned their lack of interest in the traders, who undoubtedly had some fine stories to tell. Down the road at the Four Corners Monument, where Native People were selling jewelry, sand paintings, and pottery, they took my criticism seriously. Their questions were direct and probing—and extended. I finally bought lemonade and fry bread dripping with honey and butter and sat in the shade as they carried on lengthy interviews.

We drove on to the town of Shiprock and, seeing a sign for the Navajo Youth Recreation Center, decided to stop by. The center was housed in an old BIA school with wooden porches and a dusty courtyard. Terry immediately sought out the director and arranged for us to meet with the young children in the morning, pending confirmation by our group.

It was "high noon" and the sun blazed down relentlessly as we tried to reach consensus on whether or not to meet with the Navajo children.

"We don't know what we are doing."

"We might harm them."

"I'm not prepared; I don't have my teaching materials."

"You have what you have each day as you enter your classrooms—yourselves!" I replied, impatiently. "What more do you need?"

Someone suggested we go for ice.

During the few blocks to the ice stop, I remembered similar situations where I had abdicated to students and then was disappointed when they chose the easy way out. When we arrived at the ice stop, I announced that we'd stay the night and meet with

*the children at the center in the morning. No one said a word,
but they looked at me with a mixture of hostility, amusement, and
indifference. This was definitely not the Navajo way, where those
with responsibility act with patience and indirect guidance!*

*After lunch we visited a branch of the NCC (Navajo
Community College). We were invited to camp on the campus
and use their library and were given an ethographic report conducted to determine Navajo attitudes toward energy development
on the reservation. It expressed faith that the "White Man will
come to understand" Navajo ways and will eventually see why
"they [the Navajo] hesitate" and the "reason for their not making a
hasty move." It is because, it explained, "they have been born at
this very place" just as "their late grandmother and grandfather"
were. The "White Man" does not roam about as the Navajo do nor
does he understand that "their sheep are like their mother, father,
grandmother, and grandfather." He will come to realize that the
Navajo are attached to "those endless lonely ridges . . . though they
seem bare and lifeless . . . they have become attached to the land
. . . and really like to live in this particular place . . . . He [the
White Man] will come to realize."⁷*

*This evening we drove over bumpy dirt roads through the
Chuska Valley to the foot of this giant volcanic rock that rises dark-
ly out of the desert scrub and dry, golden remains of grasses and
flowers. After circling the rock, some returned to camp on the NCC
campus. Three of us remained here to sleep and watch for owls.
The unilateral decision I made earlier weighs heavily. I am weary
and my head throbs.*

Sunday, July 8   Chaco Canyon National Park, New Mexico

*A scarlet mallow anchored atop a mound of discarded shards
from a vanished culture sways in the breeze that refreshes the hill-
top. Crumbling doorways frame azure sky. The Anasazi who lived*

46

here were opportunists, using rainwater to mix the mortar and adobe plaster for these structures or to irrigate the corn and squash grown along the Chaco River and Chaco Wash. We obtained backcountry permits and hiked in early this morning to avoid the heat of day to find rock glyphs that are thought to depict the 1054 Super Nova. Unsuccessful, we rest in the shade of the crumbling walls and write in our journals.

The Chaco River below meanders through mud and sand, seeking base level. At times it flows gently through lowlands, feeling its way carefully, cutting a bank here, leaving a sandbar there. To the undiscriminating eye, it looks sluggish, aimless, and dominated by its environment. At other times, contained by sidewalls and pulled by gravity, the stream cascades, cutting into its confining borders, carrying huge burdens with it. Then it appears to be a stream filled with energy, actively changing its surround. Similarly the flow of our lives in responding to inner and outer forces—conforming to what exists, avoiding what resists, changing what yields—is often a mystery to the outside observer.

I remember my first visit here. Exhausted after that workshop in Arches, I floated the Colorado River in the Grand Canyon on my first commercial river trip. In a group of strangers and relieved of planning and teaching, I passed each day in silence, tracing time on the canyon walls. After ten days on the river, I emerged from the canyon and drove into the visitor center on the South Rim. It was about midmorning. Sipping a cup of coffee and watching Mr. and Mrs. America taking photographs of each other, I realized something was missing: I couldn't hear the river. I jumped into my old VW bus and headed east. As I passed First Mesa on the Hopi Indian Reservation, the sound of the river returned.

For the next weeks, my fantasies carried me on through the Navajo Nation from ruin to trading post. The pattern for the tapestry woven in this field seminar took form. It was then that I decided there was much to learn from the Tribal People of this

47

continent. It was also then I determined to devote my energies to graduate students dealing with special questions in human ecology and environmental education. I complete another circle here in Pinasco Blanco.

Friday morning at Shiprock I awoke to the mourning dove's call, raindrops, and a waning moon. The night had been strange, with alternate deadly calm and howling winds that blasted us with sand. We drove to the recreation center, where we joined the others. There were no children in the courtyard, but about forty youths from the NYCC (Navajo Youth Conservation Corps) were milling about. When I asked the director where the little ones were, she said, "They don't come on Friday." As I contemplated another disappointing change of plans, graduate students moved out to the youths, who seemed amenable to taking part in the activities that had been planned. We helped them clean the center, their task for the day, and then teacher teams began with clusters of students. In one group, earth objects from a leather pouch (feathers, stones, shells, and turquoise) were handed around. Then with oil pastels, the youths depicted their ties to the land as each volunteered an explanation. Finally they wrote down their thoughts and volunteered to share them with the others.

A young woman talked openly about her life: She had attended BIA schools all her life but felt no bitterness—she accepted the way it was. She lived in a hogan high on the mesa top and ran down to the river each morning to bathe; the water was cold but made her feel alive. She followed the traditional beliefs taught by her grandfather, who, she said, rode the bear that came through each year and called rattlesnakes to a tree where he hung a rattle. A copy of Crime and Punishment *was tucked under her arm; she had enlisted in the air force. Quiet and shy but with a keen sense* of humor, she answered our questions in parables. She was a child of nature in spirit and one with the animals, she declared, and always looked for guidance to "our mother, the earth, the beautiful woman" who adorns the trails we travel.

In another group, rocks gathered at Shiprock were brought out in preparation for some "earth science activities." When the youths were asked how many had been to Shiprock, they replied that Navajos don't go to Winged Rock, a place of mythological emergence. "The air there is thin." I recalled my sleepless night and realized too late that we should not have collected the rocks. Painfully aware of our ignorance, we forged ahead self-consciously.

A counselor talked to Fred about the spirit that exists in every-thing and how when we take rocks from Mother Earth "we are dig-ging her insides out." He said that the Great One was really smart in putting power in nonhuman things like rocks and plants, because, if the power had been given to humans, they would proba-bly use it in a bad way against each other. He asserted that the Elders are worried about the way things are going and are thinking of what they can do, since white people have lost their way. "They come asking for help." He is thankful that he grew up in a tradi-tional family, because he has ceremonies, and because of them wher-ever he goes he can "always be strong and not lose his way."

Following the group work, Rich and Stella organized games in the gym and volleyball and basketball in the courtyard. The meaning of "contact sports" took on a new dimension in the com-petitive pushing and vying for the ball between graduate students and Navajo youths. Based on physical skill and condition, the games closed the distance between student and teacher typical in classroom settings and, in some cases, reversed their roles, making students the leaders. The youths, in excellent physical condition, played hard and rough but silently. They did not compliment one another on good shots or chide each other about errors as we did. Young women who joined in were as athletic as their male peers.

After the games I sat on the porch and watched the graduate students mingle with the NYCC youths, who, in spite of our bungling, had received us generously. They were wonderful teachers, recognizing our sincere desire to learn from them. I regretted that I hadn't handled the situation with the graduate students in a more appropriate way. Nonetheless, the experience had been rich and positive, and they had grown in confidence and enthusiasm.

That afternoon we traveled here from Shiprock. Yesterday, exhausted from the previous day's activities, students slept in. I waited for them to emerge from their tents and then brought them together. I expressed my positive feelings about the Shiprock experience and reiterated the limitations of our studies that had now been confirmed: lack of time for complete immersion in the culture, the linguistic barrier (none of us spoke or understood Navajo), and our personal biases and interests that filtered and clouded what we saw. Anticipating their reluctance to write and research in the midst of experiences that dominated their thoughts and energy, I focused again on final projects and asked each to describe briefly to the group the topics they had chosen for individual research. These included sex roles of Navajo women, Navajo attitudes toward competition, similarities between Navajo and Anglo cultures, the role of the child in the Navajo family, Navajo perceptions about land, Navajo perceptions about what is important to learn in school, and a curriculum unifying science and mythology.

We then joined a guided tour through Pueblo Bonito, an extensive restored ruin that may have been a trading and religious center for the dwellers. The ranger/guide, an informed anthropologist, expressed the National Park philosophy for preserving such sites: As we look into the past he said, we are able to more critically assess the present and may identify in advance the causes and remedies for cultural disintegration. He took us into the central plaza, asked us to imagine that we were in the past, and then asked us how we felt and what we saw. His pedagogy proved effective:

The pillars rose and the white adobe courtyard filled with people, dressed in garments woven in earth tones, bartering for goods displayed around the perimeter. They had come long distances over roads paved with stone to share goods and ideas in this religious and economic center.

Tuesday, July 10   *El Moro National Monument, New Mexico*

The tapestry here is woven with deeper hues in verdant juniper forests interspersed with flaming magenta and orange blossoms of cholla and Indian paintbrush. El Moro National Monument, where we are camped, is serene and beautiful. To the east is the sky city of the Acomas; to the west, the Zuni Reservation.

The design and color of the circular red brick school building with turquoise metal roof blends with clay and juniper. The Ramah Navajo Reservation sits apart and isolated from the main Navajo Nation as well as mainstream America. A feeling of separateness and independence is prized and nurtured.

The Ramah School Board was incorporated and began its struggle for self-determination in 1970, we are told, with a couple of condemned BIA buildings and a hogan or two. Now the complex represents a community enterprise. Health and social services, the development of an agrarian economy, and Navajo as well as English literacy are the goals. Our guide put it this way: "We want our people to possess the 'combat' skills to get along in either the Anglo or Navajo culture."

We were given lunch, a place to shower, a tour of facilities, a meeting with the superintendent, and observation and teaching time with Navajo children in their classrooms. As we followed our guide from place to place, he talked about his life: As a child and youth he had attended BIA schools, where they were punished if they spoke Navajo, and then a mission school in Albuquerque. Upon graduation, a friend talked him into enlisting in the army. His friend was rejected; he was sent to Vietnam. He walked through the battlefields as in a dream. He could not (would not allow himself to) feel the death and misery of war. But after the experience he could relate to the pain of defeat suffered by his ancestors. When he returned from war, he educated himself as a teacher. Navajo children are naturally quiet and do not need to verbalize or rationalize their feelings, he tells us. When frustrated, they turn their aggressions inward and become passively hostile, a side they exhibit more to Anglos than to Navajos, he added.

This morning after the children were served breakfast at the school, teacher teams met with all age groups, from preschool to high school. At first classes were dominated by "teacher talk." The "pouch" and pictures drawn by NYCC youth were passed around as Terry and Fred asked third and fourth graders to name things they saw on the desert. After a long silence, and encouragement from Terry, one brave soul spoke up, and before long Fred had transcribed a long list on the blackboard that included everything from "dust devils" to "skin walkers," hogans to snakes, and windmills to owls.

The preadolescents were more self-conscious and more withdrawn. Nonetheless, Jackie and Susan felt they had succeeded when one of the youth whispered, "Come back," as the teachers closed the session. In the courtyard Rich and Stella played a marvelous sheep game with young children. And Gordon found himself in his element teaching earth science to high school students as he began the fundamentals of map reading by asking them to sketch the area where they lived.

Friday, July 13   *Wheatfields Lake, Arizona*

Some of us sat around a campfire talking until late last night while the others went off to dance at the community college. This morning they are all sleeping in. In my hammock, my sleeping bag for a pillow, I welcome this quiet time in the gentle morning sun to bring my journal up to date. Calls of nuthatch and woodpecker rise from giant ponderosa standing against the mountain backdrop. Volcanic rocks and cones and columnar cliffs dominate the horizon.

After leaving Ramah on Tuesday, we drove through Gallup, the jewelry capital, Window Rock, The Navajo capital, and Chinle, a typical border town, to a campground at Canyon de Chelly National Monument. Early the next morning we headed for the demonstration school, where we had an appointment. An administrator took us on a tour of the facilities and then explained the Navajo view of life and the philosophy of education at the school:

The Navajo is always aware of the environment. You get up in the morning, step out of the hogan, look east. There are open spaces all around you. No fences. Few trees. Wide open spaces. Livestock. The livestock represent responsibility. When you are a child, you always ask, "Where are the livestock?"

The Navajo children have high visual discrimination. They are already motivated to the environment. What they aren't motivated to is an isolated, self-contained classroom surrounded by books closing them in. [He walked to the board and drew one circle within another.]

The children and parents and sometimes grandmother and grandfather live and work together in a hogan. They live within a closed circle. Circles that go in their own direction, go into the American mainstream, float out into space. "One Circle" is our school theme. We want to fit floating circles back into one circle. We want to maintain the land and culture as one circle.

When I teach, I make comparisons. I motivate through comparisons. I start with individuals and name things, feelings around them. But I always end up with the individual again. You always have to accept the student's background and life.

I herded sheep until I was thirteen and then was sent to a BIA school in California. We were not allowed to speak Navajo. If we did, we had to eat soap or stay up all night and scrub the "johns" with a toothbrush. I was not motivated to study. Then one day we went on a vocational field trip. I saw a boy feeding a printing press. He was so skilled! I kept watching him. I decided to take up printing.

When I came home and got off the bus in Chinle, my parents were there to meet me in the wagon. I felt clean and distant from them. My parents felt dirty. The wagon, the dirt roads, the sheepskins on the floor, the dirt floor all felt dirty. I wanted to walk on sidewalks. I was floating in space.

Then I went to college in the Ozarks and through a friend came to know the common folks in the backwoods. They would take their children to the Baptist church meetings. The kids were crying and running around. I saw the commonality, common interests, a way of sharing.

We are losing our culture. It has to be taught and carried on by the elders. But they don't teach the ways anymore. They have a feeling that if you can't lead the life in a pure way, with sheepskins on the floor and no electricity, the culture cannot be maintained. The culture is dying.

Legendary stories are told at night—stories about the brave men that survived the enemies, the government and other Indians. Children are taught many things by the elders through stories in the winter, the coyote night stories. Children are disciplined to always be careful, to always be looking for tracks, to be aware of other animals. To whisper around snakes. Not to whisper at night because it wakes the ghosts and enemies. To step over tracks. To never listen for owls, for you should never be out for any reason when owls are calling. You should be in a hogan listening to night stories.

His talk moved us deeply. At one point when he was describing the cruelty of the BIA schools, we asked how he could accept Anglos after such experiences. He answered simply that those days were past. He seemed to carry no hostility or bitterness. He did not rationalize his feelings or create happy endings for us. He allowed us to draw our own conclusions.

While I made arrangements for showers and camping, the others went with a Navajo teacher to an area of colored sands. Upon returning, they recounted the stories this woman told of her childhood when her mother was killed in a car accident and she, at six, had to learn to be a mother to the children left behind. She explained how she is committed to the traditional ways, how after school each day she gathers plants to make foods, medicines, and drinks as her grandmother taught her. She recited a genealogy of clan members that was astounding in its complexity.

The next morning, I sat on the steps watching the children in the playground. Music, exhilarating and rhythmic, was broadcast from a speaker as they kicked balls and wrestled good-naturedly.

Danny, a preschooler, came to the steps and sat beside me. He was joined by several others. Manuelita was swinging from the rail on my right, toying with coming closer. Danny was nursing a skinned knee, fighting tears and being brave. I asked if it hurt. He nodded. I opened my pack, took out the first aid kit, and found a band-aid. "My mother has some, too," he said as his face flooded with relief. With his consent, I applied the band-aid that magically healed the hurt.

Needing something further to mediate interaction, I lifted my binoculars to my eyes and scanned the hillside. A small, plump, brown hand tapped me on the shoulder. "What about me," asked Danny. I placed the strap around his neck. He mimicked my actions precisely, scanned the landscape. Suddenly I became a part of a preschool organism. Tugs, pulls, taps. Steady brown eyes staring into mine. The question in husky, soft whispers was repeated by others over and over. "What about me?" My joyous flight at the center of this pulsing flock was disrupted abruptly when teachers corrected the bottleneck we had created. I retrieved my binoculars and followed Danny and Manuelita into their classroom, where they began language development with an ABC song.

The graduate students had been assigned to observe or participate in classes, and after these ended I found them once more gathered around the Navajo teacher as she explained some of the social protocol of the culture. When visitors come, she explained, you should never sit down and visit with them. That makes them feel uncomfortable. Instead you should just go about your work and ignore them as much as possible. That makes them feel more welcome. Also, if you are an uninvited visitor, you should sit outside in the car until the woman of the house opens the door and invites you in. That gives her time to make herself and her home presentable for company. She then went on to explain how, within clans, Navajos use relationship terms (sister, brother, grandmother, grandfather, uncle, aunt) rather than their given names, which are sacred and never used.

As the visit ended, our group divided. Some went on to the trading post. Susan and Fred offered to take me to the place of colored sands. Traveling through the Navajo reservation had been a walk through a multitude of rainbows. Now at my feet in little hummocks were the familiar colors that had been reflected over and over in the landscape, from distant mesas meeting the sky in muted tones to vegetable-dyed tapestries. The colors graded from deep sepia and burnt umber to shades of ochers, tans, and golds, and from rich mauve and madder to the softest pink. I walked from one color to another, dropping scoops of sand into an old whiskey bottle I had found and washed the night before. I cherished the final product, a reminder of the journey and the connection with the land.

We drove back to Chinle to the laundromat, where I offered to "watch the clothes" as the others shopped and ate. I welcomed the time to observe the women. I had been doing a lot of "woman watching" of late. It had started in the mercados *of Guatemala,, where the stamina of the "weaker sex" was a revelation to me. Carrying babies on their backs and in their wombs, they also carried huge loads on their heads and what seemed to be the major burden of providing for families on their shoulders. Sitting in the laundromat, I wondered if it were the same here. Downcast eyes and seemingly hostile glances kept them apart. The women did not want to meet me directly, either with speech or glances. But their little ones stared at me unabashed.*

I was the only Anglo in the laundromat, one of the largest I had ever seen, built to accommodate families, many without running water, on this part of the reservation. I glanced surreptitiously at the woman sitting next to me in her traditional dress of tiered lavender satin skirt, navy velveteen blouse, and dark kerchief borrowed from the Spanish. Her face was bronzed and ageless. Our eyes met briefly, looked away, then met again. I smiled. She smiled back as for one, brief moment her face radiated warmth and friendliness. I did not press on, but looked away at a young woman in jeans with long, black hair hanging to her waist. Her baby, secured in a cradleboard, contentedly watched her. The young woman was pale and thin and looked ill. Under her thin blouse, I traced her curved spine. Feeling the strain of the new baby, I empathized with the young mother. Her husband, standing next to her watching her fold clothes, was vigorous and robust. Although I tried, I could not exchange places with him, a problem I had experienced lately that kept me from understanding the other half of the human race.

The washing and shopping done, we headed for the Navajo Community College at Tsaile. We visited the bookstore and the beautiful windowed cultural center, whose circling walls enclosed a hogan for meetings and, on the second floor, an incredible collection of eight-foot reproductions of sand paintings. We bought snacks in the comfortable union and sat before windows framing pine-covered hills. Then we drove to Wheatfields Lake for a swim. Just as we were getting out of the water, a Navajo ranger came by to tell us that swimming was against the rules. Secretly, I was relieved that he had confronted us after and not before the swim. I suspected that he had planned it that way.

Sunday evening, July 15   Navajo Community College,
                    Tsaile, Arizona

We are back at the NCC library at Tsaile. The graduate students sit at tables buried in reference books, seriously attending to their final papers. After our first visit we returned here again on Friday evening, descending like a cloud of locusts on the Native American Collection. I sat yoga-fashion among the stacks, looking at the volumes, not knowing exactly where to begin, when I saw a book whose title drew me.[8]

I took Spider Woman to a table and began reading. Soon a voice announced that the library was about to close. I showed the librarian my university faculty card and asked if we could check *out books for the weekend. We were delighted when she consented without question. I tucked* Spider Woman *under my arm and left with the students with armloads of books.*

The open time in the itinerary before we headed northward toward home provided a window for reflection. That evening I went over the remaining itinerary. It was doubtful whether our last scheduled stop at a community school with an exemplary bilingual program would materialize, since I had not received confirmation from them. I reminded the group once more that their papers were due Thursday, the day before we arrived back at the university, and I suggested that we plan on arriving at Capitol Reef National Park at midafternoon that day, sharing our papers in the late afternoon, and then going out to dinner that evening. We would conclude the field seminar with a five-hour drive to Salt Lake City the next day.

As I spoke about the ending, their mood changed perceptibly, as if I had pulled a plug and drained their energy away. It was time for them to face a difficult intellectual task: to bring together experience, readings, and interview and journal notes into a definitive statement. Anticipating their present state of mind, I had reiterated my expectations across Navajoland. Their responses were not unexpected:

"How is it possible to write a paper after all we have experienced?"

"The time is too short to do any kind of valid study!"

"A short paper will not capture all we have learned."

"Years are needed to do ethnography!"

"It is impossible to separate our perceptions from the Navajos'."

"How can we reflect upon an experience when we are still immersed in it?"

Acknowledging the difficulty of the task, yet sensing the need for closure of this uncommon experience, I would not yield to the strong pressure to delay the paper deadline until after they had returned to campus.

That settled, they began discussing alternatives as I removed myself from the decision making and let the students debate where to go and what to see. For the next two days I went along with their plans, following them with the book under my arm, reading it at every opportunity.

We drove the rim of Canyon de Chelly, getting out at each overlook for panoramic views of present-day Navajos living in a traditional way. We hiked down into the canyon at White House Ruins in the heat of midday. (I would never have planned a hike at this time of day.) The last stronghold of the Navajos against the government's planned genocide, this canyon was where they fought Kit Carson before finally being defeated (mostly by starvation), captured, and forced into the "long walk" to Fort Defiance. How did they survive that long walk and almost a decade of incarceration and cultural disruption and the long walk back to self-determination? I felt deep respect for the Navajos who had shared their lives with us on this journey and for their courageous struggles to reclaim their past.

After the long, hot day, I was ready for the cool Wheatfields campground, but the students were determined to go to a rodeo and powwow at Lukachukai that they had seen advertised. They couldn't get a definite answer to their queries concerning the exact time and place of these events. At a trading post, the white trader, when asked if he had ever attended a powwow, replied that he never had nor would he ever want to. "The Indians just beat drums and scream."

We stopped at Lukachukai for gas, water, and information. Off to the east a cloud of dust rose from the rodeo grounds, where, we learned, afternoon events were in progress. We were told that the powwow would take place there in the evening. We headed out to find a campsite. When a bumpy, dusty drive ended unsuc-

cessfully, the cooking group decided to prepare the evening meal under a cottonwood that had shed a blanket of fluffy catkins on a badly eroded field of cheat grass and tumbleweed. Pickup trucks filled with families drove by. Children waved. Clouds of dust settled over us as the two women forged ahead, making the most of an impossible situation. (Why don't they just suggest that we get out of this dust cloud and buy fry bread at the rodeo?)

I was completely out of sorts. The midday hike, the drive, the constant stopping and waiting had depleted me. Not being in charge was not easy. My head throbbed. I washed down a couple of aspirin with yellowish lukewarm water from a gas station spigot. If the evening became unbearable, I decided, I would retreat to one of the cars.

We ate, loaded up, followed the pickups, paid our fees, and parked the car in a field next to the rodeo grounds. We learned that the rodeo and powwow would begin at the same time—the first good news I'd had all day. At least I wouldn't have to attend both.

We walked around the grounds to the circle of stands, where we bought cold drinks, and then headed for the "shade," the rama-da-like structure with juniper boughs on top, where the powwow would take place. Two young, robust men who looked like brothers were brushing fur leggings. They were clad in bright red jogging shorts and T-shirts; their hair was jet black, short and straight. As we passed, one remarked, "Where did these refugees come from?" Amused, I looked at our assortment of shorts, halter and tank tops, Guatemalan blouses, and baggy jeans. I was wearing dark glasses, a kerchief, and a straw hat from Ibiza. We presented a stark contrast to traditional Navajo dress or contemporary neat-fitting levis and shirts. Additionally, we were the only Anglos at the powwow and we stood apart.

Dressed in white shirt and black pants and looking very important, the announcer and master of ceremonies took the time

*to talk to us about the powwow: The powwow, he said, is really a
meeting of many Indian Tribes who often come from great distances, from Oklahoma, the Northern Plains, Montana, and
Wyoming, as well as from the Southwest. Each region has a typical
style of dance; for example, the northern tribes have faster steps.
The powwow is a combination of competitions, divided by age and
sex and usually preceded by a practice dance and intertribal dances
that are open to all. If during a competition any part of the attire,
such as a feather or a bell falls off, the dancer must disqualify him-
or herself.*

*We asked if it was appropriate for us to sit around the imme-
diate circle. He assured us that it was and moved on as he was
called to begin announcing. The light was quickly fading. The
spectators, clad simply in contrast to the spectacle unfolding at their
center, where dancers were preparing meticulously, formed a silent
circle of anticipation around the perimeter. We joined them. I spotted the "brothers" across the way now ready with painted faces,
wigs with long braids, and magnificent feather head and tail
dresses.*

*Three groups of singers, tom-toms in hand, took their places
around the huge drums, two groups facing each other on the
perimeter and one group in the center. Several young men were still
rigging lights around the shade and microphones for the singers.
The entrance across the way framed red sandstone piled high with
pink-rimmed rain clouds rapidly losing their momentum. The long
rays and lengthening shadows intensified the colors of cliff and cos-
tume, rainbows of feathers, red painted faces, silver bells, flaming
satin, supple buckskin, multicolored beads.*

*As the sun dropped behind the horizon, a hush fell over the
crowd. The announcer welcomed the tribes and complimented the
people of Lukachukai for working hard to make the powwow, their
first in three years, possible. He emphasized the importance of the
tribes' coming together and welcomed the contestants from long*

distances. *After speaking in English—I presumed for our benefit—*
he repeated everything in Navajo.

The Sun Singers began. The drums. A piercing falsetto was
joined by others in a chant of thanksgiving. For the next four hours
I sat lost in a blur of rhythmic colors as movement and sound
ebbed and flowed. Dancers dispersed and drums ceased momentar-
ily, then picked up the song that was always there, had been there
from the beginning.

Dancers flowed together. The shawl of fox skin thrown over
the arm; the tomahawk dangling from the wrist, swayed to the
same rhythm. Tinkling silver bells accentuated the drumbeat. But
each pair of feet danced its own dance, interpreted the song in a
unique and individual style. The "brothers" circled with energy
and vigor. The beautiful Navajo woman was as precise as a pen-
dulum. The sprightly Hopi floated on cushions of air. A little one,
not over four, mimicked his father with a blur of tiny legs. One
dancer wore a crown of porcupine quills and feathers, beaded
armbands, an apron of beads and bone, a loincloth, and a pipe
dangled from his wrist. Movement rippled through the muscles of
his body from toe to head. He stalked the perimeter looking left
then right.

The powwow drew to a close. We left quickly before hundreds
of pickups began vying for the opening in the barbed wire fence.
We drove back to the Wheatfields campground. I laid my sleeping
bag out on a ground cloth and crawled in. Colors swirled about me
and drums muffled the voices of the others as they prepared for
sleep.

Wednesday, July 18   Natural Bridges National Monument, Utah

The students have been working diligently on their final
papers since we arrived here yesterday. They are silent and intro-
spective as they find private places under the shade of conifers to

*write and think. We are on schedule and will drive on to Capitol
Reef National Park tomorrow for our last stop.*

*As we expected, our appointment on Monday did not materi-
alize. Leaving Round Rock we rode along in the heat of the day,
lost in our own thoughts. We drove north across Chinle Wash,
where the tall red rocks stand on either side of the highway, and on
to the notorious Black Mesa Strip Mine where environmentalists
from all over the country had made a strong stand against development but in the end had lost. From the top of the mesa, we looked
down on the mine spreading before us, its vastness punctuated by
huge cranes and clouds of dust. They say the landforms when
viewed from the air resemble the contours of a woman. Her head is
Navajo Mountain, one of the sacred mountains. Black Mesa Strip
Mine eats away at her bowels.*

*At Navajo National Monument, where we camped for the
night, we sat apart writing and contemplating the journey. With
the end in sight and with increased thoughtfulness about their
papers, the students have been defending their viewpoints and
becoming more honest with each other. At night before I drop off to
sleep I can hear them confronting each other on such things as taking bits of pottery from the ruins or engaging once more in the
heated science/spirit debate that has continued from one end of the
reservation to the other. If Robin and Tonia Ridington's assessment
is valid, that "myth portrays reality as it is experienced while science postulates a reality that is thought to exist but can never be
experienced"[9] the debate is futile. Both sides are partially right and
partially wrong.*

*This morning we hiked down into Betatakin Ruins through
an inverted ecosystem in which plants, usually found on canyon
rims at higher elevations where water is more available, occur in
the bottoms of canyons along seeps and springs. On the trail we
saw varied thrushes, blue-gray gnatcatchers, turkey vultures, red
penstemon, silver-leaf buffalo berry, hawks' nests, giant aspen, and*

feathers left in offerings by those descending to the sacred spring. At the ruins were cubic kivas, foot- and handholds, ladders, poles, manos, matates, mountain sheep petroglyphs, and the sacred, sparkling spring. In the visitor center was Floyd Laughter, the medicine man whose poetic statement at the Glen Canyon hearings remains a testimony to tribal self-determination. A tall aspen, his roots are fed by sacred springs.

When we began this summer adventure, I considered the time allotted sufficient for the undertaking, but I was mistaken. Our understandings, limited as they are, are written not in the bold patterns that were at first apparent, but rather in gentle earth tones that blend one into the other. Distinctions and dichotomies have faded into a stream of ambiguities. What do Navajos see themselves doing? Has intentional perspective-taking helped us develop deeper understanding of their worldview? Have we grown in reflexivity and developed the capacity to stand outside ourselves and view circumstances with more appreciation of complexity? How long does it take to understand deeply another's viewpoint? A lifetime, or many?

Friday, July 20   *Salt Lake City, Utah*

Tonight I am back in my old house where the city heat, unlike the heat of the desert, is stifling. Nonetheless I conclude my journal of the field seminar that ended this afternoon when Susan and I delivered the others to their homes and the vehicles to the university and then caught the city bus to our homes.

We left Navajo National Monument yesterday morning and drove north across Monument Valley. After we crossed the bridge over the San Juan River into Utah that marked the end of our journey on

*the Navajo Nation, we stopped, and some of the students walked
down to the river and sprinkled water over themselves. To say that
much water had flowed under the bridge since we entered the reservation was no mere aphorism.*

*We arrived at Capitol Reef National Park in the afternoon,
found an empty campsite, and immediately arranged ourselves
around a picnic table for our final class session. We agreed that
rather than questioning and critiquing each other, we would listen
attentively and open ourselves to what others had to say.*

*Students read their papers when the moment seemed right.
Voices quivered; eyes misted. There were long pauses. After each
paper, we sat in silence and contemplation. Except for brief inter-
ruptions by an inquisitive ranger and a crying baby nearby, we sat
through the afternoon listening intensely to what had been
learned.*

*Fred began. Mainstream American and tradtional Navajo
values seemed to clash as throughout the reservation he had asked,
"What is important to learn in school?" A good-paying skill or pro-
fession for their sons and daughters seemed to be of primary concern to the Navajo parents. In part, he said, this pragmatic concern
had grown from the teaching in BIA schools where "they were
made to feel that they would be nothing unless they abandoned traditional ways." But it also grew out of "experienced futility" in the
lives of many adults who now*

want something different and better for their children.
. . . The Navajo . . . see a need to retain their own culture,
tradition . . . [and] identity as a nation. . . . they want the
spiritual aspects of their culture taught. . . . To these people the Earth is indeed Mother and there is a spirituality
in the rocks, water and all things. . . . Harmony is the
emphasis and interrelatedness is the concept.

Listening to Fred, I realized how completely I, a romantic outsider who did not have to "earn a living" on the reservation, had been drawn toward the traditional–spiritual aspect of Navajo life. In the heart of the reservation, where the Navajo appeared to be strong and self-sufficient, they seemed to have achieved a balance between the pragmatics of daily survival and the need for traditional ceremonies. But in border towns and urban areas, the tension between these two values manifested itself in alienation or dependency and posed complex problems for educators.[10]

Rich, openly touched by the moment, paused intermittently to gain composure and steady his voice. He had chosen to examine Navajo attitudes toward competition. "Acceptance," he said, "is the foundation of their feelings for others."

Contrary to what I was taught in school, these people, the Navajo, are not savage renegades. . . . A Navajo respects his opponent in competition whether he is winning or losing. . . . To win a game by taking unfair advantage is not to win at all. . . . Very often a Navajo competes for the glorification of his clan or tribe and individuals do not like to shine because it makes the opponent look bad.

He ended by saying that if the Navajo are to compete with Anglos, they will probably have to change their orientation toward competition. He hoped, however, that in the process they wouldn't lose the unique aspects of their culture but instead would pass their beliefs of "fairness, rightness, acceptance and cooperation" on to us to be incorporated into our ethics of work and play.

Stella set out to study the role of women in Navajo society and asserted that Native women are liberated and have no need for a women's movement. She emphasized the matrilineal nature of the culture as well as the matriarchal influence in the extended family. Although "they have specific duties, some governed by tradition, . . . immediate needs . . . or simple expediency more often dictate what a woman will do." Unlike us, they are proud to become old. "Navajo men, women and children alike deeply respect and love their grandmothers" who "run the show." The Navajo woman "does what she has to do—her every act is permeated by the rhythm of life. . . . She can see and feel herself woven into the pattern of life the way she weaves her intentions into the pattern of her rug."

Although my association with Indian women had led me to agree with Stella, I wondered silently if acceptance of role was the result of reflection and choice, or whether it was obedience to the role set out for them in their matrilineal culture. Here was something I needed to understand more fully.

Tears ran down Terry's cheeks as she described experiences she had assimilated into her previous extensive knowledge of the Navajo. Her project had been to understand how mythology and science come together for the Navajo, but her final statement spoke more to her own emergence in a mythological sense. Borrowing from the Navajo creation myth, she described her emergence through four worlds, through the land, through its animals, through the culture, and through the women she had been watching and talking to. "Into the fourth world I emerged. I am different now. . . . I have been touched by their great acceptance and their ability to move forward in the face of many shadows." She concluded, "I was moved by their knowledge of self with no need to be other than they are. . . . I find a sense of place within them . . . it is their ability to read the land through mythological eyes which sings out to me." Terry's knowledge and capacity for empathy had placed her at the heart of Navajo life. I wondered how this emergence would unfold as she returned to her city life.

Gordon pursued his inquiry into the "similarities of Navajos and Anglos" by asserting that human beings have certain innate characteristics that make all "men brothers." Differences, he said, stem from isolation and cultural evolution, not from innate characteristics.

I believe that the worst attitude an Anglo can have toward the Navajo or any other ethnic minority is the condescending belief that these people are something different, an alien phenomenon, an object to be studied. We definitely should recognize the differences and as educators teach to these differences, but we must recognize that these people are human beings like us with feelings and desires like ours. Also, we should remember that they have the right to preserve their culture if they wish—or to let it disappear. We have no right to interfere either way.

Gordon's thesis uncovered the complexities in doctrines of pluralism. Can one who is truly "other" and at variance with dominant values really be accepted as a brother or sister? How much difference can we tolerate? And what does this all have to do with equality of opportunity in this great land of ours? Is noninterference in the destruction of culture or people by themselves or others a "right"?

Jackie's statement reflected the depth of her questioning as she revealed not so much what she had learned about the role of the child in the Navajo family as what the study taught her about herself. A single mother, she had found the decision to be away from her family a difficult one. After initial panic, she realized that "one goal was to get above the mechanical things on this trip and gain harmony within myself." The main body of her paper was a letter to the Navajo teacher to whom she felt a particular affinity.

69

We're not so different, you and I. Our children, at home and school, are our catalysts. They provide our goals, needs, desires and drives, frustrations and rewards, pain and comfort. They almost become our whole life. Almost. Yet we seek harmony within ourselves. Harmony to the Navajo is closeness to family, land and sheep. To me harmony is also closeness to myself.

A single mother faced with continuing responsibilities to her children as well as a desire for personal growth, Jackie dealt with the similarities and differences between her and the Navajo teacher. Although her concern for her children followed her throughout this journey, the time away accentuated her need for autonomy and freedom. She was caught between meeting the needs of her children and satisfying her own struggle for fulfillment.

Susan, who had been looking at the relationship between the Navajo and the land as an economic resource, pointed out the dilemmas facing the Navajo:

Ways of making a living reflect the limited economic potential of the land . . . and the values of the culture. Herding and dry farming have been practiced for hundreds of years and continue to dominate. . . . I have come away from the experience with the impression that the power of the Navajo people lies in their ability to adapt to change and still not lose touch with the parts of their lives that they consider crucial. The strength of the clan system, the mythology, the real closeness to and dependence on the land, Navajo language, ritual ceremonies; all of these are very much alive in the Nation today.

Cultural practices and environmental concern clashed head on in traditional sheep-herding practices that had depleted the land in parts of the reservation. Susan had identified the crucial problems threatening both the health of the land on the Navajo Reservation and the survival and spiritual health of the People. The question was, how would they recover a land ethic that had been overridden by material need?

We celebrated the ending of the field seminar that night with dinner, and early the next morning we loaded the vans and headed back to Salt Lake City.

Friday, August 16   *Salt Lake City, Utah*

A month has passed since the field seminar ended. When students drop by or call, I welcome them like family. Since our return we have spent an evening together viewing slides that to an outside observer could have been taken on different journeys that, in a graphic way, accentuated our different views.

City messages, unlike desert tones, wound my spirit and throw into question my reservation experiences: A news item in the paper casually mentions that a radioactive containment pond broke, possibly contaminating water on the Navajo Reservation. (Who will tell the maidens who run down to the river to bathe?) The Indian man ahead of me in the grocery line is drunk and giving the checker a bad time; the Indian woman waits for him outside the door with puffy blackened eyes, holding her hand over her mouth.

In quiet moments, sensations and sounds return. My body cannot forget what my mind still has difficulty questioning:
. . . colors mirrored over and over, in the sands at our feet and in distant mesas that meet the sky in muted tones. . .
. . . dust warmed by the sun for fluffing feathers. . .

71

. . . giving *in return for what one takes or to one who asks—and never stopping...*

. . . corn, *needing human planting, but giving food and ceremonial pollen in return, mummified in ruins. . .*

. . . circles—*hogans, kivas, powwows, clans, sun, moon, earth, faces, community schools. . .*

. . . sounds, *of ravens calling, flies buzzing, chants echoing in dreams; of the radio announcer's Navajo interspersed with "50% discount" and "Midas Muffler"; of coyotes and campers whooping in celebration; of white-throated swifts chattering over red rims and canyon wrens calling from collapsed kivas in flutelike descending notes. . .*

. . . bronze skin, *weathered, wrinkled, ageless, framed in turquoise, setting off penetrating eyes scanning the horizon seeking lost sheep . . .*

. . . powwows, *continuous, circular, timeless rhythms, endless chants. Original dancers blending in one pulsing movement . . .*

. . . lizards *doing push-ups under junipers and sandstone overhangs . . .*

. . . green things—*pinyon, juniper and ponderosa; snakeweed; pinkish blue and scarlet penstemon; sagebrush and rabbitbrush; orange-red paintbrush and flaming cholla; vivid greens, soft luminescent grays, and slate-blue juniper berries; and a single scarlet mallow swaying in the breeze . . .*

. . . preschoolers *with firm, brown hands tugging, eyes looking deeply, and soft whispers asking, "What about me?" . . .*

. . . black widows *in white ruins . . .*

. . . melodies, *timeless, harmonious, improvised with no beginning and no ending . . .*

. . . NCC *with magenta sunsets, giant sand paintings, and a womblike library to comfort restless minds . . .*

. . . trading posts *with cold pop, enamelware, washtubs, Pendleton blankets, and rug rooms . . .*

. . . A Trail of Beauty—sky-reaching buttes, Changing Woman, houses made of dawn and darkness, Monster Slayer, nightwalkers, houses made of blue sky and yellow evening light, black-horned rattlers, dewdrops, and pollen.

This afternoon I worked in my kitchen and its adjoining garden. I sucked the sweet juice of tomatoes warmed by the afternoon sun as I listened to the sounds of the neighborhood. Laughter rose from the rooftop pool of the condominium down the street. Exotic music along with the smell of garlic and braised shishkabobs filtered over from the apartment across the way where several Lebanese families live. A Navajo family occupies the lower apartment.

Back in the kitchen, seven-year old Mindy visited with me.

"You know what those kooky Navajos did to my friend Eileen?" (Long pause as I gain composure.)

"No what did the Navajos do?"

"Well, we were playing and this gull flew over and a feather dropped out of it and Eileen picked it up but the Navajo lady came running over and said, 'Oh, Eileen you have my feather!' and she took it!"

"Do you know what I learned this summer, Mindy?"

"No, what?"

"A feather that falls from a flying bird is a very precious thing to Navajos. From now on I'm going to save all of the feathers I find but if Navajos are around, I'll give the feathers to them."

Preparing to leave, she paused at the door with one last question: "Flo, does a bird know when it loses a feather?"

A few moments later she came running back to tell me that brother Jason had caught his head in the railing at the Navajos' apartment. We ran across the street just in time to witness a rescue by the Navajo woman. She had poured baby oil on his head, which then slipped easily out of the rail vise. We all giggled at the humor in the situation. I thanked the Navajo woman, and Jason wiped away tears and baby oil and ran off to play. Through the buildings at the end of the street I could see pink hues in the western sky. Why is it, I asked myself, that here in the city I never know when the sun is setting?

As we crossed the street, Mindy slipped her warm little hand into mine. I held it gently and looked down into her blue eyes.

"You're right, Flo," she said. "Navajos are nice."

Sensations and thoughts from the desert experience well up into my consciousness from time to time. Sometimes they keep me from sleeping. Sounds filter in through the open window. A walnut hits the patio with a thud and reminds me of the season. Snarls and growls of combat arise as cats vie for territorial supremacy in my backyard. Across the way a "night owl" calls it a day, shuts down the engine and blaring stereo, and walks with clicking heels into his apartment. A baby's cry pierces my bosom, releasing a wellspring of empathy. The crickets' chirps, once a frantic chorus, slow to a rhythm in time with my heart.

I get out of bed, step to the window and look down at my backyard. A chill wind rustles the leaves and carries the scent of grapes growing sweeter. In the garden, clumps of marigolds flicker like golden candles, and the last bloodred tomatoes cling on drying vines to summer's memory. I look down on a central courtyard that once housed carriages and is now surrounded by garages.

When at the turn of the century my walnut and cherry trees were planted and the house built, this knoll stood bare and rocky above a settlement, a cradle of refuge that had grown steadily for fifty years. But before settlement, this cobble knoll rose above the floodplain of the stream now called "City Creek." The stream meandered uncontained, changing its course with each spring flood, as it sought its base in Great Salt Lake. An occasional trapper or Indian migrating through looked down on bison grazing on the grassy valley floor or scanned the mountain above for mountain sheep.

Long before, during Pleistocene times, cobble knoll, valley, and region were covered by a huge inland sea whose level fluctuated as its waves lapped at long tongues of glacial ice inching down the canyons. And before that time, the cycle of evolving forms and floods repeated itself over eons of time. The cobble knoll itself is the remnant of previous mountains downwasted by water and ice.

When this area was colonized, thousands of years of use by aboriginal people had not significantly altered the ecosystem. Bison roamed belly-deep in grass. In little more than a century, the valley has been turned into a farrago of concrete and pollution. What of those First People? Did they carry their secrets with them? Is there hope that their descendants and the land they held sacred can inform us? Chief Seattle asserted that this might be so:

When the last Red Man shall have perished, and the memory of my tribe shall have become a myth among the white man, these shores will swarm with the invisible dead of my tribe, and when your children's children think themselves alone in the field, the store, the shop, upon the highway, or in the silence of the pathless woods, they will not be alone. At night when the streets of your cities are silent and you think them deserted, they will throng with the returning hosts that once filled them and still love this beautiful land. The White Man will never be alone.[11]

The spirit of the past arises on such nights. Waves lap at the door. The old house creaks and groans as past residents walk through. And out there in the shadows, someone leans against the walnut tree.

Mindy's assertion returns, and, although I still agree with her, I attempt to go deeper into my interest in American Indians. Although I have yet to wear a headband, go on a vision quest, or enter their sweat lodges, I listen when they speak and still find great appeal in their words and practices.

I ask myself why this is so and wonder if my interest stems from childhood experience. The ground under sandstone over-hangs, where I sometimes played as a child, was littered with charcoal and flint chips and old firepits still intact. Arrowheads and their fragments were scattered across the sagebrush hill-sides nearby. Once, on top of a sandstone outcrop, I found a human constructed rock shelter with three skinning knives hid-den within. Is it possible that the landscape gives rise to super-naturals that touched me, as Paula Gunn Allen has suggested[12] and Chief Seattle predicted? Or is it that common childhood activities bonded us in some inexplicable way?

Notwithstanding the romantic appeal of "participation mys-tique" joining me to American Indians, another explanation for this affinity may have to do more with differences than with commonalities. As Other, they enter my psychic ecotone and dis-rupt my usual assumptions. Their words arouse ambivalence, a point of view that is not necessarily opposed to my way of think-ing but is different enough to cause me to stop short and recon-sider what I have held in great regard. In so doing, they prepare the ground for a change of mind and heart.

I hold an example close to my heart. One day over lunch with my friend Nola Lodge, an Oneida Indian, I was explaining the dilemma I faced with choosing a name as I prepared to remarry. With many reservations since my divorce, I had kept my previous husband's name for identity and convenience for myself and children. I could not see taking another man's name. My maiden name, which was my father's and in no way identified me with my mother, would only bring more confusion to my life. As I elaborated the conundrum, Nola looked at me with increasing bewilderment. When I asked her if she had not also encountered this problem, she replied forthrightly, "Of course not. What difference does a name make? It wouldn't matter what name I took. I know who I am!"

We walked back to our offices that day in silence and since then have reexamined that moment repeatedly. It was not that suddenly each of us had become aware that someone else was seeing what we also saw. To the contrary, the experience confirmed vast differences in socialization and called into question our commonalities as women. The meaning of my own selfhood and its attachment to name has perplexed me since then. I am still wondering who I am. And until that time, caught up as she was in helping to solve urban American Indian problems, Nola had never reflected on what it meant to be a woman apart from her tribal identity. She had taken her role for granted, as did the Navajo teacher who stirred questions of identity in Jackie. Nola and I are both borderline creatures, but our uncommon particularities accentuate rather than homogenize our differences, differences that in no way keep us from being friends.

4 ⁓ Indwellings
with excerpts from the journal of
Carolyn Frerichs Benne

It is an absolute rule that one never thinks alone. . . . This is the
way minds are formed, and no mind ever gives birth to itself.
—Catherine Clement[1]

I think in depths and dimensions traveling over the prairies and
plains of the Midwest. Geometric croplands of Iowa and Nebraska
gradually succumb to the grasslands of the sandhills and the
sagebrush plains of the Wyoming spaces. Denver. The mountains
abruptly rise, stand in bold relief with snow piled high. Soon the
Great Valley and the Salt Lake appear. There she is, Flo, bright-eyed
with excitement. My bags are heavy as we carry them to her rust-
ing VW. Steering wheel swinging from side to side, we drive
through the disappearing salt marsh.

C. F. B.[2]

"What about me?" Danny's question followed me through the
next year as I began plans for another exploration of American
Indian territory, this time in Alaska. Images of sea cliff and blue
glacial ice replaced red rocks and colored sands as my next excursion with students the following summer approached. An activist
in the preservation of Alaskan lands for almost a decade, I longed
to see the places I had studied and visited briefly before as a tour
guide for the Audubon Society. How had the pipeline that we

had failed to stop affected the Native Alaskan tribes? Filled with anticipation and joined by two graduate students, I prepared to follow the light northward.

June 18   *Airlines Flight, Salt Lake City to Anchorage*

Carolyn arrived yesterday and spent the day preparing for our departure while I saw to last-minute details at the office. We met Fred at the airport this morning. After the "busyness" of preparing to leave, I am relieved to be with these friends, momentarily suspended in space. Fatigue and tension are replaced by excitement and anticipation. Airline psychology works: It removes us from earthbound reality and propels us at hundreds of miles per hour in a metal box thousands of feet above the surface of the earth. Our senses dulled, we are persuaded that the pleasure of food and drink is all that matters.

As we flew near Mount St. Helens, passengers rushed to windows and stared in awe at the gaping, fuming chasm and the surrounding landscape washed chalky beige with spewed ash. Herb Blatchford's words returned, "The Earth is being strained beyond its means." Part of a "Circle of International and Traditional Elders" called in order that shamans of the Earth might inform world leaders, he spoke quietly:

We should look to primitive life for a guide to nature, for the accumulated knowledge of these participants who understand their mother, the Earth. Present persons too studious in certain aspects have lost touch with the Maternal Earth, upon which life depends. They are more authority/power conscious than concerned with others. Confined to strict patterns of behavior, they have lost a world view. Locked in the mentality of politics, they seek the greatest good for the greatest, but they should not move until the least is cared for. . . . Unlike tribal people, they have lost the greater perspective; their attention is drawn away from the total circle to spots on the circle, hot spots, power spots. They have no knowledge of cyclic obedience to the Earth or of the capacity of tribal people to possess their own autonomy while respecting others. . . . We had to inform the international community that grave violence is being done to the Earth. . . . Industry uses up not only their own resources but others. It has no right to do this. Sacred places where spiritual powers converge are being desecrated. . . . The Earth is being strained beyond its means.[3]

The scars on the Planet below are probably related to something I buy. What ultimate impact does my coming have upon the land, resources, and planet? What are the costs?

As I begin this journey, my mind is like a ball of tangled string. This is my own private search for understanding my independence, my loving.

C. F. B.

June 19   *St. Paul, Pribilof Islands*

Despite the long hours of daylight, there hasn't been time to experience the beauty. We fell into bed late last night only when our legs refused to carry us one step more.

Strong winds prevented our getting to St. Paul on the Pribilof Islands on our first try. After a terrifying landing in Cold Bay, a refueling point and old military base with a runway, unlike that on the Pribilofs, which accommodates aircraft for landing in adverse weather conditions, we waited out the gale-force winds. As we emerged from the plane, we were literally picked up by the fierce winds and slammed into the Quonset hut terminal that shuddered in their wake. We spent the next five hours watching what the wind blew in: wayfarers like ourselves, oceanographic researchers headed for Dutch Harbor, employees of a fish-processing vessel, Alaskan Natives headed for St. Paul.

Carolyn talked to the son and daughter of government employees, who mirrored the values of their parents, a frontier, "conquer the wilderness" attitude similar to the small-western-boomtown mentality in the "lower forty-eight." I watched Carolyn as she interviewed. Her blue eyes were like mirrors as she listened attentively and questioned occasionally but showed neither approval nor disapproval.

Our flight to the Pribilofs canceled, we boarded the plane for our return to Anchorage. We occupied separate window seats and kept our foreheads pressed to the windows, where below a topographic text had been laid open with snowfields, glaciers, dendritic drainage, tidal flats, muskeg, and volcanic cones.

Native man, oblivious of the sight outside the window, what pictures are in your mind? Do you see your people? Yearn for their sound, their touch? You smoke. Where have you been?

C. F. B.

Arriving back in Anchorage in late evening, we were too tired to find a place to stay and decided to spend the night in the airport terminal. We found benches, threw out our sleeping bags, and turned in. I slept the night peacefully, only vaguely aware of glaring lights, flight announcements, and occasional surges of departures and arrivals.

The flight this morning was smooth and uneventful. The second try was a charm. We dropped out of the mist and, separated by *a breath from the cold Bering Sea, landed miraculously on the lava cinder runway. Since my last journey here as a tour leader four years ago, St. Paul has dwelled within me, the intensity and clarity of the experience beyond comprehension but not beyond the understandings of my heart. I am completely taken with the island and all its residents. Eight hundred miles east of Anchorage in the cold Bering Sea, it is a tiny microcosm of interrelatedness shaped by the past, constantly recreating itself. It is the home of a hundred or so Aleuts, thousands of seals, and 2.8 million seabirds.*

June 21

    The solstice! My original plans were to spend the entire day and night in celebration. But I am too weary. For two days we have hiked the beaches and windswept cliffs, our warm clothing protecting us from the cold and rain. Likewise the hotel where we stay and the bus we ride insulate us from tribal life. Fred, in the informal atmosphere of the pub, makes more contacts than Carolyn or I. It is partly a matter of choice.

    Since my last visit, St. Paul has grown considerably. A multi-colored housing development, contrasting sharply with the old, white frame government houses, has sprung up at the edge of the village near the cemeteries. There are still two, one for Russian Orthodox church members and one for others, including bodies that wash ashore. The white picket fences and wooden markers are wind-blasted and weathered. The church, with its steeple and contrasting yellow color, still dominates the village. But the beautifully hand-sewn baidarka has been replaced by several machine-sewn versions of this indigenous fishing vessel. An Anglo woman manages the cafeteria, efficiently satisfying the tastes of the international tourist clientele. Although the island is only forty-five miles in circumference, with limited roads, most families now own

automobiles, motorcycles, and snowmobiles. The bright-blue hotel is
being remodeled to accommodate more tourists. St. Paul is growing.
We have read that the aboriginal culture of the Aleuts no
longer exists. According to linguist Richard Geoghegan,

> the Czarist Russian conquest of the proud, independent
> sea hunters was so devastatingly thorough that tribal tra-
> ditions, even tribal memories, were almost obliterated.
> The slaughter of the majority of an adult generation was
> sufficient to destroy the continuity of tribal knowledge
> which was dependent on oral transmission.[4]

This statement, however, does not address the original role of place
in shaping culture. Perhaps these people, conceived, born, raised,
loving, and dying on this island, like the Navajo are reinventing a
new culture out of the devastation of genocide, displacement, and
despair wrought by Russians and Americans alike. Perhaps self-
determination and the freedom to recreate will solidify the strands
that tie these people to this volcanic heap and to the sea mammals
and pelagic birds that converge on this dot in the Bering Sea
where storms are born. Perhaps, as Loren Eiseley insightfully
expressed it,

> out of order and disorder
>   perpetually clashing and reclashing
> comes the world.[5]

On the long hikes on beach and sea cliff, Carolyn and I walk
separately. She stands on the beach for what seems like hours, star-
ing into the crashing waves. At times she seems transcendent,
removed.

In the days on the Pribilofs, millennia have passed. I have a new perspective of time, place and planet. . . . I hope to be wiser when I return. I am looking for humor and wisdom, color and design, music and love.

C. F. B.

The seabirds are nesting on the sea cliffs; the seals are coming ashore. Wrapped in dense fog, the cries of these sea mammals build in magnitude each day as we watch the drama of reproduction unfold.

The huge beach masters set up their territories and harems in strategic spots and fight viciously with each other for females as they come ashore. After these battles, they sit on black lava boulders, nursing deep, red gashes in their skin. Dominance is a burden they cannot reject. Attack, endure, attack. They have no choice; they must be on top. Rocklike, they look continuous with the black lava pedestals on which they perch. They are the first to arrive, sometime in April, on the island. Until September, when they ease back into the oblivion of the icy waters to spend months eating and building strength for the next breeding season, they will have no peace. They will neither eat nor sleep soundly. Victims of the Earth cycle that feeds their aggression, they must obey their instincts.

The harems are steadily building. The black, shiny females ride the crests of waves, sliding into troughs and silently slipping ashore to where they themselves were born. Young bachelor males, psychologically castrated and cast out from the group by the beach masters, wait offshore for an opportunity to enter the hierarchy as death or old age takes its toll.

Among the boulders on the beach are birthing females and newly born pups with red afterbirth clinging to them, struggling to find their first meal. Females, who have just pupped, ovulate and are immediately pursued by beach masters. Copulation is intense *and long, sometimes leaving the new pup crushed. Although fertilized, the egg does not implant for several months. Gestation takes nine months, and the following year, at almost the identical time and place, a new pup will be born, a new union will occur, and a new egg will be fertilized.*

Imbedded in the black lava boulders are pods of pups, clustered together for security while their mothers, after birthing, go back to sea for several days at a time to feed. When they return there is immediate recognition. The young gorge on the rich milk, only to be abandoned again temporarily.

The gulls and arctic foxes are the beneficiaries of this bloody drama. Foxes scurry among boulders as their young play on hillsides. They eat the remains of afterbirth, dead pups, and dead beach masters. Gulls thrive.

Today I watched a female seal, ready to give birth and a tenth of the size of her master, try to escape to join another harem. He blocked her way with body, snarls, and sharp teeth. She persisted. Finally, furious at her contrariness, he set his sharp teeth into the skin on her back, lifted her off the ground, shook her viciously, and then dropped her at his side. The little female lay whimpering and helpless. The borders that separated me from this sea mammal vanished. She looked up at the huge beach master with large brown eyes reflecting emotions with which I could identify.

Might made right. Dominance prevailed. It is the way of the animal world. The beach masters towered above the scene. And yet out there among the boulders, imperceptibly, females were behaving in subtle but significant ways to protect their young and insure their own survival.[6]

What if the females were to grow to ten times the size of the males? What then? Would they then become the aggressors as they seek mates? Or is it the natural plight of those that birth and nurture to be less aggressive and less conspicuous? Can dominance and nurturance be combined? Sociobiological musings aside, the bitter aftertaste of the scene left me doubtful of my own capacity to survive in a world dominated by struggles for control and power. I, like the tiny female, felt fearful and subdued.

The Aleut tour guide has become our friend. We talk to him about his life and the future of his tribe, which, he says, has not yet received payment from the government mandated by the Native Claims Settlement Act. How should the funds be distributed? His reply is emphatic: The funds should be divided equally among Aleuts, whether they live on the island or not. Those on the island really do not need the payment; they have almost everything they need, he says. His sister in Seattle can use the money more than he. He rejects management and investment of the funds by the tribal corporation for long-terms goals. What would he do with the money? He smiled. He had always wanted to go salmon fishing on the mainland.

"We kinda got stuck with Russian names. I don't know what my grandfather's name was. He probably was a number."

C. F. B.

Helen from Australia shares our room. Seasoned and thickset, for ten years she has followed the routine of working six months as a sheep shearers' cook and traveling six months. When I asked her if there was any place on Earth she had not visited, she replied that there might be a couple, but most places she had visited twice. To Carolyn's query about what she thought of people in general, she said without hesitation, "They are savages." Unable to accept the answer, Carolyn probed. Helen backed down a bit. "I'm civilized when I'm with the likes of you, but when I'm otherwise, I'm a savage too."

Helen, grizzled old "savage" in your green knit sweater and sagging knobby mottled pants. Oh, "silly negative," you are keenly alert. Nine years on the city council, you give it up when your travels begin. "Quite civilized? Anyone mooching about? What did you have for dinner?" "Pinching" bread for your morning tea.

C. F. B.

Helen provides a striking contrast to most visitors here from around the world, although there are some with deep sensitivity to the environment. Many are photographers who seem more concerned with bird and seal than with Aleuts and their problems, and most Aleuts seem to have acquired typical American attitudes toward the environment.

Last night I spoke to the young German professor, a member of "The Greens" in Germany. He spoke with disgust of our gas-guzzling station wagons. He is concerned with tiny habitats fed by natural springs where a diversity of plants can be found.

The young Aleut I've seen drives by in the little yellow Chevy pickup with wife and child, drops by the store to buy $17.00 worth of Pampers, Coke and cigarettes.

C. F. B.

June 24

We are waiting for the plane to depart St. Paul. As usual, Helen is at the front of the line. My hopes that weather might prevent a landing have dissipated with the fog. We will leave on time.

We were able to secure permission to stay in a fox hunters' cabin last night at Tsammana Point on the north side of the Island. Yesterday afternoon the guide dropped us off four miles from the cabin at the southwest point. This morning we hiked seven miles back to the Zapadni Rookery, where we met the bus, *came back to the hotel, showered, packed, and are now awaiting departure.*

As we left the hotel yesterday with our backpacks, a gentleman tourist questioned our sanity. "Why would you want to spend the night in a cabin without water or room service?" The depth of feeling in those few hours lingers in an emphatic answer to his question.

The fog blows in from the Bering Sea
blanketing the tundra in a cloud of mist.
The solid, salty wall of air
muffles the cries of kittiwakes,
and the growl of murres.

Foxes slither over the cliffs,
capture kittiwakes, steal
pear-shaped eggs of murres,
disappear as we approach
into dark, damp dens to
crunch bird bones and
listen for our fading footsteps.

Their musk tells us where they've been.
It blends with the scent of reindeer
whose signs are everywhere:
shed hair, tracks, browsed plants,
bleached white skulls and antlers
adorned with moss and lichen.

Rafts of auks rising off the sea
alight on the towering sea cliffs.
Flocks of kittiwakes fly to and fro

gathering mud for their nests.
They face the wind, stall,
land backward on the cliff,
pushed to nest by the fierce sea wind.

Carolyn sits on the edge
of the cliff, facing north.
Mime-faced puffins
stare at her wonderingly.

I walk on by to the cabin.
It sits on a small peninsula,
its back to the wind and sea.
The door faces a small lake,
a jewel nestled in the tundra.
Volcanic cones, decapitated
by clouds, stand guard.
Carolyn joins me. We sit
on the doorstep and eat dinner,
then we enter the cabin.

A musty smell and a dead bird
splayed on the porch greet us.
Driftwood piled under a shelf to dry
and coal in a bin provide the basics
for a fire that soon crackles, drives
out the must and brings warmth.

We light candles.
Icons flicker on the walls.
Generations of fox hunters join us.
We sit around a tiny table
covered with red oiled cloth.

They tell their stories, laugh,
drink strong Russian tea.

The draft set, I crawl into my
sleeping bag spread on the
bare springs of the top bunk.
Carolyn reads aloud.
I fall asleep to the sound of
her voice, rosy finches running
on the roof, and the howling wind.
In the morning, we wake
to the bark of foxes,
replace the firewood,
close the door, and head back.

June 26   Homer

    Sitting on the deck of Land's End Restaurant, I have been
thinking about home and my children. A pale moon, nearly full,
rises over mountains stratified with mist. Folk music filters out to
us from the bar. The shoreline below is lined with fishermen.
    Our plane from the Pribilofs landed yesterday in a rainy
Anchorage, and we decided to spend one more night in the airport.
We made arrangements for a car with Rent-a-Wreck, which, they
said, was "for transportation, not ego trips." That settled, we placed
our sleeping bags in a carpeted area downstairs, took off our boots,
sat on our bags, and settled down to journal writing and reading.

We're like three beach masters lying here on the airport floor, each
with our own space waiting for things to come.
    God, this hideous airport music. Alaska rain is beating
against the window, a rhythm quite apart from the trash that

seems to come from everywhere and nowhere. I wish I could find the switch to turn it off.

I feel I've been Skinnerized. Four days in airports is like Walden II revisited. The confinement reminds me of a prison. The vibrations of this terminal never cease, a facade for the energy coursing through its bowels. A gate, a starting out and returning place. I'm a refugee.

Lots of women in lovely dresses and high heels teetering by after men carrying heavy bags. Men in business suits. Financial strategies worry me. What are the costs of lifetimes of making deals and spending money?

The Natives, their culture, like the land, birds and animals are commodities. Their features are mimicked in images for sale to well-intentioned sentimentalists while the People drink liquor in the cities.

C. F. B.

We picked up the "wreck" early this morning. The claim of the company was absolutely correct. The car, a minute, chartreuse Le Car with a license that reads "UGLY," does nothing for our egos. We somehow stuffed our backpacks in and headed south on the Kenai Peninsula.

Lupine flanked the road and snowcapped peaks shone in the distance. Bald eagles fed on the mudflats of Turnabout Arm. We stopped to watch a cow moose and her calf and a Dall sheep on the mountain. Where the Russian River joined the milky blue Kenai, the banks were lined with people fishing.

Although the quarters were cramped, I enjoyed the closeness to Fred and Carolyn. We had time to discuss what we had learned and to reiterate the problems we faced in studying "others." Even birds, Fred insisted, do not want to be watched.

Later in Homer we shopped, washed, and lightened our loads by sending home the cold-weather gear needed in the Pribilofs. I *had more trouble than Carolyn detaching myself from the things that I might need. The result is that her pack swings on easily; mine is cumbersome.*

Watching birds and people, we walked down the Homer Spit and, finding a suitable place, set up our tents. Here, where the climate is remarkably mild, life is easy. Clams, shrimp, salmon, and halibut are abundant, camping is unrestricted, and driftwood for firewood is plentiful. As a result, the beach is lined with unique temporary shelters, a combination of colorful plastic and driftwood. Over the entrance of one, written on a piece of driftwood: "The Homer Hilton." On the hillside, condominiums rise as land is "developed." Offshore the breakers crash.

Tomorrow we will return the car. Fred will set out on his own as Carolyn and I head for Valdez via the Alaska Marine Highway and then on to Fairbanks and Denali National Park.

July 1   *Anchorage*

Determined to plan more carefully in the future, we find ourselves back in Anchorage as we await the train to Denali National Park. Early this morning we walked down Fourth Street to the station. That first night in Anchorage some two weeks ago, the clerk at the hotel warned us to avoid it. "There are a lot of drunk Natives and freeloaders there."

This morning Native Alaskans were gathered in little pods. Some lay helplessly drunk on the sidewalks. On a street corner, a young woman staggered up to us, put out her hand, and asked, "Sister? Sister?" in a barely discernible slur. We nodded. She put her arms around us, we responded in turn, and for a brief moment the three of us stood together swaying in the morning light.

Anchorage is a hideous place. Tourists shop for jade, ivory, furs on one side of the street. On the other side, Natives hold each other, destitute and drunk.

C. F. B.

Our first experience with the ferry system on our way to Valdez was extremely enjoyable. Through the foggy, blue-gray day, killer whales cut the air with black fins. High glacial walls of the Columbia Glacier "calved" into the bay. Harbor and fur seals floated by on blue ice. In contrast the shoreline at Valdez stood violated by outrageous storage tanks that marked appropriately the end of the catastrophic pipeline.

Finding transportation out of Valdez was difficult. We finally located a bus service, run by a couple. It being Sunday, the woman had the day off and had joined her partner so that they could "be together for a change." They came to Alaska to work for Alyeska, the company that laid the pipeline. They had made "big money" but, because of exorbitant expenses, had saved nothing and still lived in a trailer.

They dropped us off at Glen Allen, where we hitched a ride with an Alyeska petroleum engineer and his wife on a weekend trip so that they too could "be together for a change." She was quiet as he interpreted geology for us. But at one point she expressed concern for the "Natives" who froze to death on the streets in the winter. Carolyn spoke with them earnestly as I listened. When they dropped us off at the hostel where we were to spend the night, we thanked them sincerely and removed our packs from the trunk carefully in order to avoid crushing the dried flower bouquet the woman had collected.

Carolyn and I interact in ways that suit our temperaments. Most mornings we set out separately to explore our own questions and

*interests. I am more an observer; she is more an interactor. We meet
back at dusk to review our findings and for dinner and conversation. There is a lot of "going back into" and "working through" our
pasts in these long twilight evenings.*

*We have traced our origins: hers, from Denmark to the
Midwest prairies; mine from the Italian Alps to the mountains of
the West. The portraits of family members are viewed tenderly and
lovingly. We ask each other questions that need to be asked, confront each other when necessary. Once when I tried to get sympathy
concerning a faded romance, she replied emphatically, "Things do
not have to last forever, Flo." We have no need to manipulate or
change each other; to the contrary, an implicit understanding has
emerged between us, to accept each other as we are. We listen
intently to each other taking great care not to interrupt the other's
dialogue with herself.*

*Repeatedly in these conversations she has said, "Flo, I don't
know how much longer I can continue with this education business." The bureaucracy of the education agency she works for trou-
bles her, and she is stifled by the paperwork and justifications necessary to design and initiate environmental education programs.
She has freedom to innovate and work creatively with teachers in
the field, but when effecting implementation or policy change, she
encounters resistance on all sides.*

*I share her frustration. As chair of our secondary teacher edu-
cation program, I have found administration exceedingly difficult.
I use travel and environmental studies, where my interests have
grown and my autonomy is uncontested, as a way of recovering my
bearing. With each return, however, I find myself farther removed
from the ideological center of academic life yet more deeply
enmeshed in the politics.[7]*

July 2   *Denali National Park*

I am sharing a bench with a fellow traveler and photographer
on the nature trail at the visitor center and am catching up on
journal notes. Later this afternoon Carolyn and I will board the
train for Fairbanks and then will continue south through the interior by bus.

When we arrived at Denali National Park yesterday, we were
delighted to encounter Fred, who was about to leave. Disappointed
that since his arrival Great One had been shrouded in clouds, he
decided to spend one more day and joined us on a crowded school
bus, provided by the Park Service, for excursions into the park. My
seatmate was an eight-year-old girl from California. She informed
me proudly that she was Jewish and asked my faith. I hedged, saying that I had faith but didn't go to church, which did not satisfy
her curiosity.

"But you believe in God, don't you? After all, we had to come
from somewhere, you know. We couldn't just drop out of the sky!"

I agreed that we couldn't just drop out of the sky and diverted
her attention to the huge grizzlies along the road. Their backs shone
golden in the sun that had just broken through a thick cloud bank.
After two weeks of rain, they and other forms of wildlife—caribou,
moose, Dall sheep, rodents, birds—emerged into the open, fore-
grounding the vast glaciated terrain. The air was clear and pure.
We kept checking on Denali. At our last stop the clouds slowly dissipated and we saw her towering immaculately above the fourteen-
thousand-foot mountains at her base. Later when we arrived back
at headquarters, Fred, satisfied, said good-bye and headed south.

July 3   *Beaver Creek*

We find ourselves once again close to vacationers on a tour
bus out of Fairbanks headed south into the interior. Only five of us

are not tour members: a firefighter from Idaho, another backpacker, a man who seems to be sleeping off a hangover in the rear of the bus, and Carolyn and myself.

The bus ride has been restful for me. I alternate between sleeping, reading, writing in my journal, and watching the changing landscape of muskeg, lakes, and stunted trees in this strange permafrost landscape. Unlike me, Carolyn suffers through this leg of the journey. She cannot abide the mindless conversation of tourists and the canned monologue of the bus driver. If I were not along, she would get off and hitchhike.

Bus driver, who sold you your bill of goods? Don't you question? Don't you wonder? All I wanted was a ride, not your interpretation. You innocently/intentionally divert our attention from the issues of survival. No thank you, I don't want your Santa Claus buttons.

Tourists, middle-aged Americans in your polyester suits, tennis shoes, baseball caps with your bulging bellies and mouths to feed. Don't you see what's dragging behind you? Highways, Burger Kings, motels.

C. F. B.

Passing by the most scenic areas, the bus driver stops occasionally at rest stops for picture taking, shopping, or food. I try to humor Carolyn into posing for a "typical" tourist snapshot, but she will have none of it. She can see only the tragedy of mindless souls. She continues to frown.

We stop at a monstrous "tourist trap" filled with antlers, mounted heads, stuffed animals, knives, and the skins of bear, ermine, fox, and wolf. The message is clear. This is hunting country.

Wholesale production of crafts, now meaningless, to decorate coffee tables of travelers. Plastic lilacs hang from moose antlers nailed to the fence. Inside, ermine weasles hang along the walls with thumb tacks through their heads.

C. F. B.

While the tour group shops for bargains, we go next door to chat with a woman in a crafts shop. She admits proudly to being a "wolf lover" and to activism against their indiscriminate killing by "protectors of caribou" who hunt the wolves in snowmobiles and planes. As we leave, she asks if I can recommend a good book on wolves, and I suggest Of Wolves and Men by Barry Lopez. Carolyn jots the name in her green journal.

The "wolf woman" asserts dogmatically (as is the way with most Alaskan women) that she is not against hunting but will not eat a young animal, for example, a veal. The trophy hunter in the Pribilofs insisted that he hunted for "heads, not meat," but refused to kill an immature animal. Each of us chooses an ethic to live by that satisfies our whims or fills our bellies with as little guilt as possible. But our common plight is that biologically we are defined as consumers, and in order to exist we must kill and devour some other part of our living community. Whether we do it directly or indirectly is beside the point.

Among ancient Tribal Peoples, killing another animal was a serious matter and the implication clearly understood. The people presented ritual offerings of thanksgiving to the animal in atonement for the life that had been given. Now, for the most part, the animal is seen as a rightful bounty that comes to us. Responsibility and thanksgiving are removed from the act. The Earth becomes a cornucopia infinitely overflowing with food or trophies to satisfy our needs and greed. Anything interfering with the flow of gifts becomes an enemy. Thus the wolf, the ultimate predator, is hunted relentlessly. The caribou/wolf controversy hits this deep chord. The "bounty" offered to predator hunters is a misconceived reward for the perfect gift of the wolf.

And as Lopez has reminded us, we have forgotten what the Ancients knew about the agreement, the agreement between prey and predator regarding life and death that allows them to kill and be killed. The pact no longer holds. We no longer ask permission; they no longer give it. The hunt continues, violent and mindless, but, removed from our proximity, like war, it becomes lethal and violent.

July 4   *Haines*

As we approached Haines on the unpaved Alkan Highway, the topography gave way to high glacially carved mountains and slopes with occasional clumps of cottonwoods and stands of conifers, the ground thickly carpeted with equisetum. The sky was clearing. I anticipated the ocean, when suddenly it opened before me:

> *Coming down over the pass into Haines,*
> *you can see aqua blue water*
> *outlined with forest green and glacial ice,*
> *harbor and houses washed clean.*
>
> *Peaceful old Ft. Seward*
> *glistens white in the sun.*
> *Bald eagles soar over the harbor,*
> *cocking their heads and checking on things.*
> *Ravens sit in discourse on empty clam pots.*
>
> *Wooden fences that mark*
> *territories of the dead*
> *lean against gravestones.*
> *At one hundred dollars per foot*
> *they carve totem poles.*

From the ears of tourists
silver lovebirds dangle.

Coming down over the pass into Haines,
you can see aqua blue water.

A soft, refreshing breeze blew over the town, marvelously quiet for
the Fourth of July. We located a campground near a rustic hotel
and the buildings of old Fort Seward, washed clothes, showered, ate
dinner, and then headed down to the waterfront to watch people.
We met the man who had been sleeping in the back of the bus. He
was an itinerant fisherman, logger, and construction worker. We
spent the evening with him.

He had been separated from his Tlinget wife for about a year
and was still nursing a broken heart. They had lived in a village
on an island and were active tribal members. He was perfectly
happy with subsistence, but, according to him, she wanted to get
away from it. They had smoked salmon and seals (each Native was
allowed to kill three), hunted deer, had their own clam pots, ate all
the shrimp they wanted, and gathered firewood. A few staples and
some vegetables were all they had to buy. They carved totem poles
and worked to bring the village to self-sufficiency. But she wanted
to leave (he hinted that he had mistreated her). She was presently a
bartender in Ketchikan. He was returning from salmon fishing to
St. Petersburg, his present home. He observed:

The birthrate is high in Alaska (the winters are long).
The Natives love children. It's too bad that they don't
treat them better. They weren't civilized until the turn of
the century, if you want to call them civilized now. . . . I
should get off my duff and make something of myself,
but life is too easy this way. Work a little, play a little.

Alaskans hate Sierra Clubbers. I like the bumper sticker "Sierra Club, Kiss my axe." I put it on my pickup truck.

He insisted that Alaska could not be harmed by development. I argued that very little of the land was truly "tied up." I reminded him that two centuries ago most of the land in the United States was pristine. A century ago, the land west of the Mississippi was relatively untrammeled. If development is allowed to continue unchecked, what will remain a century from now? I asked passionately. Showing amusement with my emotional outburst, he chose not to reply although he knew the answer. The three of us walked together on the beach until eleven o'clock, when the sun had set and festivities began:

> *Fireworks go off along the waterfront.*
> *An eagle flies over, wheels and looks down.*
> *Multicolored sprays explode around it.*
> *It starts.*
> *Ravens scold, groom and pick at each other.*
> *People talk.*
> *Children throw rocks into the harbor.*
> *Teens drink beer, act tough and flirt.*
> *It's the Fourth of July in Haines, Alaska.*
> *God Bless America.*

July 5   *On the Ferry*

We are headed south on the ferry on the Alaska Marine Highway with a round-trip ticket that allows unrestricted layovers as long as a boarding pass is presented to the purser. Firmly resolved

*never to ride on another "tour bus," Carolyn set out early this
morning to hike the seven miles to the ferry terminal while I road
the bus. For the past days, she has been buried in the ferry schedule
as she weighs alternatives and considers different routes.
Occasionally, she emerges to ask my opinion, then she returns to the
schedule, which presents infinite opportunities and challenges. My
only requests are that we visit Sitka and a Tlinget Indian village at
the end of our journey.*

*I spent yesterday afternoon in the museum talking to an elderly
woman who at one time ran the trading post in Haines. The beautiful Chilkat blankets, called "dancing fringes," were on display.
Unlike the Navajo, the Tlingit use no looms, only their hands, to
weave the blanket and "spin" the wool. The latter, provided by the
men from hunted mountain goats, is combed with the fingers and
spun by the women into yarn by rolling it with cedar bark strips
across their thighs. The men construct a pattern board showing half
of the symmetrical design and a crossbar from which the warp is
hung. Spruce or hemlock roots provide black dye; copper boiled in
urine, blue-green; and wolf moss, yellow. Along with white, these
are the basic colors.*

   *The love birds—the Raven and the Eagle—represent the
major clans, I am told. Although the tradition has broken down in
recent years, members are not supposed to marry within their own
clans. Eagles should marry Ravens, she asserted. Houses or tribes
are included under each major clan: the whale, coho, and frog
under the Raven; the killer whale, the bear, and the wolf under the
Eagle. As with the Navajo, clans are matrilineal. Women are protected by ownership of property, since if they lose their spouses they
are less likely than men to remarry and less able to fend for themselves.*

Tlingets believe that they are Polynesian in origin and did not arise from Athabascans. Some anthropologists believe that they did arise from Athabascans, but that they first migrated down to South America before coming back up along the West Coast of North America.

July 6   *Juneau*

We arrived in Juneau at three in the morning and walked the streets up steep steps and paths to houses clinging to cliffs, past the governor's mansion and then back down to the waterfront. The bars were just closing, and people were heading home after a night of "celebration." Some appeared to be street people, and I wondered where they went when dawn came.

Alcohol removed all barriers at this time of the morning; interactions were direct and explicit, and the human condition with all of its beauty, pain, hope, and despair was laid bare. Couples staggered home quarreling, making love, clinging to each other in care, dependency, and desperation.

As the bars closed, night people vanished like mist in the morning sun, and shopkeepers prepared for the tourists.

The bars close at 5 a.m. in Juneau in time to clear the streets for the tourists to begin their trips through shops. They fondle each piece oblivious of the lives around them. Red lips and fingernails, beauty shop hair, cigarette coughs, puffy faces.

A "well-groomed" woman has just spent three weeks in Alaska. "I would have enjoyed it but it rained every day except two." She bought an umbrella (her hair looks glued in place) and $25 of booze in little bottles. . . . She empties a carton of cigarettes of its last three packs, places them in the booze bag, sits back, crosses her legs and lights up a five-inch Merit Filter.

C. F. B.

We are following a complex ferry schedule designed by Carolyn for seeing as much of the Alaska panhandle as possible in the time that remains. We board and depart at odd hours, with layovers ranging from two to eight hours, and sleep sporadically wherever there is time or an available place in reclining chairs, in our sleeping bags thrown out on the carpeted floor of the observation car, or on cots on the open deck under the "solarium," where there are heat lamps and cover from the rain. Our heartbeats seem to have synchronized to the foghorn and the throb of the engines that vibrate through our bodies.

At the interface of the two worlds of water and land, we are never out of sight of mountains, fiords, and glaciers spilling into the sea. As evening approaches, and with it the long rays of twilight, the sparkling whites, forest greens, and aquas turn to pinks, purples, lavenders, and deep blues. Colors continue to fade until around midnight, when all is shrouded in a misty cloak of whites, grays, and blacks.

We travel on a variety of ferries that work their way slowly through passages among islands. Some are large luxury liners with many amenities for tourists; others that visit the Indian villages are smaller and crowded with Tribal People with large families wherein children are active and parents are patient but firm.

We docked at Sitka this morning at 3 A.M. and, after a bus ride into town, hiked the trails of the National Historical Park, where the towering totems tell their tales. Complex cosmological narratives unravel with raven, frog, bear, salmon, whale, and wolf intertwined in powerful animistic forms. Huge Sitka spruce drip condensed mist onto a carpet of duff, and giant black and green slugs leave mucus trails on chipped wood paths.

Last night we sat in the diner talking until midnight. It was a time for Carolyn of "going back" into youth and family: growing up on the farm in Nebraska, college days, her trip to Europe and Denmark to visit relatives, her courtship and marriage. At the end of the evening, I felt that I knew each member of her family so intimately that, should we meet on a street of strangers, I would recognize them as brothers and sisters.

I threw out my sleeping bag on the floor of the observation car but awoke at three. Stepping carefully over sleepers, I made my way to a window. The ferry was close to shore, cutting carefully through the flawless reflection of forested, steep slopes. As passengers slept, one of the crew on watch guided the ferry inch by inch through Peril Straits.

Refreshed by a walk and a short nap on a park bench, I am sitting in the lobby of a drab and worn hotel waiting for the bus back to the ferry. The people walking by seem to be workers concerned with making a living and bear little resemblance to the tourists with their wash and wear slacks, instamatic cameras, plastic raincoats, and tote bags stuffed with bargains on their quick trips through museums. I am starkly reminded of the great range of people included in middle-class America, from which I supposedly removed myself some years ago.

July 7   Midnight in Wrangell

> Shimmering in the midnight rain,
> Wrangle is silent. The harbor
> reflects the sawmill with plume of
> smoke and wastes gushing forth.
>
> Men in hard hats, hickory shirts,
> black Lee pants and red suspenders
> go quietly on night shift
> carrying their lunch in buckets.

Past Shaky's tribal house,
a fisherman repairs his nets.
He removes a dead fish,
looks at it wistfully,
drops it into the water.

We follow music to a bar,
buy sandwiches and beer,
watch bearded men and
long-haired women moving
to hard rock, life and lust.

The ferry sounds off shore.
Two women walk away
combing and braiding their hair.
"They're hiring in St. Petersburg."
Love can wait.

July 9   *St. Petersburg*

The smell of the cannery blows over this point where eagles perch. On our way from the terminal we stopped to breakfast on sweet salmonberries ripening along the road. The people of St. Petersburg pretend we don't exist. Rosy-cheeked, industrious, and aloof, they have a reputation for ignoring tourists as they strive to retain their Nordic homogeneity. A sign reads, "No camping within 23-1/2 miles of the terminal."

Homeward bound with the journey's end in sight, Carolyn talks more and more about her dwelling place, which she considers "the most beautiful place on earth." She looks forward to the family fishing trips to South Dakota in the fall. She recalls how in the tiny boat on still waters surrounded by stars, shining above and reflected below, she feels absolutely at the center of the universe.

Today she bought and mailed home heavy woolen pants for these fishing trips.

Last night on the ferry I watched a dozen killer whales feeding near the ship, their white undersides showing as they breached, cutting the water with the singular black fin and sleek backs. Visible only momentarily, they slipped back into the icy depth. I stood on the deck for a long time anticipating their return. Then, giving up, I went to the bar to take off the chill with an Irish coffee.

I sat at the bar next to a woman who was returning to her village after reconciliation with her husband. She smiled, remembering. She thought perhaps they could make it now. As I nursed my drink along, she drank six beers, admitting, "I drink too much." Yet she was shocked at the drunkenness in Juneau. Her husband has been a logger for twelve years. He works the season from March till November and then is off the rest of the year. "The season is too short, but the pay is good. It's a good life,'" she declared. "Better than fishing."

She is impatient with the Natives of her village, who, unlike many others, have refused to sell their forests to Japanese lumber companies. They fear that the destruction of the forest will bring an end to their deer herds, which they rely on for subsistence. She feels the timber should be sold and, like our guide on the Pribilofs, that the money should be distributed to the people.

July 11   *Hoonah*

We came ashore late last evening to the village where the Eagles and Ravens dwell. We will stay here several days before heading homeward. We walked the dirt road from the terminal through the village on to Totem Lodge, owned and built by the tribal corporation. After eating a good salmon dinner, we inquired about camping. The manager advised us not to sleep out. "The bears are too dangerous," he said. Instead he offered us the "Forest Service Room" for five dollars a night. Delighted, we deposited our packs in the room that had been stripped of all furniture to provide room for sleeping bags and headed out to explore the village. The houses were peaceful and quiet; the children were asleep. Down the road near the waterfront, music poured from a jukebox. Three young men walking down the road asked if we were "Fish and Game." At 1 A.M. we returned to our room.

Unaccustomed to quietness and privacy, we slept in this morning and then headed out on our own with plans to meet for lunch. I headed down to the beach, where smoke rose from a small wooden building where a woman was smoking salmon. As she sliced through the fish that had hung in the smokehouse all night firming up, she explained how Tribal People fish cooperatively at this time of year and distribute the salmon among themselves . She draped huge sheets of pink meat over racks in the smokehouse, placed alder leaves in the tin stove, and detached the stovepipe. The little frame house filled with smoke that seeped out through the cracks. In twelve hours, when the fish are thoroughly smoked, she will replace the pipe and continue feeding the fire for twelve or more hours until the fish are thoroughly dried. The salmon will be stored or frozen for chowder during the winter.

She has only recently learned to smoke fish. Now in her retired years she is returning to traditional ways of her people. She has always been a community leader, involved in tribal and village matters. Unlike the other Native Alaskans we have talked to, she believes that some of the money from Native claims should be returned to the corporation for the future good of the people. The Hoonah Tribe is doing this, she said, but there is opposition. Most Tribal People are too impatient and want immediate payoff.

She asserted that the land is rightfully theirs and explained the problem: When homesteading took place, they did not file. They assumed the land was theirs. Now there is great pressure from

Native Alaskans to sell their land, and most corporations are not looking to the future. Some are selling the timber in small parcels that are clear-cut and rotated on a hundred-year plan. Under such a plan, the timbered lands must be carefully managed. After the initial growth, the trees require thinning to fourteen feet to prevent thick stands of spindly and stunted trees that are good only for chipping. Actually most wood sent to the growing Japanese market is chipped anyway and fabricated into pressed wood. Undoubtedly, in the end, unmanaged clear-cutting is the cheapest form of harvesting and serves the largest market. Maintaining the habitat and species for subsistence is a secondary consideration, as are old-growth forests and the ecological secrets they carry.

Leaving her to her work, I walked up the hill to the cultural center. The woman in charge told me that at first the elders would not place their treasures there. They were afraid that tourists would take their things and sell them for profit. They had no trust, as the memory of exploitation persisted.

The Seal of Hoonah was painted on one wall. It was flanked on either side by Raven and Eagle. On the top and bottom of the mural were animistic representations of Mount Fairweather and of glaciers. In the center was Kasteen, the young woman who according to mythology stayed behind and sacrificed her life when the people fled the advancing glaciers from Glacier Bay and migrated south to occupy this island. The seal depicts the spirituality of mountains, ice, animals, and humans as well as the history of the people. To this day, the Natives return to their original home in Glacier Bay for hunting and fishing.

Carolyn and I met to eat lunch on the steps of the White Russian Orthodox church high on the hill overlooking the bay. Then we walked down to visit the wife of the chief of the tribe. Her husband was eighty-six and crippled. He sat by the bay window that overlooked "Main Street" and the harbor. She was a Raven and a skilled craftsperson in beadwork, leatherwork, and basketmaking. She lead us into her living room and we sat around a table as she laid out her handcrafted beadwork, moccasins, gloves, leggings, and baskets.

The room was filled with mementos of her life: family portraits, a shrine, gifts given to her. We stroked the moccasins of supple white moose skin and soft seal fur as she spoke of her life: Her entire family (father, mother, six siblings and three relatives) capsized in a fishing boat and drowned. When she lost her family, she became so ill she thought she too would die. Since that time she has survived the death of six of her eight children and two husbands. For brief moments sadness engulfed her, but she recovered her composure each time by brushing the pathos away with humor and wit.

She was seventy-six, beautiful, and respected in the community for her wisdom. She regretted the loss of tradition. "People are too busy. No one wants to learn the crafts." She doubted that she could continue making baskets, since there was no one to help her gather and prepare spruce roots. She had cataracts and feared blindness but, because of surgery the previous year, could not afford to have them removed.

Our conversation was interrupted by children from the village bringing her a bag filled with salmon heads, a delicacy reserved from the day's catch for these two respected elders. She said she would either bake them or cook them in a chowder.

Carolyn bought moose leggings and gloves for her fishing trips. I bought a beaded raven and killer whale necklace and a pair of sealskin moccasins and left her reluctantly as I fantasized a return to the village when I would help her gather spruce roots for her baskets.

Leaving her, we hiked through the village toward the old cannery four miles down the road. The village and its residents were becoming more familiar to us: children playing in the streets, women walking to the tiny market, fishermen going to and from the dock.

The Anglo fishermen seem poured from a mountain-man mold—tough, grizzled, and somewhat antisocial. We watched them each evening as we ate dinner. Many came straight from their fishing boats, took off their boots, ate heartily, drank heavily, and danced until late with waitresses. The older ones, after running a rough and stormy course, come to shore, limping and graying, and find a young Native woman to nurse them through their final years.

The road hugged the shoreline. In the distance beyond the water was Mount Fairweather and Glacier Bay. Wooded slopes rose steeply on our right. An old black Labrador, limping, joined us. We passed the charred remains of a boat that had burned in dry dock and a crumbling, moss-covered cabin with rope for niching.

The old cannery, closed in 1954, now serves as a repair shop. We peered through open doors into the cool, dim interior where men were repairing nets. Docks and building were weathered, and wooden benches, carved and whittled, were polished to a patina finish by years of fish oil applied with the seats of pants.

A barn swallow, apparently tamed, sat quietly as I photographed it. A young worker asked if I had gotten a good close-up. To my nod, he replied, "What a beautiful bird! It has no shame."

We sat for a while at the edge of the water watching the dog-salmon jump offshore. Flocks of ravens on pilings were feeding overgrown young. The old dog with breath of dead fish licked my cheek. Members of the rock band from Santa Barbara that had been playing at the lodge were out for an afternoon hike. Music blared from a cassette player. They stopped to throw rocks at the ravens. An eagle high above in a spruce cried out. We headed back to the village.

July 12

We stayed up late last night eating, talking, listening to the rock band, and enjoying our last night in Hoonah. At breaks the leader of the band joined us. He had no idea why his agent booked him here. No one knows that Hoonah exists. Tourists do not stay over. Next time he will know better!

This morning as I left the lodge, I startled a man at work. "Oh," he said, "I thought you were a bear." His fear reawakened a preoccupation that had followed me through the village and prompted a question repeated many times over: "Are there really bears here?" To this inquiry came these emphatic replies:

Housewife: *"I never go picking berries unless my husband comes along with a gun."*

Lodge manager: *"Yes! It isn't safe! We saw one over there last night."*

A guide: *"They only come at night after seven. If you see one, just take it easy. Don't run or holler or throw things. Let them know you are there, but don't frighten them. Just move away slowly."*

Second grader: *"Yes! And I'm afraid of them. But I never saw one."*

Waitress: *"I won't hike any of the trails without someone with a gun."*

An elder: *"My husband and I went to the dump last night, and bears were there, and there were tracks at the first fork of the road at the entrance of the village this morning."*

But where are you, bear? You have stalked me since I arrived in Alaska. You follow me on the trails, hide in the shadows at night. I am always watching for you, fearful. Do you really exist, or are you the projection of what I can't face in myself?

July 13   *On the Ferry*

We are aboard a ferry heading back to Juneau. Tomorrow we fly home. Last night we stood on deck a long time talking to a

*young police officer who was on his way to Juneau for special train-
ing. He was a carver and explained to us that before beginning he
checks with the elders to be sure his representations are accurate. He
was reflective about his life and articulated authentic traditional
values. Like the bird, he had "no shame," no self-consciousness, no
awareness of his perfection.*

*The young man from Hoonah has tremendous feeling for the land,
the fish, the mammals. He loves the seawind, knows each bay, each
inlet. He calls the sea lions, watches the whales. He seems more self-
sufficient and whole that any person we have met in Alaska.*

C. F. B.

July 13

After docking, we spent the afternoon at Mendenhall Glacier,
hiking the loop trail that took us high above the glacier and then
down Steep Creek. I stopped at an overlook to enjoy the colors
intensified by the rain that was falling. Two couples came stum-
bling and puffing through the brush.

"How did you get here?" one of them gasped.

"The way you did."

"We have to go back the same way we came?"

"No, this is a scenic overlook. The trail continues on to the
left and down the side of the glacier."

"Is that the shortest way down?"

"I don't know."

"This *I* could have done without! Well, as long as we're here
you might as well take a picture of the blue ice."

I was left with the aqua-tongued glacier below inching to meet its milky melt. Mist rose over the outwash and drifted by. Black schist cradled tannic acid pools where raindrops splashed. Layers of feathery mosses and lichen cushioned the impact of dripping rain from straight Sitka spruce and droopy-topped hemlock. Delicate, shy maidens, flanked with pink pyrola, bowed their dewy heads. Burnt-orange mushrooms and red broomrape nestled in the roots of black alder.

The salmon were spawning in Steep Creek. Blood-red, they dashed for life, leapt out of the water against the rocks, swished their massive tails along the bottom to make pebble nests, laid their eggs, and spread their milt. Spent by this glorious finale, they will feed the infamous bears.

July 14   *Juneau*

We are waiting for the flight that will carry us home. Throughout the journey Carolyn has suffered intermittent bouts of homesickness. Since leaving Hoonah, however, she has been single-mindedly anticipating her reunion with her husband. Although I assured her last night that my internal clock would awaken me at 5:30 A.M. in plenty of time to catch the plane, she feared sleeping in. Misreading her watch and believing it was time to leave, she woke me. Not checking on the time, I dressed in a daze and followed her past the clerk at the hostel, where we had beds for the night, who stared at us incredulously as we left only two hours after we had arrived. At the airport, we peered in disbelief through locked doors at the clock on the wall that said 1 A.M. After discovering the error and a moment of laughter bordering on hysteria, we decided to spend the night, she in the atrium of the airport, I in the car we had rented to get us to the airport on time. I have been teasing her about her error, but she, like the bird, has no shame and makes no apologies. She just laughs, totally amused with the absurdity of it all.

On the flight back we sat separately lost in thought. Clouds covered the land until Seattle, when it cleared and we could see below. Roads raced around mountains. The natural flow of the land was interrupted by a crazy quilt of development: strip-mined squares, straight-as-an-arrow power and pipe lines and patches of clear-cut vegetation. Dendritic flows bled from a ridgetop scar. The valley floors were carpeted with angular pieces of vegetation and housing. A scalloped roadcut encircled a muddy, blue-brown lake.

The steward and stewardess continued the passenger ritual. They pushed the cart, opened bottles, poured, asked the scripted questions and looked at us with the same impersonal stares. In the distance, Mount St. Helens continued to belch.

San Francisco appeared with its haphazard mosaic of houses. A great coliseum sat festering, green at the center and ringed with red bleachers and white concrete. I swallowed hard. As we landed I looked back in dismay at Carolyn.

San Francisco from the air looks as if it had been purged of life-giving support systems. No green hills, multi-colored chemical dumps, concrete. Petro planes as large as buildings. Tiny remnants of trees resemble cellophane-topped tooth picks. My eyes burn. Piped-in music, the roar of engines, cigarette smoke. The water tastes of chlorine. Cement tiers support the human multitudes in their youthful façade of luster and vitality.

C. F. B.

On to Salt Lake City. We deplaned and agreed things were beginning to look up a bit. Larry, Carolyn's husband, was there to

meet her. My daughter arrived. We picked up our packs, and
Carolyn and I headed our separate ways.

The next day she stopped by to return a few of my things. She
gave me a hug, thanked me, and promised to transcribe her jour-
nal notes. "There'll be a paper," she assured me as she headed out
the door. As usual, she wasted no time on good-byes.

Summer quarter had just ended. Things were winding down. I
was looking forward to the break and time to get back to my
journal notes.

The telephone rang. It was Steve, Carolyn's older son.

"How are you, Steve?"

"I'm all right."

A long pause.

"Is something wrong?"

"Flo, my mother died this afternoon. They say her heart
stopped beating."

I talked to Larry, assured him I'd be there as soon as I could,
made plane reservations, took the file marked "Carolyn" from
my cabinet, drove home, and cried through the night. A few
nights previously, I had awakened with a feeling of foreboding.
Unable to attach it to a family member in need, I concluded,
somewhat impersonally, that perhaps I was about to die.

Heavy-hearted, I boarded the plane the next day for Iowa.
Even in the toughest times, life had always held all possibilities
for me. Death I had accepted as a part of life. But now I found
it absolutely irreconcilable. I took out my journal and began
writing bits and pieces to try to gain some comprehension of
what had happened.

Continuing our quest for an ethic to live by in these ecolog-
ically difficult times, we had journeyed to Alaska, hoping that

glimpses of aboriginal life would inform us on how to live. We had sought moments and images to help us reconceptualize our place in the Earth community. Perhaps the project was misconceived, as Barry Lopez once expressed it: "We always seem to be turning to the Japanese or to Indians for clarification on points of spiritual order, and it is a habit which works against us, for it erodes self-respect."[8] Perhaps we should instead have looked closer at hand.

Early in the journey, I suddenly realized that walking at my side was a modern-day Artemis, goddess of wild animals, forest, and the hunt and patroness of childbirth. I began studying Carolyn as much as the territory.

I decided to do a series of photographs that would document her journey for her and her family, a Christmas gift to them. In so doing, I observed her more closely than I had any other human other than my children. As I framed her time and time again, I listened to the questions she asked the authors of the story we were reading and watched her interactions.

She walked on the Earth in beauty and harmony but never for a moment lost touch with her place. It dwelled within her; she, within it. Her cornsilk hair was intertwined with the tassels on cornstalks and with prairie grasses. Her eyes were the same blue as the sky. She understood and appreciated the complexities of the grasslands where humankind got its start.[9]

But wherever she traveled, she found a common ground with the beasts of the ocean and land, the birds of the air, the plants and the people, but especially with the children. She met them all in the same authentic way. Her blue eyes could soften in acceptance or become impenetrably steely. Her silence was disarming.

She was pantheistic and mystical, able to transcend the limitations of human consciousness. As we hiked along, she would suddenly stop, like an animal picking up stimuli beyond my senses. She would point or motion to me to listen. At other times, she would stop for long periods in silence and stare into the waves, clouds, or glaciers. At those times, I would stand silently awaiting her return.

Since the time we first met we had hiked many trails together. She asked me to chair her graduate committee and accepted me as a mentor. She always came pencil and notebook in hand. She listened with intensity to all that was said but said very little. Words were not her way. It was as if language was insufficient for what she felt. She would often respond with expressions of emotion rather than words: frowns, smiles, gestures, a wrinkled brow, little sounds emanating from the heart, murmurs. When she spoke, I listened.

Special memories return: One night sitting on a ridgetop at sunset, she pointed to a tree where she had focused on something with her binoculars. Through my glasses, I followed the line from her finger and found a drop of resin dripping from the ponderosa pine. For one brief radiant moment in its journey back to Earth, it had captured all of the energy of the setting sun and was shining like a star.

At another time when we were hiking with a group out of a hot desert canyon, we came to a tiny emerald pool in a sandstone basin. The others, intent on "getting out" did not want to stop. Carolyn stood by the pool. Under her breath I heard her whisper, "I don't think I can leave." I convinced the others that we would only be a minute and would meet them up the trail. The four of us who stayed behind quickly stripped off our clothes and ran into the shallow icy pool, laughing and splashing like children. The contrast with the desert heat was shocking. I insisted we all become "completely immersed." As we dried and dressed, Carolyn said, "You know why this is so wonderful? Because at this moment I know exactly how each of you feels."

Her quest in life was for common experiences that joined her to the Earth and its creatures. But she was discriminating in how and with whom she spent her time. Expending energy on mindless people or a heavy pack were one and the same for her. Time was precious and not to be wasted. At times when she disagreed, she set her jaw firmly and walked away. She showed a selectivity that bordered on intolerance. She was not prone to polite or idle conversation.

Hiking on the beach one day, she picked up a mussel and tried to pry it open. It wouldn't budge. She looked at me with amusement and said, "I really understand now what 'clamming up' means. I need to be more open." We looked at each other and smiled, knowing that "to be really free is to have no choice at all."[10] She would continue to be as she was. Like the cormorant in tune with the wind, like the bird with "no shame," she had no choice.

The plane landed in Sioux City as the setting sun accentuated textured patterns across fields of tasseled corn. I knew her home must be nestled somewhere in the wooded Loess Hills running along the Little Sioux River.

Her husband, Larry, and sons, Steve and Paul, met me. Although we had met many times in passing, we were united at that moment in our common grief. I asked to view her body but stayed only a moment. She really was dead. Then we headed to their home and to the family who waited. I knew them all. We had met before over coffee on long twilight evenings in Alaska. Now we planned the memorial service that would take place the next day.

Just as I knew them, they knew me. But similarly we knew very little of the ordinary events that transpired between Carolyn and each other. She rarely spoke of such things. When she spoke, she talked of people and relationships, not of events. When we had completed plans for the memorial, in response to their need to know something about the summer, I added my slides to Carolyn's, set up the projector, and explained where we had been and what we had done. I added passages from Carolyn's letters, papers, and journals.

At midnight, we went to bed. I asked to sleep in the living room, where she loved to spend long winter evenings by the wood-burning stove. Paul brought me the sleeping bag she had purchased especially for our first field studies in Southern Utah. I lay there in the darkness—numbed and uncomprehending. Larry, Steve, and Paul returned one at a time. We talked until dawn broke.

The burial took place at ten. Larry had chosen a plot on the crest of a knoll at the edge of the Loess Hills she so dearly loved. The graveside services were appropriately simple. At the end, we stood together not wanting to leave. A few drops of rain fell. Larry remarked that he must identify the prairie grasses and perhaps plant more. (Don't worry about prairie grasses, Larry. She won't be confined here.)

The minister came up to me and whispered, "Are these the Loess Hills?" Quietly, I explained the ecological significance of the formation that had its origins in windblown glacial sediment. (Don't laugh, Carolyn, a little geology never hurt anyone. Who knows, perhaps we have a convert to your "civil religion," those celebrations of life you created here in your Loess Hills Seminars.)

Following the services, I went to Carolyn's office to locate a paper she had written in one of my graduate seminars. The halls of the state education agency where she worked were lined with enlargements of pictures she had taken of children reflecting the "sense of wonder" about which Rachel Carson[11] had written and that Carolyn so cherished in children.

Filed meticulously in huge cabinets were environmental resource materials. One contained ten years of "Utah" notes. The file marked "Curriculum and Consciousness"[12] took me back to that summer seminar. Later she told me it had been a turning point in her career. But where was her paper from the Dark Canyon field studies? I picked up an unmarked file, opened it, and found here essay "The Quality of My Life." My final tribute to her would be to read her own words.

The memorial service was simple and beautiful. Friends recalled her dedication to children, womanhood, environmental awareness, and conservation work. Steve stood tall reading a beautiful message sent by Sylvan Runkell, the retired naturalist who worked closely with her throughout the years. In closing, I read excerpts from her own reflections on her life:

I gave of myself, frankly and honestly. I tried to be in touch with my feelings and intellect and acted accordingly. I accepted from others took the love they were willing to share; took of their time, their wisdom, their excitement, their values and the help they were willing to give; pondered with them our questions—and breathed a thank you. I gave and accepted their feedback.

Giving and taking has meaning for me. Sometimes I feel I have little to give but my friends tell me I give much, and by accepting this, I acknowledge and recognize the existence and importance of what they give to me. I am always struck by the underestimates we have of ourselves—people not realizing their potential, not understanding the tremendous value of the gifts they have given.

Stability, gravity, uplifts.
Lives and landforms are
momentary holding places
each a vantage point—
a resting spot.

I am what I am—
ancestor of my ancestors
of the earth and spirit.

Nurtured by the wind and prairie—
seeing through the eyes of my grandmothers,
nourished by my mother—
following my father's steps.

The waiting trees
complete without adornment
are my mentors.
Completely cyclic
nourishing and being nourished.

Adolescent
feet upon the continents
awakened by surprises
life-blood, energy
emerging
my mind and body one
gift of the universe
rebirth.

Loving shared
beyond my understanding—
duck-blind in wintery dawn,
oil on canvas, paintings in caves
to contemplate
talking under starry skies
in summer breezes
beside him on the river bank
playing, laughing, becoming
we are.

INDWELLINGS

Paul and Steve
born to us in cities
"I'm different, Mom."
nurtured by communities
the big city
the atomic bombs we're going to drop
the plastics!

And yet holding humanity in our arms
you walk away
we watch you grow
witnessing surely
evolution of the mind and spirit
toward perfection.

Eating broccoli
I feel the sand between my teeth
remember its origin
akin to my own.

Hey, woman. Hey, man.
Ponder with me the journey's map
about humanity
the universe
and our connectedness.

I, like the canyonlands,
ageless process
of quiet, continual change
source of energy
to enhance or defile

Relationships
so much a part of me
in stratified layers
and boulders strewn
shaping.

Seeing more perspectives
with a purpose
overcoming the forces
that thrust me into
indifference and inertia

sharing wisdom
I must care.

C. F. B.

A string quartet played a spirited melody that stirred our hearts and brought hope as hundreds of us filtered into the reception hall where two projectors were showing Carolyn's slides, one with slides of children, the other with slides of her Alaska trip, among which I had interspersed my slides of her. Displayed on a table were recent drawings by Paul, and Barry Lopez's book *Of Wolves and Men,* the last and one of the "most important books" she had read.

Afterward the family gathered back at the house. The adults visited, the children played on the lawn with "encounter bats." I walked up the hill into the woods behind the house and sat alone. Later Larry and I opened hundreds of letters and contributions that would make possible the nature trail and guidebook she had planned.

It was dark. The good-byes were over, and Carolyn's mother and siblings had gone home to Nebraska. The house was quiet.

I lay in the sleeping bag listening to the call of a whippoorwill. Paul came in and sat in the rocker. "I'd like to talk to you. The Carolyn you spoke of last night was not the Mom I knew. Flo, let me tell you about Mom. . . . "

The next morning Larry called me to the window to see the doe and her fawn at the edge of the clearing. (I agree, Carolyn, this is "one of the most beautiful places on Earth.")

On the way to the airport, Larry and I stopped by the wood-shed. Stacked neatly were the huge cut logs she and her family had salvaged for firewood when a wooded area was destroyed to make room for development. Since then, it had provided fuel for their wood-burning stove. The neatly stacked logs were symbol-ic of Carolyn's devotion to things of consequence. In the wake of destruction, she would not allow the trees to be wasted. During the cold winter months, she relished the warmth that each piece brought her, like the friendship of a dying friend.

On the plane heading back to Salt Lake City, I took out the little green journal she had carried in the pouch on her belt. Larry had offered it to me so that I might trace her footsteps and compare them with my own. Bits and pieces, out of sequence, they would continue our dialogue when juxtaposed with my observations.

Carolyn was gone. Yet she walked beside me as she did with Larry in Iowa and with her mother on the plains of Nebraska. Dispersed, nonetheless, she spoke to me, dwelled in my heart and mind. An authentic person, true to the Earth, true to her Being, true to Others, she forced me to reconceptualize my dwelling in place. "A flush of rose and the whole thing starts again."[13]

∾

In the years since Carolyn's death, I have continued to feel her presence and influence and am still completely mystified by her untimely death. At the time her passing devastated me. For months I could not talk about her or think about her without a flood of desolation sweeping over me. At first I tried to rationalize my feelings, I suppose the way most people have faced this great mystery once they have become conscious of it. I placed it in an ecological framework: In the cycle of life on this planet, death is a necessary part. There cannot be birth or regeneration without it. It fuels new life.

The rational explanations did not erase the loss. My response to her death was a surprise even to myself, since I had always been able to face death with courage, acceptance, and faith in the natural course of life processes. It was even more surprising since ours was not a close friendship; that is, we were not in constant day-to-day contact, sharing life's problems and joys. Involvement, time spent together, ideas shared, and expectations were limited. Rather than leading to more involvement, it was a hands-off affair, respectful, with no demands, dependency, or intent for mastery or exploitation of the other. How then could such a relationship, which in fact avoided deep ties, have been so important to me? Reviewing those moments, I now read the text and context of our friendship and its lasting influence on me rather than the heartfelt loss.

Most psychological theories of development place great importance on the influences during childhood and adolescence of parents and "significant others" who by their actions and example greatly influence the course of our lives. If books in the popular press reflect developmental theories accurately, growth in maturity and understanding are dependent on early nurturing experiences and are reinforced later by relationships in love, marriage, and career. Little is said of adult friendship, as I experienced it with Carolyn, that furthers mature understanding of the innermost self and its continuity with the outside world. Jungian psychoanalysts offer interesting explanations that speak to my experience.

"There lies a wilderness," says John Layard, "in which complete separation from the womb of the mother must be made before one can enter another plane of union. And this wilderness is life, conscious and active life overhung by the shadow of death." According to Layard there are two choices one can make in life: In one the path of individuation is shirked, because the "spiritual umbilical cord" is never cut; in the other the task is accepted "whereby the union with the internal *anima* or positive mother-image is gradually formed" in which "the *anima* acts as a bridge, thus leaving the individual free to conduct life without negative projections due to unrealistic dependence on human love."[14] It seems to me that in this way, friendship that nurtures and challenges the growth of participants is itself a manifestation of the *anima* about which Layard speaks.

In such a friendship, ego boundaries, which are said to be more permeable in women than in men, dissolve, and we are able to share a psychic ecotone that borders on the virginal territory of the other, a domain where differences mingle. Walking away from it, we feel changed. Our vision is overlaid by that of our friend's. In my case, I became more aware of the relativity of my ethics that stood in contrast to the purity of Carolyn's. Facing up to her unflinching criticism of American materialism and bracing my body against the great seawind were one and the same and cut through my uncritical orientation with a penchant for compromise. Because of her influence, I determined to be more thoughtful and critical of my actions and their impact on the Earth I claimed to love.

Others have suggested that hidden within this friendship was, in fact, a homosexual attraction that I repressed. I do not deny that this might be the case, knowing as I do that we can

127

hide from our deepest emotions. But whether or not sexual desire is repressed, such a friendship puts into perspective the "sacrificial principle," suggested by Layard, "which aims, so far as human affairs are concerned, at the ultimate transformation of instinct into spirit."[15] He suggests that this is how the religious are able to transform their human desires into love of God, or Goddess, I may add. I propose, furthermore, that this may be how humans extend their physical and emotional desires into a spiritual or mystical love of Nature.

By some immutable force, this friend has access to that place where, as M. Esther Harding described it, we are "one-in-ourselves"[16] and by example, or through sincere interest, questions the very essence of our being. She comes to the threshold of our psycho-physical self, to which we return in creativity or for restoration when we haven't had time for ourselves, have forgotten where we are, don't remember who we are, are depleted for having given too much, or become defensive because we haven't been given enough. As the Other, this friend remains distinct and separate and does not give herself over to us. She stands on the boundary for only a brief moment, looks in and then leaves us to our own thoughts, which are no longer our own.

Our journey permitted contemplation, uninterrupted by familial concerns or career demands. We stopped midstream in our lives "to smell the flowers," to explore that creative core that fuels our souls[17] and went neglected as we established ourselves as working mothers in man's world. In some of the most pristine land on Earth, we explored the outer landscape, the undefiled body of the Great Goddess, that fecund resource of wisdom that flows from purity of being and balance of forces, our perfect model of interrelatedness. We shared empathy and unconscious identity with each other. These experiences tapped our spontaneous, creative impulses, and mythopoetic language filled our journals.

Carolyn's death momentarily overshadowed, but did not erase, our original intent for the journey, to learn what we could about living on this Earth from Native Alaskans. Images of their authentic being and sounds of their voices, which had often contradicted their rational interpretations of rightful claims as seen through the mist of consumer society, intruded into the daily grind of administration that once more became my preoccupation. The tension between the veracity of actions and native patois, in Native Alaskans as well as in Anglo fishers and wolf-lovers, and the posturing for power and the abstracted language of academics, led me to assert publicly that grassroots movements seemed more vital and viable than contemporary structured political ideologies or social theories that were anthropocentric and discounted nonhuman components of the natural world. This proclamation was not taken as good news by close colleagues, who were divided into two camps exploring developmental and critical theories. Ladd Holt, my friend and collaborator for years, whose remarkably astute vision had been a backdrop for my increasing understanding, bid me farewell and joined the others. Isolated intellectually, I poured myself fervently into increasingly frustrating administrative duties, on the one hand, and, on the other, into spiritually restorative work with an exciting group of graduate students. As with many endings, the conclusion to my schizoid existence came unannounced and unwanted. The grand finale sent me reeling. When it arrived, I returned to Alaska to the heart of wildness for comfort and healing. This time the bear was there to lend a helping paw.

5 ~❧ The Shape of Things

Body and spirit express each other and cannot be separated.

—Maurice Merleau-Ponty[1]

When Jeff Soder stopped by my office to invite me to visit the Henry Moore exhibit with him, I accepted readily. We had been working hard at our desks in the quiet of a spring weekend—he on his final master's project, I on departmental affairs. Little did I suspect that this break in the day's routine would bring with it a lasting change of mind and heart.

The day was clear, cold, and still. Bare branches covered with buds anticipated spring. A few brave daffodils called down the sun to the brown lawns washed with a tinge of green. We walked briskly down the path to the Museum of Fine Arts.

In the foyer we were greeted by a huge poster of Henry Moore in his eighty-seventh year sculpting yet another maquette. I glanced at it briefly, surprised and impressed by the wisdom and vitality his figure suggested. Until that moment, appalling as it now seems to me, I had neither heard of Henry Moore nor seen one of his sculptures. I walked into the first exhibit room with curiosity and without any presuppositions about what I was about to see.

The soothing museum ambience with its dark carpets and subdued lighting enticed me into the first hall, where maquettes in glass cases and full-sized sculptures were arranged engagingly. His drawings were hung on the walls, as were large blowups of his words describing his work.

131

The first tiny figure in a glass case drew me in and then mush-roomed, massive and grounded in repose. "Do not touch!" the signs read. One can be touched without touching. One can be pulled in, can pour into gray pitted concrete, black African won-derstone, white plasters, coarsehill stones, and travertine marbles, or into bronze, polished black, or iridescent green. One can crawl in and curl up and then follow the curve from inside support to outside and back into swellings erupting from within.

Tracing the contours around and into and out of the figures, I peered down into eyes bored through the skull, into slit mouths conveying satiety, grief, indifference, pain, and fulfillment in blaring understatements. The strong curve of backs, broad and solid, were juxtaposed with concave chests, crushed, but with perpetual breasts. The form left a painful knot in the pit of my stomach. Evisceration. Dismemberment. The eternal attachment of the child, feeding. All was laid bare.

We moved in silence to the room holding his most recent works. In these he had returned to the eternal landscape: he had separated body into limbs, breasts, trunk and had concentrated as much upon the spaces in between as upon those parts. The stark white plaster standing before its replica in dazzling bronze played on the theme of space and form and their inseparability. He provided this explanation:

> You see, I think a sculptor is a person who is interested in the shape of things . . . and it's not just the shape of any one thing, but the shape of anything and everything, the growth of a flower, the hard tense strength of a bone, the strong, solid fleshiness of a beech tree trunk.[2]

Like the sculptor, I too became possessed by the shape of things. Over the next few weeks, I returned again and again to the exhibit as the doorman eyed me suspiciously. The reclining figures invited me back each day. Form and space were sufficient to fascinate me—but there was a deeper mystery that drew me to them that had yet to emerge.

Henry Moore had ignored the male, and with purity of intention and will, had created repeatedly the monstrous beauty that is primal woman, the essence of death, rebirth, and life. The eternal wisdom and limitation of the body incarnate—desires satisfied and unsatisfied, aloneness and inseparability, limits and possibilities, reality and dreams—he molded in messages all the more profound because Henry Moore really didn't *know* what he was doing. His hands responded unfailingly to the abiding question in his heart and mind: How does one create a reclining figure, eternal and powerful? How does one set in concrete all that it means to be human?

When Walt Prothero's letter arrived that spring inviting me on an Arctic expedition, I accepted without hesitation.[3] His invitation came as I was facing the wrath of faculty over what they considered my inappropriate autocratic manner of administering the department. Alaska once more beckoned in complex and obscure ways.

Amidst preparations for departure later in the summer, two fears gave me pause to reconsider: doubts about my ability to withstand the demands of the harsh Arctic wilderness, and a dreadful fear of *Ursus arctos horribilis,* the grizzly bear. The integrity and purity of untouched tundra was inviting, but to reach it this time I would have to leave behind the very edge of civilization. The opportunity to observe Walt, an ancestral hunting type, at close range appealed to me. But more than anything, it was the dream that lured me there, the dream that had visited me two long years before:

*I was walking with a man, carrying a child in my arms. Vast
expanses of tundra fell away in all directions around us. The man
walked slightly ahead of me, and as I followed him, I kept a wary
eye on two young bears following behind. Noticing, he assured me I
had nothing to fear. We stopped on the crest of a ridge; the sky was
beginning to lighten. Anticipating a sunrise, I was surprised by
shafts of light flaring up and undulating like curtains in a breeze
across the entire horizon. I turned to speak to the man, but in his
stead was a magnificent bear with a head so large it filled my
entire field of vision. Looking into his close-set eyes, I was unafraid,
assured by some primordial faith that we should be there together.
We stood side by side, he on his hind legs swaying back and forth,
witnessing the spectacle of the sky.*

A longing for repose and escape from the stress of academic
life enticed me toward the pristine ambience of the National
Arctic Wildlife Refuge, some three hundred miles north of the
Arctic Circle. With summer school and administrative duties
behind me, I was packed and standing self-consciously in line at
the airline baggage check-in counter with my well-worn walking
stick in hand. The ticket agent and people in line stared at me
with curiosity and amusement as I checked my baggage, a thirty
gallon steel drum that I had purchased according to Walt's
instructions and had filled with warm clothing, camping equipment, and 180 dehydrated meals that I had prepared and pack-
aged, my share of the food we would need for the journey.

Day 1   *Circle Alaska*

*"This is the End," the sign reads as you enter Circle, Alaska.
Walt met my plane last night in Fairbanks, and we drove the 150
miles over the graveled Steese Highway to this Kutchin Indian vil-*

lage where he has built a cabin and makes his home. The sign refs to the most northern point of the U.S. highway system on the banks of the Yukon River, but with my unrelenting fear of bears, I take the message literally. I am prepared for any eventuality. Before leaving home, I updated my will, and in my pack I carry a white bear fetish with shell, turquoise, and sinew given me by Terry for protection.

We have been busy all day preparing to fly out tomorrow with Roger Dowding, a bush pilot. I have been writing letters and trying unsuccessfully to eliminate and lighten the contents of my backpack. I cannot leave behind the books that I carefully selected for this journey: Simone de Beauvoir's The Ethics of Ambiguity, *which speaks to my present state of mind; the words of Henry Moore in* Henry Moore: the Reclining Figure; *Maurice Merleau-Ponty's* Sense and Nonsense, *which I hope will help me make sense of the nonsense of the past few months; and* The Sacred Paw, *written by Paul Shepard and Barry Sanders, on the "bear in nature, myth, and literature," given to me by Paul, whom I recently met and whose books have been primary resources for students and myself.*[4]

The neighboring families are drying salmon. The men mend nets while the women fillet the red-meated fish. Down the road the trapper, in the vest he has fashioned from caribou and grizzly pelts, is feeding the dogs that pull his sled to trap lines in the winter. They rise out of their kennels snarling viciously each time I pass by. The Yukon River flows past the cabin. Sandhill cranes that nest on its banks fly over in twos and fours, sounding as they pass.

Day 5   *The Sheep Camp, Brooks Range*

We are camped at forty-five hundred feet on a soft bed of lichen that absorbs the rain and provides a cushion for our tents.

The campsite allows a panoramic view to the southeast of tundra slopes, mostly above timberline, tumbling to the Sheenjek River far to the east. Above to the northwest the steep faces of the mountains in the Brooks Range rise majestically to eight thousand feet. We are within a valley where glacier and water have sliced through the soft sediments of a great anticline. Traces of bedrock are visible in cliff faces above where the severe climate has worn the mountains to pearly-gray, rounded contours. Nestled at the center, our tents sit within a huge reclining Mother Goddess with knees, breasts, and long ridge-limbs separated by green tundra space.

An eternity has passed since that morning only four days ago when I stood shivering at the edge of a gravel runway waiting for Roger to ready his blue and white Cessna 185 for takeoff. He was unable to get a weather report; these are usually obtained by calling various spotters on the telephone for visual observations, but that day they couldn't see the sky. Three raging muskeg fires had reduced visibility to zero at Fort Yukon and in the surrounding area. We took off nonetheless. Parts of the Yukon Flats were obliterated, and at one point we had to climb out of smoke that engulfed the cabin. Beyond the fires, Roger put the plane on automatic, took a copy of Playboy *from the pocket behind his seat, and began reading. With some concern, I watched him out of the corner of my eye as at times he leaned against the instrument panel and dozed as we bumped along over rough air currents above a jigsaw of lakes, dwarfed spruce, and caribou trails. Soon muskeg gave way to an expansive valley flanked by mountains with a stream meandering in huge sweeps across its width. Peering over the instrument panel, Roger pointed to Lobo Lake, where, he said, he would meet me in twenty-four days if all went well. We flew up the valley toward the mountains rising ahead of us, whose north face drains into the Arctic Ocean. From time to time he executed unannounced dives (that left my heart in my throat and my stomach in disarray) to check on wolves and moose. Then, as we approached the south face*

136

of the mountain, he swooped low, circled a steel-gray sandbar along the Sheenjek River, touched down on the near edge and stopped a "heartbeat" (to use a trite but very true expression) from the water on the opposite end.

Walt and Roger hopped from the plane and began unloading our gear quickly as I for a moment stood on wobbly legs trying to gain control of my stomach and bearing. Roger took off, tipping his wing as he headed south. Walt inflated rubber rafts into which we loaded the gear, and we floated to the confluence of the Sheenjek and the unnamed stream we were to follow into the Brooks Range. We cached our supplies in two thirty-gallon steel drums and hid them in the willows. Then Walt sprayed them with ovencleaner to deter bears, who, he said, had once ripped his drums apart. On the beach were tracks of caribou, moose, wolf, fox, and grizzly. I looked at the huge footprints of the bear and then placed my hands within them as I tried to visualize the animal that might have left such an impression.

It took us two days to hike to this campsite, through a treacherous mountain stream with smooth tumbled boulders, and across muskeg thick with cushions of buoyant lichen and moss that had overgrown rock and fallen trees to form hidden pitfalls into which we occasionally broke. I hiked with extreme caution, knowing the difficulty a broken leg or sprained ankle would present. Huge fresh scats of bears, tinted red and blue by the remains of berries, dotted the landscape. Walt walked ahead with his rifle and proceeded cautiously whenever we did not have an open view. When the mountains were clearly in sight, he began scanning them for Dall sheep which graze high on their tops and from the distance appear as small white dots.

We chose this campsite because it sits high on the mountainside with a view on all sides and is near a stream—and because at the time I could hike no farther. As we set up our tents, caribou from the Porcupine herd streamed along a trail above the camp, oblivious of us. A grizzly roamed a nearby ridge eating berries. High above on the edge of a cliff was a lone Dall sheep.

Shortly after we made camp, it began to rain. I watched incredulous as Walt took his rifle, said he was going hunting, and headed up the mountain. Exhausted and fearful, I crept into my tent and fell asleep trembling. Somewhere in my dreams I heard the shot, and later I was awakened by the sound of heaving and puffing and something heavy falling to the ground with a thud outside my tent. I peered out at an enormous head of a ram, with a cape of white fur flowing from its neck. I reluctantly emerged from the tent, lit the gas stove, and prepared food for Walter as he changed into dry clothes. He drank warm liquids and ate until his body had regained warmth and energy. Then he spread the cape of fur about the huge ram skull and faced it into the night sky with glassy-eyes peering into the rain and circular horns framing its ghostly face. Before turning in, he announced that we would hike up to get the sheep meat the next day and carry it back down to the Sheenjek. My firm reply as I crawled into my tent was that there was no way I would go anywhere the next day.

Exhausted from the hike and changing weather, we slept deeply and almost continually for two days. Arctic days and twilight nights merged as the rain continued to fall. Except for an hour or two in the middle of the night, there was enough light to read by. I nibbled granola or trail mix, and at times, when I heard him stir, prepared a meal with Walt. Today, on the third day, we arose from our deathlike torpor to hike to the high slope to retrieve the sheep meat. Walt removed the ribs and sliced meat from the bone, leaving the carcass for ravens and bear. Back at camp, we hung the meat in a willow near the stream, away from camp. This evening we braised ribs over a fire of dwarf willow and birch. The taste of tallow reminded me of my childhood on the sheep ranch. I felt at home. There was no more talk of returning to the Sheenjek.

Day 6   *Sheep Camp*

Today we went "hunting" with binoculars and cameras. We climbed the steep tundra slopes laced with scree, leaned into gale-force winds, and crossed the divide into the headwaters of Old Woman's Creek. I nestled down in a protected spot among boulders as Walt, with next year's hunt in mind, stalked and photographed six Dall sheep grazing under cliffs nearby.[5] The sun played across the slopes. Buoyant cumulus clouds driven by high winds created a kaleidoscope of shadow and light and changing hues. I waited expectantly in this sea of color for brief moments of sunshine and warmth. During the days we have been here, the slopes have changed from pea green to burnt umber. Berry bushes are scarlet, magenta, and burnt orange. Giant saxifrage leaves are yellow, edged with brown, and the willows are golden.

We hiked the creek bed back down to camp. Signs of Ursus were everywhere. In a huge mound hollowed at the center, a daybed for the mother bear and cubs, Walt found golden clumps of her underhair which he gave to me. It was soft as down and had a sweet, spicy fragrance.

The stream was bordered with a mossy carpet. As we descended, it grew and in places coursed under limestone into dark caverns out of which echoed subterranean sounds. Near camp we found a fresh caribou kill, probably by wolves, Walt said. The skull and vertebrae were entirely stripped of flesh; only the skin ripped in many pieces remained, and the legs were missing.

Back at camp we saw a grizzly crossing the skyline high on the ridge where we had gone to retrieve the ram. Silhouetted against the twilight sky, it lifted its nose to the heavens and then turned and ambled over the hill. It seemed unaware of two respectful humans, dwarfed, far below, staring in awe at its massive, shaggy form.

*For two days storms have repeatedly moved through this val-
ley. Each morning the snow line descends, and the mountains are
shrouded in clouds. Last night the splatter of raindrops on my tent
turned to the rustle of granular snow. At midnight, all was quiet.
This morning I awoke to a thick, white blanket of snow that covered landscape and tent. As I made a quick trip to empty my blad-
der, I saw the gray form of a wolf trailing a lone caribou across the
stream.*

*During these stormy days, we have again returned to the pri-
vacy of our tents/nests/caves. Rested, I now spend my time reading,
writing, and thinking. I roll over my thoughts as I find a new position of repose. The raindrops and stream below provide background
for meditation. I have been reading the description of how, from
the time she gives birth to her young in the den during hibernation
until they leave her side, the mother bear "licks them into shape"
and educates them as they grow. She cuffs them if necessary, and
"when they are old enough, she deliberately sets them on their
own."[6] My thoughts dwell on relationships, duties to others, and
my perceived role to form and "shape up" my children and "other
people's children."[7] Bear mother. Have I licked these children well?
I sniff bear hair, anticipate fleeting possibilities out of the corner of
my eye. I have been too busy licking others. Now I must lick my
own wounds.*

*Early yesterday, Walt left camp for an all-day hike into the
high mountains. He did not invite me along; in fact, he strongly
suggested I do a "solo" to overcome my "irrational fear of bears."
After cleaning up around camp and gathering wood, I decided to
take his advice, although the prospect of hiking without Walt and
his gun terrified me.*

I climbed straight up from camp toward a ridgeline. The tundra was pockmarked with bear diggings for roots and ground squirrels. As I walked toward the ridgetop, I kept imagining meeting a bear head-on as it came over the top from the other side. My heart raced with exertion and fear until I crested the ridge and could see in all directions. Another drainage basin fell away on the other side, joining the creek that ran through camp and on down to the Sheenjek. In the distance were the Davidson Mountains, snow-covered at high elevations. I lay in the sun, listening to the wind howl around a matterhorn to the east, an uncommon feature in this land where everything is weathered smooth. After years of reclining figures, Henry Moore had returned to this primal landscape, where knees, breasts, and hips are separated. Here the form of space becomes more understandable and more pulpable.

Walking back to camp, I kept alert, scanning the tundra for signs of movement. Having faced the bear alone, I was beginning to understand my fears. I respect the bear all the more, and should I meet her, I will undoubtedly quake, or perhaps faint dead away. But now I am beginning to deal with the bear herself and not some spectral creature hidden behind each knoll and shrub upon which I have heaped my unnamed anxieties.

Today I joined Walt for a hike up the canyon where yesterday he saw a sow and her two cubs. At one point, I left him and crossed a saddle to look down the long slopes toward the north. Rocky pools held tobacco-colored sphagnum. Mounds of cushion plants, grizzly gold, were swollen plump from recent precipitation and nutmeg-brown saxifrage smelled like incense. Frosted bearberries and blueberries that had lost their juicy turgidity left a bittersweet taste in my mouth; the cranberries growing flat on the ground were crisp and tart.

My legs grow short as I walk across the vast tundra. It dwarfs me; I become squat and stocky. As I lean over to sip water from a placid pool, I expect to see reflected the face of a crone, wrinkled, leathered, with a toothless smile and squinting eyes shining with secrets of what has been, of things yet to come.

Walt has made no mentioned of leaving this camp, and I think he has enjoyed the stay. But the time for leaving draws near. Our food is running low. He believes we are the only humans to have walked on this land since time began. The Indigenous People did not come this way, he says, and modern hunters do not come here. I accept his declaration although it is difficult to comprehend. Nonetheless it makes me tread lightly and respectfully.

Day 13   *Sheenjek River*

Yesterday morning we awoke to sunshine and, with only one day's supply of food left, decided to leave the "sheep camp," hike down to our cache, and begin our float down the Sheenjek. The temporal dimension of this mountain experience will remain eternal and deep for me. Time had substance and persistence.

Walt walked ahead with the ram's horns on his pack, like some Paleolithic hunter. We hiked hard all day, across muskeg rather than down along the creek. When finally we crossed its confluence with the Sheenjek, I felt a deep affinity for this little stream that sang to us in the mountains. It was like a child whose beginnings I had witnessed. It had grown and now joined another stream on its path to the Pacific. We set up our camp on a sandbar near it and near the cache.

Walt went fishing for grayling this afternoon. It was a sunny, warm day. I gathered wood and then decided to bathe. Unable to withstand the icy-cold waters of the stream, I filled every canteen and pan, built a fire, and heated the water. I stood on a plastic bag and lathered my entire body with Dr. Bronner's Eucalyptus Soap, shampooed my hair, and rinsed down all at once. I saved the last pan of hot water and poured it over me slowly. Although I used only about two gallons of water, it felt luxurious and was my first "shower" in two weeks.

Just as I finished dressing, Roger flew over, circled twice, tipped his wings, and headed up the Sheenjek. Walt returned, propped up his duffle bag as a backrest, asked if I'd cook dinner, lay back in the sun, and fell asleep. Using his cast-iron fry pan (now that we're floating rather than backpacking, we have more equipment), I prepared a good-looking fried quiche from his store of backpacking food. I broiled the last of the sheep meat and called him to dinner. As we finished eating, Rick, a friend of Walt's, appeared on the river in his raft. He had flown in with Roger— two weeks earlier than expected. He and Walt will hunt moose together after I leave them at Lobo Lake.

Day 15   *Sheenjek River*

We started floating down the Sheenjek early this morning. Time on the river was peaceful and restful. Huge clouds formed and dissipated in place just above us. High above, cirrus clouds rippled in windrows across the sky and altocumulus encircled the horizon. Here clouds are touchable and at times form around us as they do in the stratosphere.

A mew gull began circling and diving in order to distract us from her offspring, a gawky brown juvenile barely remaining airborne below her. I lay back on my backpack to witness her aerobatics against the backdrop of streaming cirrus clouds, her show staged and choreographed precisely. She dove, crying out loudly. At raft level, her cry changed to a chatter that sounded like talk. As I talked back to her, she would rise, dive, cry and chatter again. She repeated the sequence over and over, and each time she turned sharply at eye level and soared up into her airy world, I was carried aloft.

The fall colors have deepened. Golden willows are luminous and cotton grass and opening pods of fireweed, backlighted, stand like candles along the shore. The long, red pods of fireweed have always fascinated me since the day I gathered a huge bouquet and placed it on my dining room table. The next morning when I came downstairs, I thought I had died and gone to heaven. The pods had opened during the night, releasing seeds with feathery plumes that floated throughout the first floor of my home. It took me weeks to vacuum them all up. When the pod dries it begins parting at the top, reminiscent of its four-parted pistil that caught pollen and brought it to this ripe stage. Inside, the seeds are lined up alternately along a single stalk. As the pod dries, it splits apart, and the interlaced wings of the seeds pull each other out of their compact setting. In perfect collaboration they set each other free to float individually on the slightest breeze.

After most of the day on the river, we chose this sandbar for our new camp. It is about a half mile long. Brushman Mountain rises to the west. The terrain has changed; there are more trees and willows. We will stay here several days before floating to my final camp at Lobo Lake.

Day 15   *Sheenjek River*

The loon's call reaches me each morning on the mists of cold, gray dawns, the sound rising like a baby's wail. Penetrating and sad, yet somehow familiar, it takes me back to times that match the tones.

Rick, Walt, and I hiked up Brushman Mountain the day before yesterday to view the Sheenjek Valley, but yesterday they headed out alone in opposite directions. Walt wanted Rick to do a "solo" to prepare for the hunt. They took their rifles to protect themselves in case of unexpected encounters with bear or moose.

I stayed in camp to do chores, clean up, write, and read. I was writing in my journal when I heard the shot echo down the mountain. It occurred to me that perhaps one of them had come across a caribou, which had all but but vanished from the valley since that first storm. Later Rick returned from his hike downstream and asked if I had heard the shot. It was getting late, so we prepared dinner and ate, placing some aside for Walt.

Then I went for a stroll along the river. The sandbar was crisscrossed with tracks of the "big four": moose, caribou, grizzly, and wolf. At one point wolf and grizzly tracks ran perfectly parallel as if the two had been out together for an afternoon jaunt. When I returned to camp, I could hear Walt talking to Rick.

"Well, did you bring home the bacon?" I asked Walt as I approached.

He walked up to me, held out something in his hand, and said, "Here, give this to your friend."

In my hand he placed the bloody penis of a grizzly bear.

Day 18   *Sheenjek River*

I have spent the best part of two days helping Walt "flesh" the grizzly skin. I now appreciate the labor that goes into the preparation of animal hides. After removing all of the fat, we rubbed it well with salt. It has been hard, tedious work and made my head ache.

We hiked up above camp yesterday to retrieve the skin and bring back some grizzly meat. Last night we had grizzly steaks and spinach soufflé. Walt and I had great difficulty swallowing. Rick ate with gusto. Later in my tent, I heard Rick comment that the night before, after the grizzly kill, Walt had looked and acted differently.

I too had noticed the change. He had a strange look in his eye and was trancelike and euphoric. Walt was usually a quiet man, but his voice was now louder and more animated. Along the way I have been questioning him about his drive to hunt. When he encounters an animal, he says, adrenalin flows, breathing and heart rate increase. He is primed for action. He has to consciously disengage from the experience in order to aim and shoot accurately. Hunting, he says, is a primal instinct and as natural as eating and sex, an experience that cannot be rationalized; it is tremendously challenging and reinforces what he values: independence, power, skill, and self-sufficiency. It is a statement of what he is.

Today I questioned him further about his response to killing the bear. This time, he said, there was something more than excitement and reinforcement in the hunt. He had encountered the bear unexpectedly at close range as he came up over a ridge. He immediately engaged a shell, and the noise startled the bear, who stood up and then lunged toward him. Walt shot him in the neck at twenty feet. As the bullet hit, the bear looked Walt in the eye before falling over backward, dead. At first Walt would not say what meaning the look carried. Finally he explained: "I saw the look of death in his eyes and knew that it could have been me just as easily. If the shot had been one inch more to the right, he wouldn't have fallen. That look made me realize all the more that we all count the same. I am no more privileged than he. It was his time, but mine is coming." It was very hard to eat the bear, he added, because he realized it was just a matter of chance that the bear was the one being eaten for dinner.

The hunt seemed indeed to be a primal activity that challenged Walt to the utmost and took him to death's door in humility and thanksgiving. It called up an ancestral image that still ran through his veins. He protected and prized the heads and skins and admired their beauty. He ate the meat and shared it with others. His aim was straight as an arrow. He was fearless and independent, and he challenged the physical limits of his body. His dedication to hunting did not seem based on violence and domination but rather appeared congruent with Tribal People's respect and thankfulness to the animal for the life taken—and given.[8]

Day 20   *Sheenjek River*

Today I boiled the bear penis and removed the tissue from the small delicate os bacculum. *Penis bones, called "usiks" here in Alaska, are collectors' items. I will have this one fashioned as a pendant for Paul when I get to Fairbanks.*

My "irrational" fear of bears has been replaced by caution and respect. I am sorry Walt killed the bear; I eat him nonetheless and am joined to him in that sacred act. One cannot fear her own flesh and blood. He has taken part in the ritual of my transformation in celebration of prima materia,[9] *the "flesh of the earth" that joins creatures, rock, and vapors rising from dark caverns with resounding melodies.*

Day 22   *Sheenjek River*

This morning on a brisk walk across the tundra, I began weeping unexpectedly. Until that moment I had not acknowledged my reluctance to leave the virginal wildness and return to civilization with all of its turmoil. In the subdued morning light, a cone-shaped pingo, an upthrust of permafrost, was perfectly mirrored in a glass-smooth pond, as were the clouds and surrounding mountains. The animals were tame at that hour. A gray jay followed me, almost landing on my head as I sat to rest. An arctic ground squirrel froze and observed me as I passed. The silence of the morning was broken intermittently by piercing cries of ptarmigan and raucous quarreling of ravens flying by with heavy wingbeats.

Animals here are in place. Their utilitarian ethic is apparent in all they do. Their actions as well as their curiosity are purposeful, efficient, and aimed at harmonious exploitation of their environs. They have no questions to ask, no dilemmas to face. They do what they do without the conflict of choice. They are healers and teachers and vehicles to other realms. Thinking back on the seals, I wonder if they might also have provided the first model for patriarchal culture.

Last night in my dreams I lay in a coffin. Yesterday afternoon, lying in soft lichen on the top of an esker facing the sky, I watched ravens circle me in anticipation. Images of death are all around, as is the intense surge of life. Here the integration of death and regeneration is complete. Like a reclining figure frozen in eternal repose, a part of me wants to remain here in a dark, musky den sheltered by the bear's warmth and held in the embrace of roots. But it is time to move on. I begin the separation.

Day 24,   *Lobo Lake*

I am sitting on a blue, white, and orange Chevron gasoline can nursing a small fire with my back to a chilling wind. The can is testimony to the use of this sandbar near Lobo Lake as a rendezvous point, and to the insensitivity of humans to wilderness designation. If all goes well, Roger will pick me up here tomorrow morning. The snow line, which keeps descending and is only a few hundred feet above me, gives me cause for worry. A tiny speck in this vast landscape, I am gripped with fear momentarily. Why in the world am I here? Will I ever get out?

The tundra has lost its glow. The drainage basins are only faintly yellow, and willow leaves along the river are changing to brown. Poplars, berry bushes, and birch are bare, and equisetum is the color of porcupine quills. The season has progressed to early winter in the four short weeks since I arrived. It is frigid. I have to wear my heavy down jacket in addition to four layers of clothes in order to stay warm.

Until three days ago, I had not seen the moon. Then it rose full and orange. And last night after midnight, Walt called me out of my tent to witness another spectacle. A shaft of light streamed from Little Brushman Mountain to the north and extended across the sky toward the moon. Wavelike it dispersed to reform in an undulating pale yellow and green curtain in the northwest sky. The aurora borealis was breathtaking but familiar. I had seen it before in a dream.

Day 28   *Fairbanks*

My spirits rose and fell with the clouds that had brought more snow the night before. Without forewarning, Roger's plane suddenly appeared and skimmed the sandbar as he tested it for landing. He disappeared from view but in a moment returned, barely clearing the ridgeline as, with his magical touch, he dropped out of the sky onto the sandbar. He made plans with Walt and Rick to pick them up downstream in two weeks after their moose hunt. I said goodbye, and we took off with the usual foot to spare at the end of the sandbar, and just missing the spruce trees on the other side of the river.

We flew down the west side of the Sheenjek along the edge of the mountains, skirting storms and, when that was impossible, flying through curtains of snow and rain. As we flew south, fall returned. Red-leaved berry bushes surrounded gray stone outcrops on ridgetops. Flaming yellow drainage basins spilled like lava to the Sheenjek; the tundra had turned brown. Spruce trees cast long shadows northward.

We landed at Fort Yukon, where I caught a flight to Fairbanks. There I visited the Federal Building to buy maps, the University Museum to submerge myself in the natural history of the region, and a jeweler down on Second Avenue who knew all about usiks. He polished it to a pearly sheen and then attached a gold loop. As I looked at it, the tiny, ivory-colored bone grew in dimension and accentuated Henry Moore's explanation of scale and size:

A small thing only a few inches big might seem as if it has a monumental scale. . . . I can't explain what it is that gives monumental scale to something. . . . I think it's an innate vision, a mental thing rather than a physical thing. It is in the mind rather than the material.[10]

The foothills were brushed with the crimson of maple, and in the drainages yellow aspen, in contrast to the solid green surround of conifers, trembled in the cool, crisp air. I walked briskly up the canyon. Following the annual departmental retreat in the mountains, I had chosen not to join the faculty on their gondola ride. I preferred to walk alone up the canyon near my home.

Retreat. The act of going backward, of withdrawing, of drawing back. What a strange word for a faculty meeting that is a symbolic beginning of each year, a place where we start over. As I sit in the circle each year in the annual fall retreat, my mind plays tricks by taking the actors of the day and rearranging them in bizarre scenes:

Scene I: A huge column rises from the center of the room. Around its base in a circle and joined arm to arm are thrones facing outward. In front of each throne is a mirror. Faculty are seated side by side in the great chairs with their backs to the column, and to each other, reciting monologues to themselves.

Scene II: A battle scene, such as I've seen in old World War II movies. Above are two fighter planes locked in fierce combat. Behind the gun site of each is a man, an embodied weapon, trying to outmaneuver the other. In the trenches on the ground, we watch intently, knowing that the outcome of the battle will somehow affect what we do next.

Twenty years of retreats! Very few stand out, but I remember the first clearly. A middle-aged woman, I was nonetheless a naive and impressionable graduate assistant entering the first year in a doctoral program. The department had just hired several male professors—all young, powerful, and articulate. Threatened, the old guard made their stand, and a brain/power battle for supremacy and dominance ensued. Some walked out, swearing they would never return. The tenured women sat to the side, silent and amused.

Now, as chairperson of the department, I was to open this fall retreat. I would welcome faculty back briefly, introduce the new members, wish them well, and then step back. I had submitted my resignation as chair the previous week, effective at the end of the academic year. What more was there to say? There was, of course, much more. Walking across the tundra, I had said it all to myself repeatedly, but what could I say to colleagues that wouldn't be a defensive justification of my past actions? Could I speak without the revealing quiver in my voice, the tear in my eye, without causing others discomfort?

When I first occupied the chair, I knew it wouldn't be easy and that my tenure would be short-lived. Those were hard times. Yet I had confidence in my ability to make a difference. I was eager to initiate changes in a department that for years appeared to me to be stalemated, incapable of accepting change, mired in complacency and self-protection, and unable to overcome the deadening power of the status quo. Focusing on the bright possibilities for change, my eyes were blinded to the political reality that no amount of hard work and innovation would overcome.

At the time, the department was recovering from a six-year "receivership" during which the graduate council had placed us under the governance of an associate dean. Scholarly work was the emphasis. "Unproductive" faculty were encouraged toward changing roles, phased retirements, or resignations. Rigorous assessment and evaluation procedures were initiated for teaching, merit pay increases, and reviews for tenured and untenured faculty. Morale was understandably low among many senior faculty, who under changing expectations became bitter and entrenched for survival.

The meaning of "scholarship" was ambiguous. It was clear, however, that publishing was directly related to scholarship and was mandated for the granting of retention and tenure. New faculty, hired for their research potential, were the best scholars that could be found for our money. Aggressive, competitive, and bright, they exemplified the individualistic ideals of the institutions that had honed their intellectual skills. Threatened by overwhelming and unrealistic expectations that they should save the department, many, in spite of impeccable academic credentials, became insecure in their roles and uncertain about how to carry out their research agendas.

When governance was returned to the department, a chairperson had to be selected. An outside search was not approved, and one interested person surfaced in the department. Deciding that I was ready for the challenge, I also threw in my bonnet. After all, hadn't I learned a few things as secondary division head? Besides I felt somewhat safe since I saw very little chance of winning the election. By my count, one-fourth of the faculty supported me, and one-half the other candidate. The rest of the faculty were uninvolved. When the final count was tallied, however, I had drawn a narrow majority, with part of the faculty indifferent to me and about half of them clearly in an adversarial role.

The administrative assistant, who had a long and loyal tenure in the department and handled all finances, died the month my tenure in office began. After her death, when I finally worked through the morass of papers that had accumulated during those last months, I discovered that the budget was written heavily in red ink. When I objected to the out-going dean, I was told that nothing could be done about it; the budget was in.

I had been given no discretionary funds, and, with the deficit facing me, I found myself repeatedly saying no to faculty who came to me with financial requests. My first priorities were to eliminate waste and limit expenditures. Barely holding the department together that first summer, I entered the fall term with an inexperienced administrative assistant, secondary and graduate chairmen on leave, searches to initiate, a difficult resignation in process, a new and energetic dean at the helm, and the disappointment and mistrust of the faculty.

Nonetheless I forged ahead with plans to change the department. Expectations from all levels of the university, from the new dean to the central office, clearly conveyed the same message: If we were to expect any support—in fact, if we were to maintain faculty positions and our present level of funding—we had to continue drastic changes in our review and hiring of faculty, our research agendas, and our graduate and undergraduate programs. I favored strong, field-based programs with room for experimentation and innovation. The faculty I envisioned would be diversified in terms of research orientation and minority representation. I was primed to make those changes.

I scrutinized university policies and began a literal demarcation of my duties from faculty responsibilities. Having worked my way through the department as a graduate assistant to professor, I determined to emancipate myself. I would not ask permission to make decisions clearly within my purview; certainly, I would not go to anyone for help. Neither would I try to manipulate and coerce others. My commitment was to making changes that would strengthen departmental standing. I would treat everyone as fairly as possible without showing favoritism or buying support, and I would not place myself at a personal advantage. I would be short on words and long on action.

The new dean and I worked well together, and I found his ideas congruent with changes that had already begun to take form in our department and my mind. Good working relations were established with the academic vice-president, the ethnic studies program, and the office of equal opportunity as my plans for affirmative hiring were forged. As new positions opened up, they were debated by the executive committee and faculty in terms of priorities. To counter repetition of past practice, of taking the "best person," who usually turned out to be white and male, I sat on all search committees and took an active part in defining the meaning of "affirmative action." My involvement in searches met with considerable opposition from the faculty, although at the university level our department was seen as an exemplar in affirmative hiring.

One of my top priorities was to mentor untenured faculty and to support as well as to monitor their professional development. I reduced teaching loads and gave extra support for professional development of newly appointed professors. But I also insisted that untenured professors be clear and accurate in their documentation for retention, promotion, and tenure. I wanted no more criticism by the college council about inflated vitae. Since I was responsible for recommendations to the dean on such matters, I read manuscripts diligently and in interviews tried to come to understand faculty research agendas and intellectual orientation. My recommendations for tenure and retention were shared with them before they were sent on, and in cases of disagreement I negotiated changes. In the end, all of my recommendations for retention and promotion were supported in the reviews at the higher levels of the university hierarchy, but they met with particular animosity in the department when I went counter to faculty recommendations made to me.

According to university mandates, all senior faculty were reviewed by a faculty committee and then by myself. I tried as much as possible to ease long-standing faculty into changed roles or retirement that allowed them to maintain their dignity and usefulness, but I didn't hesitate to maneuver resignations from tenured professors who were not meeting institutional or departmental expectations.

Caught up in the power of decision making, I went busily about my plans, implementing the changes in the department. Midway in my second year, a tide of dissatisfaction swelled, as more and more I found the executive committee, which served in both a decision-making and an advisory capacity and had become more "interest group" oriented, more uncooperative and unsympathetic to my views. Although faculty did not come to me to express discontent, members of the executive committee repeatedly reported faculty complaints about my lack of communication and undemocratic procedures. Unsure of who was speaking for whom, I became more isolated and felt more mistrusted with each week.

One decision that I reached seemed to represent the proverbial "straw." Office space in our college was at a premium, and we lacked conference rooms and a curriculum lab for students. When a newly renovated suite of offices became available on the third floor, the dean offered them to us if we would move the administrative offices and convert the old central office space on the first floor into a curriculum lab and conference rooms. Since he was being pressured by other departments for the new space, the decision had to be reached quickly. I took the plan to the executive committee, but they disapproved of the move. I then polled faculty. No one favored the move. Since the benefits to the department were clear to me, despite overwhelming opposition, I decided to make the move. In the end the decision opened the way to more offices, the curriculum lab, and alleviation of a critical space problem, but it emphasized my "autocratic, top-down" style. More importantly, it disrupted the traditional configuration of the department and placed the central offices, which had previously been readily accessible to all, out of sight and removed to the third floor.

As pressures built that second year, two impressions washed over me: The first was a sensation of being crushed; the second, a feeling of being swept away. In both cases I felt I was at the mercy of powerful forces beyond me. Twice before in my life I had felt the hot breath of destruction:

It was a typical summer day in Wyoming. The heat of the day had set cumulus clouds building in a sea of magnificent blue that cast a patchwork shadow on the sage-green landscape. In response to Dad's request to "run in" the band of horses from the pasture, I had bridled my horse and ridden off bareback. About five miles out, I spotted the band and began running them toward the ranch and the open corral gate. Suspended in a cloud of dust, I galloped along behind them, my long hair flying like a tail, in a splendid moment of puissance, oblivious of the gathering storm. Suddenly a bolt of lightning and crashing thunder disrupted the flow of energy, and I found myself at the center of a circling cyclone of wind and rain, beating hoofs and animal strength that threatened to crush me. Caught up in the exhilaration of the herd, my "trusty" steed began to balk and buck. Trembling, I dismounted, pulled off the bridle, turned my horse loose and made my way to safety. I walked the five miles back to the ranch, tears of anger and betrayal mingling with the steady rain that had begun to fall. From that moment on I would carry a deep fear of brute force and unbridled power.

*I was hiking in the heart of the Wind River Mountains
where the range is laid open by physical forces that shaped this
Earth. Climbing along a rushing stream to above a waterfall where
water broke into crashing cascades onto huge boulders below, I
stopped to get a drink from water that churned over rocks bearing
the striations and polish of recent glaciation. As I leaned over with
my tin cup, my foot slipped on the smooth, glacier-polished rock,
and in an instant I was being carried away by the stream. A friend
at my side reached out his hand but also lost his footing. We were
swept along by the force of the current for what seemed like miles
(but in actuality was little more than a hundred feet) when the
course was interrupted by a log jam above the waterfall. Knowing
that the slightest force could release the logs and send us cascading
over, we carefully inched our way across it until we reached the
safety of the shore. Sitting on the bank, I felt neither fear nor
thankfulness, only emptiness. But when I crossed the next torrential
stream, the terror buried inside erupted.*

My spirit and determination began to wear thin. In retrospect, it
was a critical time. Given the opportunity to repeat it, I would
go south for a week, lie in the sun, and regain energy and center;
instead I initiated a process that led to my demise. I remember
clearly my feelings that morning. Discontent hung like a cloud
in the hallway as I walked to the executive committee meeting.
At the end of the meeting, I suggested that the committee think
about ways of looking at the governance structure that would
address faculty dissatisfaction and provide more democratic participation. Two days later I discovered that the committee had
formulated a letter to faculty and were planning to move ahead
independently of me on a departmental self-study. Feeling a
coup in the making, I went to the dean and asked him to set up
an external departmental review.

A pair of management specialists were brought in who interviewed all faculty and quantified comments into a report concerning positive and negative aspects of faculty life and departmental governance. As I read the report, the positive aspects supporting my initiatives were blurred by an overwhelmingly negative evaluation with such descriptions as "tenacious, authoritarian, myopic, inconsistent, personalizes decisions, unilateral in decision making, hidden agendas, sense of pressure." Faculty described each other critically as well: "insensitive, rude, patronizing, sexist, uncaring, unwilling to deal with conflict, unethical, negative stereotyping, gossipy, backbiting, moaning, petty, prima donnas, selfish, lacking in cohesion, lacking in trust of chairperson, posturing, hidden agendas." The method of study and reporting were strongly criticized by the faculty, yet they agreed with the conclusions, at least the negative ones with respect to me. No one faulted the results I had achieved, but they strongly objected to my "top-down" decisions. No effort was made to examine faculty attitudes that also had been portrayed extremely negatively.

A departmental meeting was held to discuss the report and to determine an action plan. Requested to leave the meeting so that faculty could freely discuss my administration, I walked alone back to my office. In my absence, a task force committee was formed, by volunteers most of whom were my keenest critics, to examine in detail the report and to make recommendations for restructuring the governance.

At no time was I invited to take part in the dialogue and deliberations of the task force. In none of its actions could I find the principles of communication and democratic action that they had found so lacking in me. But in my office at work, I knew very clearly how things were going out there. As my termination was being forged, energy built in the faculty. There was more animation and joking in the halls than I had seen in years.

158

I felt like a human sacrifice who would bring fertility to the barren academic landscape.

Finally the chairman of the task force came to me with a draft document and asked me to respond. I fully expected that the committee would identify me as the problem, yet I was shocked to see that their entire effort had been directed at one question: "How can the power of the chairperson be curtailed and controlled?" I pointed out that they had mistakenly confused power and authority. Their proposal went counter to university policies regarding responsibilities assigned to chairpersons, who could, if they found it advisable, delegate power to others. But faculty, themselves, could not divest the chairperson of authority granted by university policy without changing those policies through due process within the university senate. I suggested to the task force chairman that he go back to the committee and propose a more appropriate question: "How can policies and procedures of governance within the department enhance and protect the freedoms and talents of all members?"

The task force continued their deliberations, and a meeting was scheduled to discuss their recommendations, which had been broadened to cover all aspects of governance and contained a minority report supporting the duties of the chairperson as set out by university policies. The afternoon before the meeting, I met with the dean. It was clear to both of us that the faculty expected me to resign. He did not attempt to influence my decision but assured me of his continued support whatever my decision.

That evening I sat at my desk considering courses of action. An impulse for retribution for what, in my more paranoid moments, I referred to as a "witch hunt" urged me to destroy all records, resign in the morning, and spend the rest of the year watching faculty scramble to put the pieces back together. But I knew if I did so, the consequences in terms of our pending graduate review would be devastating. After hours of deliberation, I finally composed the statement to be delivered to the faculty the next morning. As I wrote, the decision emerged. At midnight, I closed the door, walked through the dark halls of the building and went home.

The next morning in the meeting after the issues and agenda were laid out, I was asked to speak. This is some of what I said.

> Hopefully the past difficult weeks will be a prelude to mutual growth and understanding among us, to the evolution of this department with realistic expectations for its members . . . with a strong sense of self-determination. Denial of personal implication in the problems, self-protectiveness, and defensive or dogmatic stands may satisfy temporarily our wanting to get back at each other but in the end will thwart possibilities. . . . We are embedded together in the life of this department; we cannot escape this fact. . . .
>
> I have been hard-driving throughout, but I believe I have been just. . . . I have bought no support and asked no favors. . . . The conditions under which I entered the chair were impossible. . . . I felt no mentoring from those who in their own leadership roles I had respected and supported. Your expectations for me under the extraordinarily difficult circumstances have been unrealistic and unsympathetic in terms of the overwhelming complexity and difficulty of the task I faced.
>
> I am very supportive of your move toward self-determination, and our present dean has shown his commitment to work with us. . . . The next years will demand great effort . . . in order to identify the true sources of our conflicts if we are to make appropriate changes. Much of the leadership and impetus should come from you

through a committee structure and through participation. . . . I welcome faculty leadership and assertion.

You say I am arbitrary in making decisions. I am not. My decision today, like the others I reach, came after serious thought and reflection. . . . I have been in solitude at the center of a tense and silent circle where glances are guarded and sometimes fierce. My decisions are informed by multiple factors including my own sense of rightness and fit. . . .

I intend completing my term as chair with dignity and integrity. In the fall, after assessment with the dean, we will decide whether in the best interest of the department I should resign the following June. If that is the case, we can spend the remainder of the year selecting a new chair and preparing for a smooth transition. . . .

Just as many of you have been offended by my style, I have also been offended by yours. On the other hand, I am constantly amazed by your human potential. My hope is that the outcomes of this meeting will be constructive and that, by working together, we can magnify rather than dissipate that potential.

I am willing to work with you, with diligence, as is my nature. On the other hand, I will not lie down, roll over and play dead.

I expected fierce and immediate rebuffs to my comments. Instead the faculty sat in silence. I looked at the faces in the circle around me for reactions and saw traces of surprise and puzzlement, resentment and hate—and here and there, a tear or two of compassion. But only traces. Most countenances were impassive, showing little feeling. I had hoped for some open dialogue, some direct statement to me by the faculty, even open confrontation to which people of my Mediterranean blood are accustomed, but none was forthcoming.

The dean, who was to follow me with a statement, asked if the faculty wanted to comment. The reply was a long silence. He moved ahead, and then work groups formed to address questions the task force had formulated: What are reasonable expectations for administrative leadership? What should be the relation of the executive committee to the chair? What is the province of the executive committee? How should the executive committee be constituted? How should the department be organized in terms of programs and divisions, faculty meetings, and so forth? What are faculty responsibilities? How should administrators be evaluated? Does the faculty have confidence in Flo's continuation as chair?

When groups reported back, the relationship of the executive committee to the chairperson received the most discussion. There was "widespread sentiment that the chair should be more accountable to the faculty." Most favored a proposal that the executive committee should be a panel for consultation, from whom the chair should solicit faculty input, and with whom the chair should share the rationale for decisions. From my perspective, that was exactly what we had been doing. The issue that had been the major concern of the task force from its beginning, the extent of faculty confidence in me, went unaddressed. Other than a letter supporting my initiatives circulated to faculty by a member unable to attend the meeting, no public declaration was made for or against me.

Back at my desk, I took up the work of the department and began planning for the coming year. Faculty filtered in, giving me words of encouragement and a few left notes or letters. But those private encouraging words did nothing to alleviate my feeling of abandonment. At the core I had been deeply injured and violated. But the greatest violence was inflicted when the faculty refused to publicly identify my deficiencies, question my motives, or address my needs. The fate they assigned me was worse than any direct condemnation. They had effectively erased me. I no longer existed as far as they were concerned.

Now, after my summer journey, I was back at the fall retreat. A facilitator took charge of the meeting, made the introductions, and effectively canceled the "nothing of consequence" speech I had planned. I briefly described my Arctic sojourn and, still feeling the bear coursing through my veins, explained briefly what I had learned of the mother bear who educates her young from their birth in the cave until she sets them free. Speaking with levity, I admitted to being a bear mother who had been a little too rough with her cubs. The faculty would have none of it. They sat sober and unyielding, incensed with the analogy. I heard someone mutter "no one is going to lick us into shape." They wanted nothing to do with bears or me.

Their continuing rejection sliced through the festering wound. The pain would persist, but the way had been opened, and my despair began to drain away. I had hit rock bottom, and the only way to move was up.

One source of human suffering arises when our words and actions are perceived, by those we serve or love, in a light different from that intended. Happiness and harmony follow us when others see us as we see ourselves. Primal landscapes had unveiled my wounded psyche, with inside and outside rent, with no congruence between how I saw myself and how I was portrayed. I had moved to art, the Arctic, and animals for consolation and stability. The experience of beauty, in itself, brought hope and reaffirmation of life. And wayfaring in some strange way grounded me as it affirmed life's journey. These were essential ingredients of a beginning cure.

I had also experienced an active period of contemplation when I faced the uncertainty of my life and attempted to integrate the experiences into a new life view. But as Simone de Beauvoir had suggested, contemplation is never detached from ambiguous emotions. "My contemplation," she said, "is an excruciation only because it is also a joy."[11] When we contemplate, says Ivan Illich, we consider and take the actions and thoughts of others into our own lives.[12] The books I carried with me into the Arctic, that I would not discard to lighten my load, provided that template for me to better consider my disrupted condition. A pillow at night and companions during rainy days, the words of the authors instructed me, as did the photographs of Henry Moore's reclining figures who spoke in simple but profound statements. They drew me out of my own particularity and carried me back to the social context where my spirit had been wounded but where my life had to be reformed. But more importantly the Arctic landscape and the bear were there to help me. The Great Mother was a wonderful teacher. She received my questions and returned them in embodied representations that were tangible and beautiful in clarity.

Like images on placid Arctic water, themes of death and transformation in my journals reflect concerns that must be interpreted in light of conditions out of which they emerged. The descriptions of my experiences contain elements of darkness, not a nihilism that turns back on itself in hopelessness and self-destruction, but a human struggle arising from failure and disappointment and the feminine psyche.

Life and death are straightforward and clear in the natural world, where we are never seduced into thinking they are separated. There are no signs contrary to subsequent actions; behavior is never deceitful. Appearances, rather than falsifying and mystifying, are thick with deeper meaning: conelike pingos rise in response to the pressure of permafrost wherein "form pushes out" as it does in Moore's sculptures.[13] The bear voraciously laps berries in preparation for winter sleep. The northern shrike hovers over me because I move and may be prey. The aurora borealis glows in response to solar flares. The gull becomes an exhibitionist in defense of her young. In these forms, we find clarity, integrity, and hope as well as delight—a soothing balm for embodied pain. But Nature carries metaphorical meaning as well and sends back to us answers to questions we have not yet asked. The bear, for example, took part in my integration.

As Shepard wrote, "From time older than memory, the bear has been a special being: humanlike, yet close to the animals and hence to the source of life.[14]

> Above all animals, the bear is considered to be the supreme physician of the woods. . . . Not only is it the animal of beginnings but also of re-beginnings—of recovery from spiritual malaise and physical illness and, metaphorically, revival from death. . . . Spiritual healing requires agitation and movement underground, in the soul's dark caves. Thus the bear represents . . . the blackness and darkness of *prima materia* that must be transmuted on the path to enlightenment.[15]

Symbolism in the dream as well as the return to the cave/tent take on added meaning in view of the bear's "many hued healing ability." On the surface, shafts of light from the horizon and the child in my arms in the dream reinforce the renewal associated with emergence. But under the canopy of hopefulness is the black despair of the soul that longs for light. The unifying theme found in ceremonies and beliefs that reveal deep respect and reverence for the bear is that of the "metaphysical mother." "A feminine principle of birth, growth, death, decay, and rebirth lies at the heart of the veneration of the bear, for the bear is the supreme model—and therefore the guiding spirit—of the theme of renewal."[16]

Facing the bear, I uncovered the real source of my fears: I would be given no opportunity for redemption within the department. My life there had ended and with it my long-standing dedication to its purposes. As Merleau-Ponty advised, "The decision we must make is to accept death, but that cannot be separated from the decision to live and to get a new grip on our fortuitous existence."[17] In living we give ourselves to new projects; we make a place for ourselves in this "world of accidents" where we are misunderstood and misrepresented. "It is simply that all of our actions have several meanings, especially as seen from the outside by others, and all these meanings are assumed in our actions because others are the permanent coordinates of our lives.[18]

When we choose life over death, the outcome is uncertain; we move as wayfarers without certainty of where our path leads. When we are called to account for our actions, we are caught between justifying them in terms of our intents, which are never entirely clear, or in terms of their effects upon others, which are never predictable.[19] Being human brings with it this double bind. We may return to the land for renewal or go to animals to be our teachers and healers, but in the end we live our lives in conjunction with other humans where we alone are responsible for our acts but where we are ultimately judged by others. The path toward self-definition is a lonely, bitter trail when what we are is unacceptable to others. "The drama of original choice is that it goes on moment by moment for an entire lifetime, that it occurs without reason, before any reason, that freedom is there as if it were present only in the form of contingency."[20] We cannot efface the agonizing evidence of our freedom, says de Beauvoir.[21] The shape of our lives is defined by our relationships to others but is achieved through our freedom and through its effects on the freedom of others.

Although there are those in the world who because of oppression or mystification cannot choose freely, most of us prize and possess the freedom that is placed in the palm of our hands. No matter what motivates us to participate in life projects, what ideology we espouse, what altruism we practice, what philosophy we live, we choose our own way.

But in dedication to our own projects there is always the possibility that we may act unjustly toward others. Even actions performed for the common good cannot be justified if they deny some the right to be. Self-determined projects may lead to the conquest of others and the destruction of their freedom or homeland. On the other hand, to live is to move in accord with our own internal truth. Caught in this human dilemma we find that to fully realize our freedom, we must constantly sacrifice our present particularity in order to open new possibilities for others. Disclosure and openness are the keys to this movement, as are self-criticism and reflexivity when we question our own goals as well as the means we use for achieving them.

Because of lack of courage, we may choose to become dependent on someone else's decisions or we may pursue covert goals by devious means. In refusing to acknowledge our freedom, in asking or demanding to be cared for, in covering up what we really are, we deny our pure and primary core and distort our existence until it lacks meaning and congruence. We become a mass of clay without the beauty of pure form, a sculpture lacking the integrity of bedrock. Not only women but men as well take shelter in the shadow of others.[22] With all of our freedom, there is scant courage among us.

Instead we often find a kind of sophism, a conservatism and paternalism, that draws up guilt and other forms of persuasion to control what others might become. Concealed skillfully in positivism or rhetoric, the "enlightened elites" practice their own kind of tyranny. "To vote is not to govern; to govern is not merely to maneuver."[23] Strong forces act to maintain the status quo, which is called into question by those who exemplify diversity in appearance, word, or deed.

Whether through authoritarianism or through sophism, to prohibit others to fulfill their existence while making their own errors is to deprive them of life. In freedom, we choose our own way without assurance that the path we have chosen is the right one. Humans, says de Beauvoir, try to mask the tragic ambiguity of their condition by reducing mind to matter, by reabsorbing matter into mind, by setting up a hierarchy between body and soul or by denying death. In so doing, they also deny life. She proposes there is no escaping this fundamental ambiguity and that instead we should realize it through free choice.

Whenever we become deeply involved in our projects, we are faced with uncertainty. Meaning is never fixed and must be constantly won.[24] If we choose not to live in a world of ready-made values, our answers and acts will always be somewhat arbitrary, and the arbitrary always involves outrage.[25] Situations in our lives become truly agonizing when we must make decisions about causes that serve the group.

Each decision is ultimately made in isolation and determined by the ethics we proclaim in our actions, but the precepts that guide us daily might not be evident, even to ourselves. We come to see the shape of things in our own lives with more clarity, as Henry Moore suggests about his art, only "with a great deal of experience and effort and struggle" and by constantly correcting ourselves on the very things we feel most intensely.[26]

Within our lifetime, and within the limits of our chosen projects, we can experiment and work to perfect our existence. Success depends on our ability to respond to the moment and movement within. The montage of life is especially evident in the season of passing colors. We share this passage, as subjective entities, always in the state of transformation, always imperfect. It would be well if, in our interactions with others, we came to understand what Merleau-Ponty discerned in his wisdom, that as unfinished projects we are more similar than we care to admit: We often take stands on trivial issues but in the end compromise our views as we settle with "outward necessity," shrink our freedom to things we can control and put our consciences to rest "by means of carefully weighed sacrifices."[27] But there are also moments, he said, "in love, in action . . . that flash of fire, that streak of lightning . . . which in its brilliance blots out everything else." These "glorias," these brief moments of human fulfillment, come to us unexpectedly "when harmony is created among us"[28] and when, like fireweed seeds, we set each other free.

With the help of Jeff and Walt, who, like Carolyn, were witnesses to a crucial, transitional time in my life, I was able to plumb the depth of wildness, the psychic space within, as well as untouched wilderness. Exploring there, I found in solitude a temporary place to pick up the pieces. Merleau-Ponty moderated my discourse with the authors I had read and helped me understand the depth of despair and ambivalence that accompanies the weight of choice and the consequence of actions. Those reclining figures, the Arctic landscape, and the mother bear were witnesses to my despair and transported me beyond it to where subterranean sounds from *prima materia* were emerging inchoate and a new form was pushing out. Most importantly these friends in word and deed had charted a new course that drew me out of reveries and introspection, forced me to face my fears, and uncovered new opportunities for interaction that were very different from my past "pathogenic" experiences.[29]

Failure had been a relentless and truthful teacher. The message was clear. My life in the department as I had known it had ended. Unlike the redemption that the bear brought to indigenous ceremonies, there was no such thing in academia. I saw no self-evident life project such as Merleau-Ponty had suggested would emerge from death. Believing that he was the bear in my dreams, I took up with Paul Shepard. With an extended leave ahead of me, we headed toward Europe. I would wayfare a bit and perhaps something would come to me.

6 ❧ Minerva's Owl

> The failure to see the different reality of women's lives and to hear the differences in their voices stems in part from the assumption that there is a single mode of social experience and interpretation.
>
> —Carol Gilligan[1]

"What are you doing?"

His tone at one time would have intimidated me. Now it raised an important question. What was I doing? The interrogation of my colleague came in response to my request for feedback on a paper I was preparing for a panel that would be examining "pain and transformation in academia."[2] I had chosen to look again at my "failed leadership" as head of the department. Was I, as he suggested impatiently, trying to vindicate myself and blame the faculty? Why was I going over this again? What was I doing?

After an extended leave abroad, I had returned to the department. Immersed in teaching and writing, I tried to remain detached from the politics of the department, yet something kept "eating at me." My observations in passing led me to believe that things were progressing much as they had in the past. Faculty were not highly involved in departmental affairs, yet someone—the chairman, I presumed—was making decisions. Although a new partner, travel, emerging interests, and time for contemplation had restored me, apparently I was not cured of administration. The suspicion that there was more to that bleak time than my autocratic nature that robbed faculty of their freedom pressed me to look deeper into that "lived" failure and humiliation which I suspected was shared with others who have suffered through the collapse of relationships, careers, businesses, or other life projects. My motive for "going over it again" was undoubtedly influenced by the need to blame as well as the need to help others, but I had developed a deeper interest during my leave, which fueled a fascination with the subject—the intriguing discourse of feminisms.

Suffused with a passion for the multifaceted subject of Woman, I had every intention of gleaning the past for all it held for me as well as for what it could say to women and men in the flow of their careers. I wanted to personalize that experience, to examine it in the particular context wherein it had arisen, as well as to generalize from it by creating counternarratives that would question those events that had grown very old to my ears. I was filled with thoughts and images from my travels and reading that I hoped would lead me to the depths of this very mundane, and in some ways very boring, experience. As I began the project, I wondered if I had the stamina to go over it one more time. At one level I wanted to drop the whole thing and let it be, but at another I felt compelled to approach that past failure, as James Hillman has suggested, as a "salt mine."

> We may imagine our deep hurts not merely as wounds to be healed but as salt mines from which we gain a precious essence and without which the soul cannot live. The fact that we return to these deep hurts, in remorse and regret, in repentance and revenge, indicates a psychic need beyond a mere mechanical repetition compulsion. Instead, the soul has a drive to remember; it is like an animal that returns to its salt licks; the soul licks at its own wounds to derive sustenance therefrom.[3]

In my absence from the department, this new interest originating in primal landscapes and reclining figures erupted full

force. In his wisdom, Merleau-Ponty had predicted that life arises from death. I was familiar enough with the myth of the
phoenix, which, D. H. Lawrence had written, "renews her
youth" after being "burnt down to hot and flocculent ash" as an
"immortal bird."[4] But my change of mind emerged imperceptibly, without sacred rites of transformation. I simply walked upon
this Earth and began looking around. And everywhere my glance
rested on the feminine form that implied a primordial, intrinsic
structure that first drew me to Henry Moore's figures.

Traveling in Scotland that first summer, unaware of the gathering storm within, I stood pensive amid standing stones. My
relationship to the Earth and to the cyclic round of seasons where
life and death were partners was firmly planted, but how this
affinity translated to women's social life was obscure to me. I was
skeptical about this "goddess stuff" as another New Age panacea
for the angst of meaningless lives. I did not believe that women,
because of the body they had been given without choice, were
any more goddesses than they were inferior because of their
anatomy.

In London, in galleries and museums, they sought me out,
those feminine forms: strange bird-faced figurines, nippled and
spouting vases, nursing Madonnas, goddesses of mythology,
immaculate virgin maidens, red-robed prostitutes and black-
robed crones and nude women lunching on the lawn with suit-
ed men. I joined the other voyeurs of the world and became a
woman watcher, not a difficult task in museums and art galleries,
where the vast majority of all representations (over 90 percent, I
am told) have women as primary subjects. But it was something
other than numbers that drew me, especially to those ancient
icons with their strange, stiff, fecund, bird-faced forms. I began
collecting slides of art and artifacts that captured my attention,
but upon closer scrutiny of them I was further confounded by
the selections themselves. What was I to make of all this?

Meanwhile, in my comings and goings, I kept one eye on the Virgin Mary as her distraction with the divine infant grew until she finally covered her breast, abandoned her son, and stood on the world in flowing blue gowns with a crown of stars and the moon at her side.

At the British Museum Library, I read Jung[5] and Neumann[6] but was put off by their underlying assumptions that women are destined to provide the energy force for men's creative work. I, for one, was done with that. As had Virginia Woolf years before, in the circular, blue-domed reading room of the British Museum library,[7] I surveyed the lists of feminist literature. Scant volumes that began in the early nineteenth century with a few books by women on grooming and manners and explanations by men of what it meant to be a woman had steadily grown to thousands of volumes written by modern women. In the manuscript room I found illuminations of Mother Earth splayed unselfconsciously on the landscape suckling animals at her breasts. I read mythology and saw it enacted in sixteenth- to eighteenth-century paintings, yet there was something enigmatic about the mythical portrayals that contradicted the simplicity of the ancient figurines.

As a result of my increasing awareness, women appeared everywhere, as sexual commodities in advertisements and films, as working women riding the subway; overresponsive in the company of men and unselfconsciously lost in thought when on their own, as caregivers, pushing prams aggressively on the streets, the staccato click of their heels trailing after them as they rushed here and there, and as punks in Leicestershire Square in emphatic, sadomasochistic statements of the day. Scattered among them everywhere were solemn, gray-faced, macabre figures who didn't bother to hide their blackened eyes or bruised and cut lips. What drew men to look, buy sleek cars, and then strike out in anger and hatred? As I stared, men and women returned the gaze, but only momentarily, as they had since I had become "older." What was it about this graying condition that caused them to pass over me and look away?

Back in the flat, I wrote long journal entries uncovering my "growing up" years, my relationship to my father, now dead some thirty years, and to my aging mother. My children and grandchildren paraded past one by one as I considered each carefully. I continued probing for a deeper understanding of the woman in me that was daily called to question in a new relationship. By some luck of fate, Paul's research had led him to Artemis and Demeter. He was looking for the bear in them; I merely wanted to make their acquaintance.

We traveled through the countryside of Greece, Sicily, and southern Italy in a labyrinthine search for Artemis and Demeter temples. The few scattered pediments identifying these temples shared one thing in common, the topographical sites upon which they had been built. As Scully[8] had documented, often a spring would be nearby. Sometimes the temple would be on a mountainside looking out at other mountains meeting in Vs in valleys below. If the temple was in a valley, in the distance the same "Mother Goddess" configuration of mountains was often seen. We began anticipating temple sites by the lay of the land and often upon closer examination found an ancient structure incorporated into a modern church.

At Eleusis I sat on the foundation of the temple to Artemis and looked up the pavement where great gates, opening to a cave beyond, had left grooves in the stone. Labyrinthine pilgrimages of initiates came from Athens, carrying offerings and preparations for the sacred "mysteries" of death and rebirth that would take place.[9] And at Brauron, bronze dragonflies danced in the sun by the spring and standing pillars marked the place where once young girls dressed as bears celebrated puberty rites.

Museums, most very unlike the British Museum, where everything was beautifully displayed and labeled precisely, turned up some unexpected treasures. In the disarray, I began recognizing recurring types: stiff alabaster corpses; obese, full-bodied figures; bird faces, owl eyes, serpentine figures; pubic triangles, meanders, and spirals; vases with breasts; and, on a good day, a birthing goddess. In one I found a wonderful depiction of Demeter, full faced, confident, joyous, and peaceful and so unlike the image created by post-Hellenic mythology, where she is forever angry and searching for her daughter.[10] A familiarity with the Goddess icons grew from those jumbled collections in musty cases.

Further journeys led to Africa, where my presupposition that Tribal People were intrinsically tied to the Great Goddess was rudely disrupted as I encountered the Masai, where, in the absolute commodification of women, patriarchy is at its most extreme. And in India, where I thought I would find a plethora of examples of the Great Goddess, I had to dig under patriarchal representations to find traces in ritual practices.[11] I began recognizing essential chronological differences in the iconographic representations: Time changed the primal figures to wives and sexual objects. It became clear to me that I would not find adequate models for the Great Goddess in post-Vedic and post-Hellenic representations.

During those years abroad, I was taken by the hand by the Great Goddess—not simply a religious icon or monotheistic deity, but that archaic, primordial feminine that represented the unifying forces of life on Earth—and led steadily to her source. She was for me a resource that, as Vandana Shiva has explained, "originally implied life" and whose Latin root, *surgere,* "evoked the image of a spring that continually rises from the ground."[12] She had flowed from strange, numinous images from the past, diminutive sculptures that released a multiplicity of interpretations and deep-seated intuition—that, rather than totalizing the feminine, revealed the vast complexity of meaning in the unifying symbol of the female body. At first it was a matter of attention, and it all began on that spring day with those reclining figures.

When I returned to my homeland, the images persisted. In Marija Gimbutus's books I found explanations for the symbolism that at one time seemed beyond my grasp.[13] A new life project was indeed emerging from my experiences of the past. The drastic change in my focus became evident when, upon attending a conference shortly after my return, I listened to women in a session on feminist issues lament the lack of adequate models in our society, that transcended patriarchal mother or commercialized sexual images. It was spring. The rain brought a freshness that swelled blossoms into bursting, brilliant fragrance. Even in the city, in the courtyards and cracks in the sidewalks, new forms were emerging. And yet not a single woman in that assemblage proposed that the Earth herself suggested a feminine model for humans. Confronted with this terrible void, this amnesia about our origins, I once more sat silent and tearful. What was the use? Why go over it again? The Earth as Gaia was a familiar enough concept.[14] I could anticipate the response to any reminder I might provide: nods of assent, silence, and then on with the discussion. The Great Goddess, reserved for cloistered covens or ethereal moments when we catch fleeting glimpses of her, was too much of an abstraction to apply to our theory and practice. Remembering similar responses previously, I determined to take a more positive route. I would look for applications of the primary feminine to my own life and its relationships with others. I would confront what was still troubling me and conduct my own self-study in my own department.

I began by interviewing thirteen people (four women and nine men) who were members of the faculty at the time I was chair. I explained to each that I was taking part in a panel on "pain and transformation in academia" and that I was going to reexamine the difficult time I had experienced as chairperson. I asked each to characterize my "failed leadership" and, if they wished, to explain what they had seen as problematic about my administration. I listened carefully, took notes, asked only clarifying questions, and avoided becoming defensive. After each interview, I went back to my office and wrote extensively on issues they had raised.

The faculty cooperated fully and were straightforward in their responses. In some cases the interviewees described how "others saw me," but most expressed their own qualified opinions. Trying to retain the original language, I combined the statements of these very different people into a many-voiced declaration from "the department":

> The department was at a critical juncture. You attempted to bring cohesion to a fragmented department, and that frightened those who were trying to hold on to their empires. The department was large and complex. It was a matter of individual domains versus the department as a whole. We function as a whole now, and we are the recipients of the changes you made. The strong stands you took made a difference. You made progress and won support in the central office, but you created enemies in the department.
>
> Faculty were fighting the leadership role as well. They are pretty selfish. Typically they think about their own needs and don't think about or see the needs of the department as a whole. There was an inability to send messages back to you. How much the history of the place fed into it isn't clear, but a problem with leadership has been a consistent one in this department. Additionally, the executive committee was unwieldy.

At the time you entered, the department was caught in a clash of visions between senior faculty made tremendously insecure and threatened by changing expectations and highly individualistic and competitive younger faculty intent upon "patricide" and gaining control. These younger ambitious people were resistant to the personality of an older person who was willing to nurture and mentor and make judgments. In the institutional shift, you were caught in a generational clash, but you were not seen as a member of either camp.

It was clear you had an agenda in mind when you entered and that you were going to make changes. You had a vision about what needed to happen, but the faculty either was not ready, didn't understand what you were trying to do, or didn't see the need for change. They didn't see the whole picture. Some of them were merely guarding the status quo.

Changes had been instituted under the receivership to make the department more research oriented. You entered and wanted to revise and improve programs, so you were asking faculty to move in still another direction. You wanted them to put effort into program revision and implementation; the faculty wanted to stay in their offices and do their own research.

The view of research and scholarship that was mandated by the graduate council was ambiguous but narrowly interpreted by most. You were not mainstream in terms of your research. You were not seen as a scholar, and your judgment was not trusted, especially by junior faculty upon whom you were called to pass judgment in cases of retention, promotion, and tenure. Your efforts to evaluate research or to give advice about its direction were seen by some as entirely inappropriate. In their view you had no right and no ability to do so. Some felt you were infringing on their academic freedom by giving feedback about careers. Moreover, you were too strong in your feedback.

You were not willing to be political. Your straightforward, honest, and confronting manner challenged the core of individualistic assumptions, where competitiveness, cheating, and duplicities were natural. You were too autocratic and unwilling to negotiate. Differences of opinion seemed irreconcilable. It would have been better had you said no to no one and given everyone something of what they wanted. You were unwilling to be political and to cut bargains and deals with individuals; as a result we felt we were unable to affect the system. You did not create a support group for your agendas. In this place you gain support and form coalitions by buying favors. Although you didn't spend enough time talking to and listening to faculty and securing allies, our claims of lack of communication and democracy were used as excuses. The real problem was that we could not anticipate what you were going to do. I operate better if I know who the enemy is.

Gender was definitely a problem. Your style was different. You refused to ask for help or delegate authority. You asked no favors and granted no favors. You were egalitarian in the distribution of resources. Clearly you were honest and fair and did nothing for personal gain. But your intuitive style created a feeling of unpredictability. There was no prior basis for trust. We probably would have treated a man the same way. We are "sophisticated cowards" in our dealings with each other.

I saw you as caught up in the cause of feminism. When we disagreed, I felt it was not so much a disagreement about ideas as much as it was a man disagreeing with a woman. You were overly defensive. This left me feeling ill at ease and guarded.

I had trouble with you as a mother figure. Projection of the mother onto you caused role confusion and turmoil in younger faculty, who were resistant to the personality of an elder who was nurturing, mentoring, and making judgments. Your style somehow triggered negative responses related to mothering. Your mentoring was invaluable to us, yet we felt you were infringing on our freedom. Your role was inconsistent with our original idea of you. There seemed to be confusion between mothering, mentoring, and meddling, and we wanted to take the mother out of administration. We expected, as well as resented, nurturance.

I should have supported you. I don't really know why I didn't. The "old boy's club" was well in place. It networked a system of nepotism and played individual interests against the common good. There was no "old girl's club." You were out there alone. Younger women were in a minority and could not network since it was too risky.

Your tough stand on affirmative action was resented by the faculty. You moved too quickly and took too strong a stand. Bringing diversity to the department was a priority with you. You wanted a diverse but cohesive faculty.

Frustration crystallized into action. Your way of personalizing successes and failures left us uncomfortable. Since you responded in a personal way, the faculty felt justified in treating you as they did. You should have stood back objectively from the problems and not taken them so seriously. I enjoyed the time with all of those changes. The faculty came together, and now we have a department.

The difficulty you faced was no different from what goes on every day in universities. On the one side you have egotistical, self-centered, specialized academics steeped in the mystique of academic freedom; on the other, you have the administration trying to accomplish something for the common good. The two inevitably clash.

Administration is a tough task and is for those who are "steely," who at night can walk away from their decisions. You were open, but it was clear you had come with an agenda and you set out to do it. I have never been with a person who worked harder than you did. My question is, why?

The assessment by faculty left me vulnerable and exposed, yet thankful for the honest and forthright assessment. During the crisis of my leadership, I considered it a misfortune to have been placed head to head with these people; now I saw it as fortuitous. I had no intention of depersonalizing the remarks nor of looking at them objectively. After all, I was the subject here, and the story told was deeply subjective. "Just like a woman," I took upon myself the responsibility for the portrayals. It was important that I do so. If I erased the comments from my computer and my mind, as I repeatedly contemplated doing, I would have removed myself from the context out of which the problems arose and in so doing would have denied my presence in the scene. Better that I understand my failure than to deny my existence. But moreso I wanted to understand as completely as posssible what the interviews had beautifully revealed: The personal was indeed deeply political.

❧

In my first efforts at interpretation of faculty responses I began by going back to my origins in the department to see if I could see myself as the faculty saw me. My career had grown like the improvisation that Catherine Bateson describes which accommodates the demands of family.[15] Arriving at the university in mid-life, I worked out of necessity and was thankful that each day brought me such pleasure. Much of my young adult life had been spent in oppressive circumstances. Now at the university in freedom, I could live my life to the fullest.

Environmental activism set me apart, more by notoriety than by acclaim. Those first years in the department were times when in a conservative state, *environment* and *wilderness* were very dirty words and activists were suspected "communists." Leading environmental field trips and starting alternative programs did not strengthen my image. I was seen as an anomaly, but I was tolerated, I believe, because I was hardworking, was successful in teaching, and carried a substantial load of the teaching. But in matters of departmental politics, I was always a bit anarchic and off-center. I was neither liberal nor conservative, and because I was seen as "unreflective and uncritical," I was totally unacceptable to radicals. Not a minor factor in my departmental image was the fact that I had received my degree in the department with a chairman who continued to maintain a strong voice.

As I circumscribe this woman that others must have seen, a figure emerges, one both strange and familiar, a caricature of a graying activist with backpack and apron scurrying about in a cloud of dust tidying up affairs of planet, department, and family, a woman who obviously did not know her place. I tried to imagine what those people who voted for me to head their department were thinking. My best guess was that most did not givc it much thought and that those who did saw only my apron. As a motherly figure I was someone who would listen to and nurture them. They probably conjectured that I would do no harm and that I would not say no to anything. But in those first days as chairperson that was about all I said. Before I could grant individual requests, I had to be assured of a stabilized departmental budget. As friend and foe flocked to me with requests and received the same negative response, the ambiguous but benign image changed.

In meetings with adversaries as they came to demand or ask favors in exchange for support, I recognized the signs of repressed fear, anger and loathing: They flushed, sweated, paled, and trembled for no apparent reason. Puzzled after such encounters, I would walk down the hall to the broom closet where there was a mirror, just to check on who I was. I fully expected to see staring back an old hag like the Indian Goddess Kali, who in drunken orgies dances in graveyards on copulating couples and eats children. My reply to all who came, friends as well as adversaries, was the same. Out of the patronizing attitude, which some used to cover their animosity, as well as out of my growing insecurity, a feeling built in me of being split into the two sides of the stereotyped woman: the one, benign and nurturing; the other, lethal and aggressive.

As I reflected on these faculty comments, as well as on my own interpretation of my emerging role in the department, I became starkly aware of the complicated processes through which leadership emerges, especially for one without previous experience or training. I entered the position of chair concentrating on the changes that I hoped to initiate, but I was inattentive to the concomitant political and interpersonal problems as they arose. At the same time I was determined to present a new model of leadership, one less prone to persuasion and less self-serving.

All previous heads of the department had been males whose leadership was more predictable and understandable, but whose methods I often resented. It was not that I didn't know how the system worked; even from the outside the dynamics were fairly clear. I knowingly chose not to go that route. I was determined to stay true to my vision and to make decisions on my own. In that process, however, I was subject to the "ethics of ambiguity;"[16] I saw situations sometimes from one side, sometimes from another, and sometimes I changed my mind. From a faculty standpoint I was "unpredictable, inconsistent, arbitrary, intuitive."

In terms of the processes of democracy, I had little to justify; I was totally naive. I approached departmental affairs as I did my household, in a matriarchal fashion, attending to matters of resources, trying to support individual projects, allowing members to come and go as they liked, but maintaining high expectations and control of the finances. Like running a household properly, administration was a great challenge that I enjoyed: Solving problems, generating funds, negotiating and collaborating with the dean and higher administration fed the overachiever in me. As I effected change, my sense of accomplishment responded to the need within the department for more change and fed a never-ending cycle of reformation and restoration. The department was an ideal place for an ambitious person; there was much that could be done, and I was anxious to get on with it.

My style of administration was seen as feminist, but actually ran counter to the feminist ideals of collaboration and consensus, which I saw as possible in women's studies programs but unrealistic in a large, bureaucratic department. Since I would not be "political," which in our department translated into "buying support and giving everyone something they wanted," I relied heavily on the letter of the law in university regulations to implement plans. I had decided to serve only one term and was determined to make as many changes as possible in the time I had. When it came, however, I was unprepared for the ending I had forged.

Entering administration as an older woman who had raised her children and mentored many students, I was a mother figure to the young faculty and perhaps a wife surrogate to some of the senior members. In rejecting both images in favor of that of the liberated woman, like a Balinese shadow puppet, I projected a blurred image. This position was not new to me; I had occupied indistinct boundaries for most of my life and had found that being different was not necessarily alienating. It generated and maintained identity, although often a negative one.

I undoubtedly called up multiple and incongruous images that fed a mistrust that is denied in our public declarations of acceptance of difference. We acknowledge our predetermining part in what we are able to see. Fusing subject and object, we insist, does not remove the uniqueness of various subjects. We believe in a pluralistic view and multiple interpretations. We are expected to put our views "in writing" so that others can "share" what we are about. Under the veil of acceptance, implicit but unarticulated presumptions guide the ways we see and listen to each other. When a person does not mesh with these hidden expectations, she or he struggles through advancement procedures, and collegial relationships.

Difference is played out most dramatically in language. Although no one can keep us from writing, our words can be used against us if they do not follow a common norm of scholarship or creativity or if they go too far afield—into Nature, for example. Agency to determine how we write and act is still not accepted as the natural realm of women. My writing, which was seen by the faculty as unscholarly and outside the mainstream of academic thought, had evolved out of a necessity that tied me to people and land as well as to my inner being. My voice had grown slowly and steadily, and with each essay I wrote I learned more and more about what I was doing and who I was. I began openly questioning the assumptions of qualitative as well as quantitative analysis that supposedly kept the researcher distanced and separate, rationality as a single avenue to solutions, stage development schemas that placed women lower than (under) men, and materialistic social theories that were no better than capitalist ideology in their exploitation of the Earth. I insisted that personal narrative was the only honest way for researchers to express their views.[17] These declarations were taken as being inappropriate from one with no firm scholarly or ideological grounding. My developing "voice" and language in feminist and ecological discourse soon lost their resonance in the world of administration and politics—those abstractions that, for motives of efficiency or power, are superimposed upon real people in all contexts without reference to place or being. In fact, my deep subjectivity, which others labeled as "personal style" was used as justification for the faculty's treating me without consideration.

As shown by the interviews, asserting power to choose how we speak and write and act is still the greatest sin of woman. Being strong, taking a stand, making decisions, refuting dependency, having an agenda in mind, working hard, moving quickly, making progress, and being innovative are positive leadership characteristics, but in a woman they are feared and mistrusted. Why would a woman work so hard?

I, for one, had always worked hard, not because I took "work" as a prescription for what one should do, but because I had always entered life projects with great commitment. Since most of my career decisions had been predetermined by necessity, I was not in the habit of evaluating my actions on the basis of merit or outcomes. I just got on with what had to be done. Although I have acquired a bit more skepticism, along with a slightly bruised ego, in the tradition of the working class, I still hold to the tenet of the underdog that effort does make a difference. What else must we believe? That we are completely oppressed and unempowered? That we can never change our lives or make a difference in our circumstances? That we are entirely at the mercy of outside forces? That we shouldn't take the one life we're given too seriously?

The labor we women learn around the house makes us good short-order cooks. To be able to keep track of many things at once, monitor progress, pick up on them here and there, is a skill we learned from our mothers and develop in ourselves as we manage our own households. This skill grows for many of us as we nurture and care for loved ones at the same time as we attend to careers. But for a chairperson, this ability may be more a disadvantage than an advantage; it is best not to see too many things.

When we are preoccupied with many things at the same time, solutions to problems come in flashes of insight, more likely at the kitchen sink than in the faculty meeting. The experience of striving to find the way and then seeing it open up suddenly is a joyous one often dampened by the incredulity of others. When we try to explain the complexity of what we see to others who demand that things be laid out in straight paths, they often become resistant and critical. Loquaciousness, rather than being the result of an overdeveloped *animus* in women as Jung proposed, may result from our having to explain too much to too many who, because of their mistrust of us, entrenched expectations, and positivistic bent, have developed selective hearing. When our viewpoint repeatedly falls on deaf ears, we become silent in defeat or defense or to avoid confrontation. Our breath is sucked from us, as well, when we deny the truth of physical abuse or the assault of rationalizing and intimidating arguments.

Communication, which was repeatedly mentioned by faculty as one of my failings, implies a relationship between two parties where neither is striving for control and where both are willing to listen. Poor communication is not just a one-way affair. Frustrated with failure to be heard, we move ahead with decisions before the moment is lost. Our actions then are seen as arbitrary and impulsive. After repeated experiences along these lines, we continue withdrawing into silence, acting when we see the need. Mistrust, combined with our socialized self-doubt, leads us to lose faith in ourselves as others increasingly question our motives.

Women are also seen as untrustworthy when, counter to the soft-hearted and full-breasted images projected upon us, we make hard decisions, show righteous anger, or confront unethical behavior. We reach decisions as men do, by balancing reason and analysis with feelings about consequences to individuals and the group. Judgments are not reached on irrational impulse; intuition feeds into the way we perceive the world. That women are capable of hard decisions is unacceptable to both men and women, not because we lack the capability, but because we are not expected to use our capacities assertively.

When we are in positions of authority and choose to nurture or mentor, we are targets as well for unclaimed shadows in those who in their paths to adulthood have failed to resolve or understand their own relationship to the feminine. For them our role becomes a confusion of mothering/smothering/meddling. For the liberated young as well as those reared in patriarchy, the unconscious is expressed as rage against the "controlling" mother, the negative side of the maternal, a projection of the person's still-dependent self.

In the passion of this moment, I have moved from "I" to "we." Do I propose to speak for all women? It might be best if I remained true to my own motives, which may differ from other women's—and adopt the kind of honesty implicit in an interview with Shauna Clark, a young secretary who filed sexual harassment complaints against a former district attorney and who suffered professionally and emotionally during the subsequent three years of litigation. When asked if she would not have complained if she'd known the consequences, her reply was, "If I had it to do all over again, I wouldn't complain. I'd jump off a cliff instead."[18] She was done with self-sacrifice for the cause of women, and she didn't presume to speak for them. It had cost her three years of her life and a career and untold suffering.

Unlike Ms. Clark, I am not done with it. I call up a "we" that speaks to a "they" that represents persistent, androcentric norms that prevent transformation of gender and professional relationships. To deny that we are still working through the same old problems is to deny a rightful place on this planet for women and minorities. Like Ms. Clark, I must acknowledge the despair, frustration, and disappointment I have felt. After all, it was my life. My motive to go back over this is driven by the belief that my experience does generalize to men and women struggling to understand themselves and each other in the context of a complex society. Thus I am led from self-assertion and self-justification to another form of interpretation situated outside the dwelling place where I have been informed by experience and the views of faculty. I borrow from minds more critical and theoretical than mine to examine the complicity of individualism and gender relations in the events I have described.

As seen through social criticism and a predominantly androcentric view, individualism upon which our country was founded has led inevitably to a "struggle for legitimation," a situation in which persons or groups are expected to exemplify self-determination as well as to justify their unique point of view. Characteristically this new view is accompanied by a strong criticism of the status quo. When groups of individuals share a new vision, they often find themselves joined in movements that frequently lead to "legitimation crises," exacerbated in part by rigid or conservative elements in society that will not allow change to evolve.

Universities have not been exempt from the legitimation crises that have taken the form of "youth unrest, energy crisis, economic recession, ecological movement, women's movement, peace movement"[19] throughout the world. In fact, as suggested by Peter Berger and Hansfried Kellner, crises may be the commodity of intellectuals who "have a vested interest in proclaiming crises, because this attracts the public's interest and gives legitimacy" to their occupations and preoccupations.[20] For whatever reasons, the crisis mentality transfers readily from ideology to individual worth.

Occupying the bottom rung of university hierarchies, departments of education in particular suffer from an identity crisis. Perhaps this place is deserved, since these departments have accepted without serious questioning the model of technological development that earns dollars for research by often forcing a specialized or reductionist view that restricts vision and elevates self over community, a very poor model in my opinion for those interested in educating children. In their defense, it may be said that educational institutions differ little from other "service" entities—from churches to hospitals to governmental agencies—where hierarchical, bureaucratic systems are adopted that feed on levels of abstraction. Although the rhetoric of the social good is prevalent in such institutions, they are designed for survival of a predetermined "fittest," and their members are often faced, in the end, with mediating inequalities they have generated through token affirmative action. The problem of legitimation, of proving oneself worthy of an institution or cause, is compounded for women, who are caught between institutional expectations for behavior that go counter to socialized roles that deny their intellectual capacities.

In academia, women as well as men are called on to justify their scholarly lives. They are expected to make names for themselves: get their word out, leave their mark, become visible, take office in prestigious organizations, get to the top of the heap, and "master" the subject. Caught in a game of winners and losers, as they are judged, so do they pass judgment. Once their careers are established, they move on up the scale, repeating successes at higher levels in more difficult (and higher paying) positions or institutions. On the one hand, they are colonizers exploiting resources and people as they go; on the other hand, they are vagrants, without long-term commitments to place or people. Moving on is not merely a disease of the acquisitive careerist, it is the route of sensitive souls who, constantly thwarted by institutional pressures, seek greater fulfillment and challenges to their human potential in situations more hospitable and open to cooperativeness and solidarity in their relations with others. In the overall picture, the system of legitimation works against establishing long-term relations in community and place.

In the game of materialism, success feeds upon success, and one accomplishment leads to another. Collaboration is sought, not just because it is a natural posture for gregarious and interdependent people, or because it is in vogue or makes sense in research, but also because one person can enhance another's position. Madeleine Grumet warns us that "collaboration is the foundation for the transformation of the space, time, and politics of schooling and yet it must constantly be challenged by another voice, if collaboration is not to degenerate to a coerced consensus."[21] Collaboration may also degenerate into exploitation. Furthermore, collaboration may not pay off. Tenure is never given to a group. Making a name for oneself implies that one name must stand out among many. Furthermore, the high cost of research may misdirect scholarly focus from a passionate question to one that brings in funds.

The United States was founded upon the premise of male individualism. Each man would be freed for life, liberty, and the pursuit of happiness. The fertile ground of the university, we are told, replicates the history of our country and is the seat of individualism, where academic freedom is inviolate and sacrosanct. Power, control, and authority are crucial issues in such a milieu where rigid lines are delineated and maintained. Leftists challenge authority that is not founded on democratic processes that "empower" individuals, themselves included. On the right, conservatives dispute authority and see themselves accountable to no one but themselves. The danger of uncontrolled authority is present not only in uncontested leaders, but in all parts of our democratic political system upon which our institutions, including universities, were founded; and it requires safeguards against what could become the tyranny of the majority."

Unfortunately, hatred of authority and total identification with authority are sometimes indistinguishable. A particular kind of liberalism that questioned all beliefs grew out of the sixties with an assault on all authority, and further inflated the cult of individualism. The majority of professors in universities today grew up in that era. Although some question authority on the basis of strong ideological beliefs, that questioning also serves interest groups, apolitical protest, and narcissism. Meanwhile little evidence is seen on either side of the political spectrum for self-limitation for the greater good. In spite of the rhetoric of emancipation, most professors have been socialized into acquisitiveness themselves and can go only so far in self-limitation— about as far as it takes to reach for their wallets.

Institutional compliance with federal mandates for "equal opportunity" can also be self-serving and can be used to prove the superiority of the dominant view. John Shaar proposes that true reformation would require self-examination and sacrifice by those in advantaged positions who "were the direct, traceable beneficiaries of past practices of racial and sexual exclusion and discrimination." He suggests that rather than placing a moratorium on hiring white males, as his college faculty voted to do, they should have required the "white males already on the faculty to draw lots to determine who among us should resign . . . thereby making openings for women and minority candidates."[23]

The self-limitation that Shaar suggests is not practiced. Instead, authority is delegated by consent to institutions to set up the boundaries and limits to individual freedom. As Samuel Weber points out,

> The question of institutionalization . . . is eminently a question of the power to *take place,* to define and to delimit a space, within which certain functions and operations can be performed. The power of the institution is the power to lay down borders, to *impose* limits, to enforce demarcations.[24]

I used university policies that defined and limited my powers and distinguished them from those of faculty to justify my decisions. In this context, the symbolism in my decision to move the central office is clarified. I had used the vested power of the chairperson to change a literal structure that symbolized the center of control of the department. I "upset the apple cart" when I removed that "central office" from the mainstream of departmental life and placed it above (three stories above) and out of sight, where my activities were more cloistered and ambiguous. I had tampered with the rigid walls that delineated departmental life and, in so doing, had questioned the beliefs that originally acted to create them. Moreso, I had initiated changes that threatened the androcentric strangle-hold of the status quo.

Still another interpretation of my "failed leadership" merits consideration and comes from feminist and psychoanalytic theory. In the struggle for academic survival, maintaining and advancing one's position often take precedence over actual research and writing or efforts to develop cooperative systems. Posits Norman Birnbaum:

> Some of the most challenging matters come from thinkers like Barbara Ehrenreich and Jean Baker Miller, who argue that the assumption by women of men's roles would betray the human promise of feminism. Competitiveness, exaggerated individualism and careerist relentlessness, they declare, are already men's diseases: why should women eagerly seek these maladies? Cooperativeness, solidarity and empathy are what they instinctively (a word in itself debatable) bring to what was a man's world—and no one needs these traits more than men."[25]

Unfortunately the so-called "men's diseases" are communicable and transmitted by women as well as men. A kind of hyperindividualism follows not only from history, politics, and economics, but from gender as well. Oedipus lives on. In order to grow up and become independent and self-sufficient, a person must overcome infantile synergism. As Jane Flax has asserted, "The strongly felt need for fathers and sons and, to a lesser degree, daughters to bond against the return of the repressed mother world has not disappeared."[26] This repression not only plays itself out against mother figures, but pits faculty members against each other. In the same way that Freud denied relationship in therapy, affiliation is denied to colleagues who may be co-workers for entire adult lifetimes. Such a stance denies human interdependence emanating from a common "prehistory" when they were symbiotically attached to another person, when the mother was their world.[27]

Feminist theorists are beginning to reveal what Flax describes as "psychoanalytic complicity in the fundamental form of domination in our society, based in gender relations."[28] She points out that, in creating a "male psychology," Freud failed to explore the extent to which the preoedipal mother-child relationships affect not only women's psychological development but the very structure of masculinity itself.[29] In a culture where gender is an exclusionary category, the son can enter the masculine world only by rejecting and devaluing the feminine world, including his own prior identification with his mother and his internalization of her.[30]

Freud did not create patriarchy, which developed over four millennia. Nonetheless he did influence Western thought in profound ways, some of them positive: He introduced us to the unconscious and broke ground for a self-centered consciousness that helped us to understand our human condition. But he also institutionalized gender polarity as well as assumptions about scientific treatment of mental and emotional disturbances (mostly in women) that set therapist apart from patient. Psychoanalysts, such as Flax, ascribe this flaw in his theories to his denial of the importance of the preoedipal mother.

Speaking of the consequences of repression of the figure of the preoedipal mother, Nancy Chodorow puts it this way:

> Women's inequality may be multiply caused and situated, but I have yet to find a convincing explanation for

the virulence of masculine anger, fear, and resentment of
women, or of aggression toward them, that bypasses—
even if it does not rest with—the psychoanalytic account,
first suggested by Horney, that men resent and fear
women because they experience them as powerful mothers.[31]

Despite the seduction of mother-daughter relationships as
espoused by object-relations theorists, daughters who are career
women also see the necessity of identifying with the father and
of rejecting the mother. They face problems similar to those of
their male counterparts in repressing their early ties with a
woman. According to Margaret Mead, since mothers remain the
primary socializers of children, the ones who give early approval
and disapproval, "the nagging voice of conscience is feminine in
both sexes."[32]

Freud's suppression of that voice and his denial of the importance of the first symbiotic relationship between mother and
child, paired with his inability to face the mother's aggression, led
him to idealize the mother/son dyad as the most perfect of
human relationships, thus promoting the institutionalized
repression of the preoedipal mother, the "spectral mother," who
Madelon Sprengnether says haunts the house of Oedipus.[33]
However, Sprengnether is also critical of object-relations theorists such as Chodorow, as well as Lacanian psychoanalysts, and
claims that both subordinate the role of the mother to that of the
father. Likewise she suggests that in the context of "discursive
androgyny," somewhat on the order of Lacan, "the interests and
writing of actual women" are marginalized. Sprengnether
reminds us that "it is difficult to give up privilege once you have
it and middle (and upper) class white males are not risking much
by adopting a discourse of subversion."[34]

In a highly competitive milieu, gender, says Gayatri Spivak, is co-opted and fetishized in a "politics of inclusion"[35] as the discourse of Others is reified and used against women and ethnic minorities. Brutality is disguised as "honesty" and "caring." Devaluation, rather than mentoring, is the hidden agenda in our "rigorous" assessments of each other where the word *empowerment* is bandied about but where one person's empowerment, rather than enhancing other positions, threatens them. Insensitivity and hardness of heart are seen as desirable attributes. Destroying a career should not keep us awake at night. To get to a goal, we must be strong, butt heads, push aside, or step on the other. Anything goes, as long as we don't get caught. Finally, and for emphasis, using a repeated analogy to which women cannot relate: Reaching the goalpost, we raise our hands in self-adulation and expect everyone to join in a cheer for our touchdown.

Not only women, but now feminisms, have become commodities co-opted by men intent on continuing the master narrative and supervising our conversations. "Commodities," says Luce Irigaray, "can only enter into relationships under the watchful eyes of their 'guardians.'"

> It is out of the question for them to go to 'market' on their own, enjoy their own worth among themselves, speak to each other, desire each other, free from the control of seller-buyer-consumer subjects. And the interests of businessmen require that commodities relate to each other as rivals.[36]

I return to an unarticulated question that has followed me throughout this chapter. Why was it that my appeal for help in restructuring the governance of the department went unacknowledged by the executive committee and faculty? Why was my request for assistance taken as an excuse to oust me? In the context of feminist psychoanalytical criticism, the answer becomes more clear. Benjamin explains it thus:

> It is easier to immerse ourselves in the power of the father than to become autonomous on our own, to accept his principle of difference rather than our difference from him. . . . True differentiation involves not only the awareness of the separation between self and other but the appreciation of the other's independent existence as an equivalent center. . . . Man/father achieves absolute autonomy because woman/mother represents dependency. Individuality, then, is constituted by what is male, by the permanent assignment of man to the role of subject, through the father's assertion and insistence on complete independence. Originally it is through this denial of subjectivity to women that men lose the mirror of their subjectivity. Recognition occurs not through the love relationship but only in the competitive struggle with other men. [37]

In order to acknowledge my request, the faculty would have had to acknowledge me, a woman asking for help in her leadership role. That would have taken them back to a place that they were trying to forget. To quote Benjamin, "The mother's subjectivity must be denied and her nurturance rejected."[38]

Another way of looking at the substitution of blind individualism for preoedipal and Earth-centered ties is to look at the consequences of this denial as it is played out in accepted university procedures and so-called democratic practices whose roots can be traced to sixteenth- and seventeenth-century Europe. At the same time as the foundations of democracy were being laid and universities established, witches were being burned (estimates of the numbers killed vary from one hundred thousand to nine million).[39] These witches included a variety of humans on the margins of society: widows or single women who made their way alone, healers and midwives who knew the herbs and spiritual rituals that bring new vitality, souls sick at heart and mind, intellectuals and scholars who saw the world in an entirely different way, mystics and ascetics who proclaimed their visions and by example greatly influenced both laypeople and clergy, lower-class peasants and the poor, and those with self-knowledge and "Earth wisdom" who ignored and transcended dominant ideologies and political systems. About 80 percent of the witches were women.

With the move toward a dominant view, which saw the world as mechanistic and controllable, came the enclosure of land that prevented its communal use by the poor and created wage labor and a destitute lower class that could not escape poverty and starvation. Attacks were carried out on healers and midwives, and the persecution of witches, who were portrayed as the ultimate evil, was sanctioned.

As Carolyn Walker Bynum has proposed, this over-reaction occurred partly because church and community authorities feared the mysterious power of mystics and ascetics, again primarily women, who lived highly spiritual lives in their humble homes on the fringes of society, untouched by the doctrines of the church and the norms of society.[40] Careful studies were made, and great debates conducted, to determine how to identify, torture and exterminate witches. The *Malleus Malificarum* was a detailed document developed by the best authoritative minds explaining policies and procedures for this purpose. In rational language it justified genocide as did Nazi, anti-Semitic rationales for the Holocaust and United States governmental policies for the eradication of Native American populations. Out of the Inquisition grew the authority that would determine what should be taught and thought and the control of education through testimony and certification.

The Protestant Reformation and the ethic that grew from it brought, rather than human liberation, a puritanical ideology of work and individuality and a shift in value from use and practice to gain and abstraction. Money became the dominant icon, and work became an ascetic discipline leveled against the enjoyment of life. Women were increasingly excluded from their productive roles in the crafts, healing, commerce, politics, and mysticism of medieval times. Witches became the scapegoats, the recipients of projected powerlessness felt by those in controlling positions. Witches were stripped nude, flogged, pierced, raped, hung upside down—humiliated in every possible way, tortured beyond belief, and finally burned in public, often in the presence of their children.

Universities arose out of the pollution and ashes of "the burning time." They grew with and out of the takeover of thought by monastic authorities responding to the divergent practices of the laity. They were honed on patristic authority and chauvinism, on one view to which all should ascribe. We are the recipients of that monotheistic legacy.

Like the *Malleus Malificarum*, university policies for promotion, retention, and tenure of professors are honed with the utmost care to insure proper procedures. The rules are clearly laid out, with all terms defined so that anyone entering knows what it means to be a professor. Yet proof for or against a person's scholarly worth is as difficult to obtain as were witnesses to the flight of witches. How many ways are there to interpret and understand a child's life in the context of his or her family, community, and school? How is each of us led to our beliefs? What visions do we have? What experiences do we value? How do we come to understand and portray our beliefs? How do we serve others and ourselves? How many times are we misled by our own ideologies?

The ambiguity of each person's interpretation of scholarship, teaching, and service to which universities are dedicated is not the only problem we face. We are also confronted with the ambiguity of individualism. In universities we are caught in the bind of individualism, which we both criticize and exalt, it is claimed by some to be a false consciousness that creates a competitive and paranoid group of intellectuals, and by others to be the ideal to which we should aspire. And why should we not aspire to enhance our differences? Doesn't unique vision that is authentic, pure, and creative portray reality to us in new ways, cause us to reexamine our beliefs, and instill in us a change of mind, practice, and heart? In all this we are morbidly fascinated with the witches' flight, yet we cannot tolerate it.

We cannot tolerate it because the Other, who is truly different and individualistic and therefore not transparent and understandable to us, calls up psychological reversals. All that we fear in ourselves—our repressions, insecurities, unnamed loathing, unclaimed anger, fear of sexuality—is projected on this person who is in a vulnerable position. Like bloodhounds we sniff out vulnerability that our self-righteousness translates into further humiliation of the victim, just as the Nazis humiliated the Jews before they gassed them, and we starved the American Indians before we incarcerated them on reservations. Killing was not enough; the persecutors' own insecurities and lack of personal understanding and power had to be vented upon a victim whose humiliation represented what was most feared in themselves, the vulnerability of the human condition and the mortality that we each face. In the same way, as Susan Griffin has reminded us, a pornographer expresses explicit humiliation and torture of a victim as a projection of fear of sexuality.[41] Similarly in our universities, the supposed seat of rationality, the processes so carefully formulated to protect the individual are transformed into sado-masochistic rituals to humiliate others and sublimate our own neuroses.

It is not surprising that we approach promotion and tenure procedures—a ritual that is clearly patristic, sadomasochistic, and chauvinistic—with a veil of "caring." We mask our unquestioning faith in our worthiness to judge others with an aura of community spirit. Just as in medieval times, church fathers under a veil of authority took from the mendicants, women ascetics, and laity the practices they had established for the distribution of spiritual food and ministration,[42] we cloak our need to exert power over others in the rhetoric of caring. We rationalize our behaviors in terms of the greater good. In most cases decisions are reached not on the basis of competence or incompetence, but rather on the basis of reversals that occur deep in our psyches and drive us to project onto those who are different an evilness that mirrors our own failed humanity. Rationales, always readily available, justify our psychic reversals.

November is the month of the dead. Shadows lengthen as daylight hours succumb to darkness. In a proper ceremony we would build fires and light candles in anticipation of that low time, after which light is once more born; instead, during the month of November our tenured faculty committee meets. This committee examines carefully the vitae, the written lives of faculty being reviewed for retention, promotion, and tenure. The merit of these written lives, detached from the living beings that spawned them, is debated long, thoroughly, and "objectively" in terms of scholarship, teaching, and service. Then a secret ballot is taken on each candidate. For some, this will be "the burning time."

Most faculty come with their vote in hand, few change their minds. Sitting in their offices close at hand are the ones being reviewed. They reach for their antacids, pray, occupy their minds with research, and visualized success as they await the decision. If they pass the test, next year the torch will be passed and they will find themselves on this cloistered tribunal deciding who will burn and who will not.

Rather than being subject to psychological reversals, we could be done with this whole "bloody mess." With clear minds about the ambiguity implicit in such categories as scholarship, teaching, and service, as well as our interpretation and enactment of them, we could set in place a new process. We could strive to understand what the Other is about. We could accept our chaotic beginning and ending, our origins from our mothers and the mother of us all, the Earth, and, facing death squarely, or as straightforwardly as is possible for a human, accept our own failings and weaknesses and end. We could make the annual ritual in the month of November what it once was, a celebration of death to old ways and of birth of new ideas and hope.

The rhetoric of criticism shifts the responsibility, or blame, to "hyperindividualism" deriving from masculine norms that through compulsive acquisitiveness encourage exploitation and humiliation, norms that I myself promoted. I was subject as well to my own psychological reversals fed by my mistrust of faculty motives. Although helpful in identifying the societal and historical context of our cultural maladies, critical analysis, like a death wish, robs us of hope for regeneration and, perhaps more importantly, levity; this I learned in face-to-face interviews with faculty. Although I wasn't prepared to hear all that I was told, the discourse of the interviews, which held many surprises, moved me from the position of victim to the privileged position of listener. What I came to understand was that we were all caught in a web that wasn't entirely of our own making. We were all being crushed and carried along by the brute force of the system. Gender was a factor, as most of us argued, but it wasn't the whole story. We were dealing with a complex picture of institutional and personal history.

To offer one more way of understanding the web of engtangle-ments of gender and power, I borrow two counternarratives from mythology; they are my Artemis and Cassandra stories. The two are closley related: The first has to do with purity, the second with persuasion. To illustrate how the two interrelate, I go back to an experience after that tough spring.

Feeling insecure about leading the department through the next year, I went to a "leadership" conference for middle-level administrators and managers. The conference was a bit too late for my own benefit, but nonetheless it helped me survive the coming year and gave me some insight into faculty claims against me. On written tests and in group participation, I scored high on creativity, problem solving, and intuition; I also had the capaci-ty to quickly organize complex data into appropriate categories. And I was surprised to find that I was a good communicator. I flunked the test on persuasion, however. In the predominantly male group, I was unable to influence group decisions. Although I pulled the highest score on individual problem-solving ability, time and again I was unable to convince anyone of the value in my solutions. Participants ignored my suggestions and worked only with each other. After presenting a solution and having it rejected, I began doubting its validity and withdrew to silence. I did not continue to find ways to defend my position.

The socialization of women partly explains this behavior. A "good girl" doesn't talk back and doesn't cause a ruckus. Even today in the era of liberation, most young women do not play

competitive games where they must aggressively assert themselves or defend a position. In school they know that "outsmart-
ing" classmates may very well make them unpopular with peers
and threatening to the teacher. Similar practices at home and
school reinforce each other. My particular socialization as a shy
child raised apart from playmates and the frank give-and-take of
peer feedback undoubtedly influenced my responses to the threat
of faculty dissent. Unnerved, I withdrew to the security of solitary and exclusive thoughts.

Something more feeds into this that comes from the inside,
not from outside social forces. Assured as I am now that my powers of persuasion were poorly developed, I nonetheless see that I
chose deliberately not to use what powers I had. Indeed, I found it
offensive when others tried to win me over with their rational
explanations. I wanted my ideas to stand powerfully on their own
merit. It was that pure Artemis within, exemplified by my Alaska
experiences, that encouraged me to remove myself from the
demands of relationships that were filled with "crucial irony and
tension"[43] in order to seek virginal territory where I stood apart. As
I have suggested earlier, this place of soul searching and soul making is the creative landscape where we are freed from the misconceptions of others, conceive new paths, and reconceptualize our
place on Earth. It is pregnant with possibilities, spontaneity, freedom, and feelings that "soar impersonally beyond the here-and-
now, above the tangles of the immediate, the mess of the petty, personal details of every day life."[44]   The problem arises when we
withdraw into our own pure, undefiled self and create about us a
"shell of self-sufficiency" that makes us "exclusive, solitary," and
complete unto ourselves.[45] This is where Artemis becomes
Cassandra and where "Cassandra needs to be misunderstood."

Her perceptions and intuitions do not lack insight. In
truth they are quite acute, but they lack effect, the power

of persuasion . . . it is not that Cassandra's words go unheard—the chorus hears what she is saying—but her words have no *effect,* her prophecies do not touch the principal characters or influence the course of action. This inability to influence, to formulate effectively, is Cassandra's purity.[46]

With respect to this "self-same, self-enclosed devotion to purity," when we become fixated on our own thoughts, we "are unable to be touched or stained" and thus "neither life nor insight is possible, only dedication, barren and pure." We walk single-mindedly out of the kitchen into our offices, shut the door, and think that we are still at home. Like Lot's wife we are turned to salt, hard, crystallized, impenetrable, self-occupied, without feeling and without fervor, solid in our purity and cut off from the tensions of life.[47] This selfsame preoccupation is the plight not only of Cassandras seeking isolation, but of intellectuals who become self-possessed with their own ideas. And I can imagine that some people who are so distressed by life's complications that they contemplate or succeed in committing suicide have followed this course to the extreme. They have forgotten to wayfare. They continue unwaveringly on one path. They forget that the psychic ecotone that is filled with tension and ambiguity is where life is the most fecund. They should tarry there playfully, even during dying. Instead they continue on into the depth of the forest where everything becomes the same and loses its meaning, and they lose their way.

The story, of course, is not ended. The owl's flight serves in transformation only if we can recreate a world whose ideas grow in the light of day. Life's force, when released, imbues new processes and forms at the same time as it disrupts the clichés of language and the banality of contemporary lives. By freeing our energies from the deadening restraints of "totalized" lives, we might bring to our actions and discourse the vibrant clarity of artistic creation and a new kind of individualism.

We may find in contemporary art forms, on the order of operas directed by Peter Sellars,[48] which many of us criticize vehemently because they defy the accustomed norms, a model for superindividualism. Like artists we could be steeped in the context of place and impassioned with the desire to act out the vision within us. Our motives would be to understand the ethos of our age and to explore appropriate actions and discourses. Our art would be expressed in multiple forms. Like a video, it would focus close up on the action, the moment, the experience. Like the filming of a theater production, it would be imperfect, slightly out of focus as the camera tried to follow the action and played on characters moving across the stage. Like a Shakespeare play or a Mozart opera, performed in the banality of the present, it would carry the deep wisdom of what is repressed. Like a painting, it would play on background and foreground and bring them into conjunction. And like dance, it would be fraught with ambiguity and with essences with vibrant centers and fuzzy boundaries. It would clarify our total interdependence—with each other, with the Earth, and with its creatures—and at the same time celebrate our uniqueness, which is both powerful and beautiful. It would carry feeling and love, solidarity and bonding between us, as with the parent and the child, and would force us to act unconditionally in favor of the less fortunate. It would celebrate both youthfulness and aging as two sides of the gift of life and would see birth and death as a natural return and continuation of what has been. Above all it would necessitate our trying to understand and clarify our motives so that we could help each other find our particular forms of expression. Our question to each other would be, "What are you doing?" And in that question would be a sincere wish to know what lies at the heart of the other person's desire.

This chapter of my life came out of darkness. The title that "seemed right" now takes on deeper meaning. Minerva was the Roman version of Athena, who grew out of her father's head just as that masculinized segment of my life grew out of my encounter with the androcentric world of administration. After several years of introspection and discourse with others, I still have no conclusions to this story. If what I have addressed here were a problem for mother figures only, we could establish older women support groups and let it go at that. But it affects us all, young and old—babies and elders who are beaten to death, children who are sold into prostitution, men and women who war against each other or anguish in unfulfilled lives—all of us caught in this tangle of gender relationships.

It has been a long night. Yet it has brought me some understanding and hope. Now with traces of dawn in the east, the owl can go back to its perch in the woods.

7 ✿ Equinox

Now: If here while you are walking, or there when you've attained the far ridge and can see the yellow plain and the river shining through it—if you notice unbidden that you are afoot on this particular mountain on this particular day in the company of these particular changing fragments of clouds,—if you pause in your daze to connect your own skull-locked and interior mumble with the skin of your senses and sense, and notice you are living,—then will you not conjure up in imagination a map or a globe and locate this low mountain ridge on it, and find on one western slope the dot which represents you walking here astonished?

—Annie Dillard[1]

The close, the far-off, the horizon in their indescribable contrast form a system and it is their relationship within the total field that is the perceptual faith.

—Maurice Merleau-Ponty[2]

The season has changed. Ice forms each night, and in the morning frost glistens and the air is heavy and clear and still. Gone are the familiar winnowing sound of the common snipe's summer flights and their frightening explosions from underfoot when disturbed along ditches. They have abandoned their hiding places in the tall brittle grass for warmer climes. The uncanny call of sandhill cranes has disappeared, and Canada geese no longer fly over, sounding. And the last pair of mountain bluebirds, dallying to the end, has headed south. Autumnal equinox. Paul has returned to his teaching, and I have been here at our cabin essentially alone for two months at that turning time when the sun at midpoint in its journey south begins its movement toward darkness. I have come home to Wyoming, where as a child on that sheep ranch, somewhat removed from mainstream societal influences, I invented my own brand of individualism. Stillness rings with summer's past and other autumns. It is time to take stock of things and lay up stores.

The first month I was not really alone; I was lonely. My mother, who is slipping rapidly from this Earth, stayed with me here at the cabin. Most days she was not present in the way I have always known her. I looked for her longingly, but the mother I once knew did not return. We repeated a familiar ritual the two of us have enjoyed throughout the years: We drove through Yellowstone Park and watched the animals, the elk, moose, and bison along the road. This time two grizzlies accommodated us on Mount Washburn. She did not want to leave Old Faithful; we watched it erupt again and again. Back at the cabin, I curled her hair, rouged her cheeks, fed her well, took her for walks, and prepared coffee breaks, repeating the daily ceremonies that she has performed for a lifetime but can no longer manage. Each afternoon we went for a ride in the car. As she pointed to landforms that took her back to the other days, she confirmed Annie Dillard's assertion:

> When everything else has gone from my brain—the President's name, the state capitals, the neighborhoods where I lived, and then my own name and what it was on earth I sought, and then at length the faces of my friends, and finally the faces of my family—when all this has dissolved, what will be left, I believe, is topology: the dreaming memory of land as it lay this way and that.[3]

In the time since her last visit, she had changed. I watched her carefully and listened to what she said, trying to grasp her vision. She looked the same yet was different, her responses vaguely familiar but out of focus. She challenged the duality of mind and body I have worked all of these years to dispel.

I took her to visit Aunt Mary, her sister, who, attended by her family and friends, lay dying in her ranch home with cowboy music playing softly in the background. Until the last few weeks, Aunt Mary was fully aware of what was happening to her, but could not understand how the cancer had come on so rapidly and unannounced, "just like that." On her last visit, my mother ran her hands caressingly over her sister, told her she loved her, kissed her, and said good-bye. She knew clearly that Mary was dying, and she mourned the separation.

All things equal, the Equinox is a good time to die. Aunt Mary was buried on the full moon in her Levis. They sang her favorite western songs. The eulogy was given by one of the many men she had mothered in their youth. She took in those boys, most of whom were facing crises, and told them they could stay if they worked for their keep. The first test was to clean the chicken coop. If they survived the ordeal, they were counted as kin. Her life history was told by a cattle buyer and friend who portrayed her as a tough, hard-working, independent Italian woman who fashioned a ranch out of marginal land on rocky banks along a small creek.

My mother was that kind of woman, proud, independent, and ambitious. The oldest of nine children, from an early age on a meager homestead she was given primary responsibility for her brothers and sisters. When we returned to the cabin from the funeral, she could not forget Mary as she was as a child and repeatedly saw her riding her horse or running through the sagebrush. She dreamed of her each night and in the morning would say, "Mary keeps running away from me." One morning as I heard her stir, I went into her room to help her into her robe.

"Who is your mother?" she asked.

"You are, Mamma."

"No I'm not. I'm Mary's mother."

"Mary was your sister," I explained as I went over her family history giving the names of her mother and father and sisters and brothers.

"How do you know all this?"

"You told it to me, Mamma."

"How could I have forgotten such a thing?"

"I don't know. Things slip away as we get older."

"Well, I guess I better believe you. You seem like a special friend. . . . I am sorry I got old so fast."

"Would you like a cup of coffee?"

"That would be nice."

Sleepy-eyed, with rumpled hair, she sat at the long table that had been hers on the ranch where I was raised She sipped coffee and looked out at the mountains and meadow bathed in morning light.

"It is such a beautiful morning," she said.

It is not my intent to deny, trivialize, or romanticize the dementia of old age that has become, along with AIDS, a plague in our day. Yet my mother's path is not unlike the medicine path that Paula Gunn Allen describes. Time for her is achronological; she and "the universe are 'tight,'" knitted together along that steadfast and authentic path back to the Earth.[4] She has forgotten most of the socialized norms that for years she taught to me; manners, prayers, and rules of games have disappeared. Yet she is very clear about her phenomenal and embodied self: She is a girl. She creates fantastic narratives, out of deep subjectivity coming from the land, that carry countermovements of wisdom. She knows the difference between life and death and caresses the morning landscape as she did her dying sister. Under the confusion of language I translate melodies of meaning that need no words, the discourse of relatedness.

Her life seems full and content. Through her needs, she brings home to her children, grandchildren, and great-grandchildren the relational work and "the healing power of 'caretaking' itself." As Flax has pointed out, in caregiving, such as my older sister gives to my mother during most of the year, is the real meaning of "woman's work" and the knowledge and power that comes from therapeutic relationships.[5] More importantly, through her presence and essence my mother reminds us of the care that flowed from her, a steady stream of love, devotion, and friendship.

I return once more to the meaning of human friendship, that mysterious interface between humans. During this equinox I attended another memorial, for Ladd, my friend and close colleague who abandoned me during my leadership crisis. We met together earlier in the summer and forgave each other for our past failures to each other, and then I headed for Wyoming, knowing that the cancer was running its course and I would not see him again. During the eulogies at his memorial, I wanted to rise and deliver a minority report, as he had often done, a counternarrative to what others were saying. I would not have idealized him. He was not entirely honest, but through his superb intellect he was able to psychologize and convince himself along with others of the right course of action, which he constantly sought. His vision was not supreme, but he was very hard to argue against. He was a flawed human like the rest of us. He did not forgive himself or others readily; he was a relentless taskmaster, especially to those he held dear. He insisted that we all be perfect.

He himself was not perfect, but he was memorable. We can never forget him. His uniqueness stemmed from openness, as one of our colleagues pointed out. As did Henry Moore, he kept reinventing the basic human motif as he struggled with that undefined side of being, the underlying tensions and ambivalences that are a part of living life intensely and thoughtfully. He laid it all before us: his change of mind, heart, soul—even his body, as it succumbed to disease. He was a psychic street person, a squatter on our personal ecotones. He would not leave us or let us be. He was always there in that pregnant moment bringing forth the depth of our painful interrelationships and interdependencies. He was both sculpture and midwife, fully involved in our continual emergence as he pointed the way to that "unitary reality" that "for our differentiated consciousness is real only as a borderline experience."[6] He did not isolate himself from others. He mined life's experiences for their salt, but he himself never turned to salt. Up to the day he died, he was involved with the full swing of life. He was in touch with the primordial feminine. He was the archetypal friend.

In comparing humanities, I think of him in contrast to Madonna, the pop icon of the nineties, who certainly chose the right name, since she is virginal to the core in Hillman's salty sort of way, pursuing the purity of her physicality. As only one face of the Goddess she misses the true polyvalent essence of eroticism and wildness and of the Earth. She has thoroughly domesticated her wild nature, flogging and chaining it and making it conform to a banal sexuality. In her obsession with difference in experience and Others, she steps over that margin, where irony abounds, into the prosaic. Caught up in her own power, she pursues her selfsame song.

Something in me wants to mother this wayward child, cut her chains and release her. She teeters on a precariously fine line that borders on self-annihilation. If she looks back too many more times, she will surely turn to salt or, more probably, gold, the "standard," as Haraway reminds us, of the "final commodification of the body of the world."[7] Pure and crystal-clear in her intent, however, Madonna does make me stop and reconsider my mother and my friends Carolyn and Ladd in the fullness of their humanity—and myself as chairperson, certainly no Madonna, yet just as pure and certain in my own "skull-locked and interior mumble."

Mamma has returned to my sister's home. As is my way, I have withdrawn into my project and into deep subjectivity. I think back on my maiden years when I considered being a nun. The cloistered life held appeal for me in those days, as it does today, although it leads to talking to oneself. To keep my center of gravity, I follow a somewhat structured, daily routine. I get up early and thankfully witness the sunrise. I don't pray. The sublime does not enter my life through formal spiritual practice as it does for Charlene Spretnak. I do not intentionally seek "happy and peaceful mindstates,"[8] although they come to me unbidden, as does sadness and, at times, despair; nor do I translate the wisdom of the Goddess into daily ceremony, nor have I joined formally the "contemporary renaissance of Goddess spirituality."[9] I write, work, walk, and watch carefully the happenings around me. On breaks I cook simple but good things to eat: heavy wheat breads, sourdough pancakes, roast chicken, thick soups, pasta. I keep the house tidy, most of the time, and each evening during dinner I listen to British radio on the shortwave with its never-ending analyses of social upheavals and catastrophes around the world.

After dark I use a bit of technology to touch base with family. I go to sleep to coyote calls.

In the late afternoon, after a good day's work, I take a long walk. Walking connects me to the land in ways that thought cannot. The familiar sights, sounds, and aromas reinstate my residence on this Wyoming terrain. I feel at home. Am I, like one of Lorenz's goslings, imprinted to childhood places and relationships? How much of my adult life has been spent trying to replicate those early childhood experiences? Am I now merely returning to what is familiar and nonthreatening? Or is my return to Nature a way to mend human failings and to reinvent human possibilities?

I cross the meadow and slip through the pole fence onto national forest land. A chipmunk sits watching me from the top of a pole as I walk into the sagebrush foothills that lead to aspen and conifers up on Clark Butte through a "text book" succession of plant communities and ecotones. Earlier this summer, the sagebrush in these foothills resounded with the songs of various sparrows, meadowlarks, and sage thrashers, but now the only sounds are the heavy wingbeats and call of the common raven as it passes over. I answer it. It seems to be a friend. Although I don't understand what it says, I had better believe that there is meaning in its call.

Yellow blossoms of rabbitbrush send out a last surge of pollen, and golden aspen on the ridgeline to the north point like a flaming arrow to the butte, where they burst into a flaming finale. The landscape will remain gilt until the leaves have fallen and reveal the crimson and mauve of bare willow branches.

The antelope have migrated over the rim to their winter grounds to the east. Earlier this summer, resting on the south-facing slopes awaiting the warmth of the morning sun, they would rise reluctantly as we passed on our early morning bird walks, the females "barking" to distract us from the kids hidden in the brush.

218

I step around coyote and fox tracks and over a mound of badger diggings and avoid a scat. On up the draw coyotes are howling and yipping in social ceremony or in pursuit of prey. I hear them from late afternoon until early morning, but they are most energetic during the nights when the moon is waxing.

A raven rests momentarily on a pole near the spring where in summer the frogs set up a frenetic chorus and red-tailed hawks hunted ground squirrels and voles for their young. The ground squirrels are long gone underground; they will live on their own fat in hibernation and emerge next spring in synchrony with returning hawks. The tranquility is rent by the repeated harsh cries of the raven, the raucous complaint answered only by its echo and me.

I pause a moment and look down on our cabin and the meadow, where the contours of newly constructed dikes and islands, constituting our wetlands project, resemble the mounds and moats of Avesbury. I smile as I remember Annie Kahn's[10] words early this summer. "Well," she said as she looked with surprise at the pocket-gopher diggings cupped in my hand, "it looks as if you want to be a bulldozer." She was right. Later in the summer I enacted her prediction as I supervised bulldozer operations as the meadow that had been established on an old flood plain was torn up and dikes were built for a wetlands and a tiny waterfowl refuge we hope to establish. If one pair of sandhill cranes alights for only a moment, it will make it all worthwhile, I reassure myself. Nonetheless the project raises questions for me about the consequences in restoration of tampering with Mother Earth.

Annie Kahn, the Navajo medicine woman, stood on a rock that morning and sent us out into the conifers to gather a plant and bring it back to her. As each person returned, she looked carefully at the plant and at the person and brought something deeply personal to the interaction. The ground was littered with pocket-gopher diggings that drew me away from the plant I was supposed to collect and took me back to the "powerful medicine" Scott Momaday had described.

> Something had always bothered Mommedaty, a small aggravation that was never quite out of mind, like a name on the tip of the tongue. He had always wondered how it is that the mound of earth that a mole makes around the opening of its burrow is so fine. It is nearly as fine as powder, and it seems almost to have been sifted. One day Mommedaty was sitting quietly when a mole came out of the earth. Its cheeks were puffed out as if it had been a squirrel packing nuts. It looked all around for a moment, then blew the fine dark earth out of its mouth. And this it did again and again, until there was a ring of black powder earth on the ground. That was a strange and meaningful thing to see. It meant that Mommedaty had got possession of a powerful medicine.[11]

Annie Kahn was not to be distracted by someone else's "powerful medicine." She had her own to mete out, which was direct and to the point. She had come to us that morning as a part of the environmental education institute for teachers of American Indian children. Most of the participants were from southwestern Indian tribes. She began the morning under the shade of conifers, where she sat on a blanket at our center. She named each medicinal plant she had gathered and explained its use as she tore off bits that she chewed, smelled, or rubbed on her skin. I took careful notes, trying to tie her Native taxonomy to the one I had been taught. As she talked about the healing properties of the plants, she added moral lessons and passed the plants around so that we could become more familiar with them.

She blessed us. She chanted, and smoke from Indian tobacco billowed over us as she puffed on the tiny clay pipe. In closing she handed each of us a bit of ceremonial cornmeal to rub on our feet. I was out of her sight behind someone and thought she might skip me. She didn't. She must have seen the skepticism in my eyes as I took the pinch of cornmeal. Well, why not? What difference would it make? I rubbed it on my tanned toes showing through my sandals.—Something entered me like a whirlwind, shuddered through my body, and sent tears to my eyes. Something unanticipated and uninvited shook me soundly. I kept my head down to hide my response. It is Annie's doing, not my own, I told myself, yet one should not be so removed, and skeptical. It is better to be humble and thankful for the blessings that come our way. Even when we don't ask for them and don't expect them, we'd better believe them.

The entire institute had been a blessing. Once more I was touched by American Indians from the Four Corners area. I came away with a basket of gifts—among them a necklace to catch my dreams and one to keep bad dreams away—and a heart full of hope. As usual, I had learned more than I taught:

What will you give to Mother Earth in return for what she has given?

"I give to the Earth one caring child."

What do you say to a person as you part after having met on a path?

"May you grow."

What is the purpose of ceremony?

"Ceremony is to make you remember."

What is the purpose of books?

"Books are to make you forget."[12]

When I asked the teachers if there was something more we could give to the Earth, apart from offerings of thanksgiving, they stared at me in silence. Should we, I asked, do something to restore Mother Earth's health when we have abused or overused Her? For example, I persisted, in places on the reservation that have been overgrazed, is there an area near your school, such as a spring, that might be adopted by children as a restoration project? Silence. One person suggested that careful discussion would have to be held with tribal elders to be sure that no sacred land was defiled. Restoration could very well be just another form of desecration.

These were not the answers from a dying civilization. These were not the answers I expected. They are the answers we need in order to start over. They are lessons of humility and thanksgiving that come as gifts from those Others. They are lessons delivered from the margins, and because of their unfamiliarity they shatter our certainty and presumptions. They are answers that question our Western views and cause us to reconsider what we hold most dear.

My wayfaring has taken a turn, and I must properly question what time it is, where I am, and who I am. Who knows what lies ahead? One thing that lies ahead that has been ever-present as a life project is "dwelling" as "right living" in place and with others. Through listening, watching, and studying I have learned much but have also doubted seriously the possibility of biocentric communities in the relativism and fragmentation of this postmodern world. Nonetheless, I will continue to try to develop a Native sensibility in my relationship to the Earth and toward others—a sensibility that has thus far been influenced and enriched by Tribal People's beliefs and stories and Western interpretations of those stories as well as by messages from the archaic past in Goddess iconography and symbolism. I will continue revising my translation of Native sensibilities into the pragmatics of daily life in several workable ways: In daily householding I will have direct engagement with Nature through gardening, gathering, watching, and sensing. Through relationships with family and friends I will strive to establish patterns of mutual respect and support that carry the meaning of kinship and bonding. As I try to understand more deeply the meaning of community, my involvement in local, national, and global issues will be guided by alternative politics and democratic patterns that strive for biocentric diversity and cultural continuity. Most importantly, I will continue to search for ways to let Earth's sacrality enter my life. Two intertwining strands will form the basis for this personal heuristic: one an ecological consciousness, the other social and political commitment. Both will emerge from greater understanding of self and place.

Direct engagement with Nature, says Stanley Diamond, is fundamental to a communal, ecological view that is embedded in "the pragmatism of the primitive."[13] He suggests that we return to the use of the word *primitive* to denote the "earliest," "primary," and "original," and that we return to primary groups for a deeper vision of our interrelatedness to the Earth.[14] One way to begin is to get to know our bioregions: the way the land falls away or rises from our homes, the watershed and where the rivers flow, the weather patterns and their signs, the changes in animals and plants attuned to the seasons, the culture and the people it spawned, our neighbors, topology as Dillard has described it:— the history of place as it relates to topography.[15] We can embrace the land in "down to Earth" activities such as subsistence gathering, hunting, and gardening. Although tampering with Nature leaves me uneasy, I accept the need for preservation and reclamation projects to help restore ecosystems to health. Contact with Nature may diminish our destructiveness and false sense of urgency and involve us in sensing the Earth as a living entity. As Diamond has so aptly pointed out, "Even now, we hardly love the earth or see with eyes or listen any longer with our ears, and we scarcely feel our hearts before they break in protest."[16] Our deracination can be mitigated by the direct engagement that Diamond suggests.

We have much to learn from Native People who differ greatly from our Western acquisitive culture concerning patterns of kinship and mutual respect and support. When we are informed by other cultures about different realities, maintains Dorothy Lee, we can look at ourselves and our own culture in less bounded, less finite ways, and we can begin to question "tenets and axioms" of which we have been unaware.[17] She uses as an example the way Dakota children were raised.

> They grew up to feel that they were a part of nature, to feel that "there was no complete solitude," because wherever they were, they were with their relatives—the rocks, the trees, the wind. They grew to feel, as Standing Bear put it, "that we are of the soil and the soil is of us. We love the birds and beasts that grew with us on this soil. They drank the same water and breathed the same air. We are all one in nature."[18]

Trying to understand this concept of "all one in nature" challenges the values and premises upon which we make daily decisions. Not only genuine engagement with Nature, but direct and authentic engagement with each other, is necessary. Kinship and generative ties become increasingly important. From birth to death, contact with others becomes more extensive and intensive. The consequences of accepting the life cycle as an organic transition—one emerges out of what one was—are profound. Children are integrated into the group and bonded to multiple caregivers. Life-cycle transitions are ritualized. Youth is not idealized; aging is not denied. Human needs are realized and crisis rites enacted by a community that allows the individual to maintain integrity in the face of change, while his or her own crisis is particularized and personalized. Socially accepted ways for the young to deviate are sought so that youth need not reject their past and present in order to fashion their own future. The "golden years" bring new commitment to the welfare of people and those "other nations," creatures and habitat. A place is made for the trickster and the clown, who act out ambivalent human feelings that, if cloaked in pretension, make fools of us all.

Each person studies past patterns of her life as a guide to what comes next. Dreams are visions of what one is and of where one is going. Passions are accepted as normal, and love is a deep, holistic emotion, not a lowering, as in "falling in love" or merely a genital act, as in "making love." Sexuality is neither hidden nor exploited nor confined to one norm. The arts allow free expression of one's sensuality and open acceptance of the human condition.

A sense of privacy and individualism, one that has nothing to do with walling oneself off, arises out of understanding and empathy for others, as does a strong social consciousness as individuals make their own decisions about different paths they will or will not follow. Freedom is defined as the right of the individual to choose ways to actualize responsibility to the group. The self is seen as an extension of Nature and of the universe. One feels responsible for and related to all things, although valued as a separate and distinct entity. Although a person lives in freedom, a sense of limits is always present. Lee reminds us that it is a highly developed structure that "makes autonomy possible in a group situation." Permissiveness in a structural vacuum leads to chaos.[19]

Lee suggests that in a biocentric community there is no minority status and no effort to make all persons equal. The inherent difference of each person is maintained through a structure that allows the individual to exercise the rights of all. The self is not opposed to the other, assessed against the other, or compared to the other. "Enabling conditions" are sought to allow the individual to expand possibilities within her own limits, not someone else's.[20]

The pragmatic politics of place greatly challenges us as we seek bioregional and biocentric orientations. Such a politics is neither on the left nor on the right; it sees the benefit of diverse views and ideologies. It is more a civil religion than a political movement. It unearths in both cultural and countercultural conservatism the seeds of totalitarianism. At base, it is revolutionary because we cannot come to such an ethic without questioning present acquisitive, middle-class values of leisure time, surplus, and scarcity. In communal politics, cultural values are conservative and radical at the same time;— conservative because present life evolves out of a past that is acknowledged and preserved; radical because norms evolve that tear down old structures that set up hierarchies, exploit members, or create dependency in those who are exploited.

Work and play in an organic community are integrated. Labor is perceived as an act of reproduction or procreation, not as an act of fabrication to bring nature under control or a burden primarily for the benefit of others. Responsible nurturance is the essence of training and apprenticeship rather than supervision and evaluation that introduce fear and insecurity into the work world as one class tyrannizes the other[21]

Basic necessities for survival, the means of production, materials, and resources are held in common so that there is no struggle for scarcity, real or contrived. Public property belongs to whoever is using it. Private property is limited to personalized extensions of oneself and most often constructed by oneself. The compulsion to consume is controlled by self-limiting accumulation of wealth; giving is valued more than holding. As Richard Lee has seen in the !Kung, "arrogance and stinginess" are abhorred.[22] Tools are "vernacular," homemade and homespun[23] and used to extend human potential and as means of achieving "conviviality,"[24] not as compulsive and addictive fetishes.

Leadership is accepted by the most skilled and most experienced persons, who may, but must not necessarily, be the oldest members of the community. Leaders act like reference books, giving advice and determining how things should be done, but need not be strictly obeyed. Diamond proposes that since we presently lack structures of evolved and grounded communities, our only recourse today is to establish democratic and fair procedures that clarify roles and protect the rights of individuals within the context of their immediate "life territory." A movement toward decentralized institutions, where individual rights and the good of the community are balanced, is possible only when individuals are willing to limit their own freedom and acquisition for the good of the group. But in undeveloped communities, he suggests, democratic procedures are a person's last line of defense, and "procedure permits the individual to hold the line, while working toward associations designed to replace the state."[25]

Murray Bookchin likewise advises us to seek new patterns of living together and exchange that will support nurturance and, in his words, the "manifold participation of individuals in nature and society." Rather than crude environmentalism that mitigates exploitation by controlling destructive forces, Bookchin suggests a social ecology that fosters and nourishes interdependence. We should strive, he says, for decentralized, democratic communities connected to their bioregions and customs where Nature is a participant that advises the community and is coextensive with each individual.[26]

In a dialogue between Bookchin and Dave Foreman, eco-activist and founder of Earth First! who in 1989 was arrested by the FBI on "trumped-up charges of 'terrorism',"[27] the two tried to resolve the differences between social ecology and deep ecology. The dialogue grew out of a heated debate in which Bookchin took to task deep ecologists who questioned the ecological validity of aiding indigenous starving populations or immigrants who have overpopulated or overextended their homelands. The in-fighting reflects conflicts in ideologies but uncovers deeper issues that cannot be easily resolved. The interaction between human-constructed and natural environments can no longer be ignored; culture and ecology are interactive.

Carolyn Merchant's astute historical analysis of European and North American environmental crises makes a strong case for an ecosystem model with "an earth's-eye view" that takes into account "human factors" that influence the "total ecosystem composed of interrelated physical and biological components." She suggests that "instead of dichotomizing nature and culture as a structural dualism," an ecosystem model of historical change "sees natural and cultural subsystems in dynamic interaction."[28] The problem does seem beyond debate. Although some extinctions of species and natural disasters such as volcanic eruptions or meteorite impacts are a part of our natural prehistory and not due to human intervention, destructive human influences on ecosystems have steadily grown out of a complex cultural context. Likewise, major global problems require not only local involvement but also international action to preserve ecosystem diversity and integrity and to prevent catastrophic worldwide suffering. Overpopulation and exploitation of land and creatures, humans included, have devastated ecosystems and life support in ways that some think are irreversible. We are now faced with the destructive tides of industrial-capitalist and material-socialist societies as well as our own past history of acquisitive and consumptive greed.

Why have we strayed so far from a sense of dynamic interdependence with other forms of life? We long for Native sensibilities that will give us clues to what we have forgotten, but we assert that we cannot go back in time. To those who say we can't go back, Shepard asserts: "The truth is that we cannot go back to what we never left. Our home is the earth, our time the Pleistocene Ice Ages. The past is the formula for our being."[29] In a recent essay in which he further contests "the four word dictum . . . : 'You can't go back,'" he suggests that there are "important recoverable components" that include the "affirmation of death, vernacular gender and fulfilled ontogeny." Reading the world as a hunter-gatherer creates resonance with nonhuman entities that give us clues to "livingness in the world" and applies to drum and song as well as to identity formation through bonding and separation. Along with Gary Snyder,[30] he sees the food chain as a "Sacramental Trophism . . . a basic act of communion, transformation, and relatedness incorporating death as life." In this changed epistemology where "place replaces space, moments replace time and chance replaces strategy . . . (s)igns of the sacred presence and the mystery of being" are relocated in the participatory role of human life. Shepard, like others, suggests that the best guides to this "archetypal ecology . . . when we learn to acknowledge them, will be the living tribal peoples themselves."[31]

Experiencing the Earth as sacred is essential to Shepard's "livingness in the world." Here, too, American Indian beliefs and stories are helpful. Paula Gunn Allen says that in her studies over the past two decades she has identified five similarities that encompass *indianismo,* the Spanish term for the "psychological, cultural, and spiritual attitude common to the people of the tribes."

Concourse with the immortals is one; the knowledge that the planet and all that dwell upon it—including rocks, bodies of water, meteorological phenomena, and geographical features—are alive is another. Powerful kinship bonding and the notion of mutual respect and interchange among spirits, animals, humans, and gods are also definitive. There is a fifth aspect of indianismo that bears mentioning, and that is the sense of fate or destiny."[32]

My limited observations affirm Allen's viewpoint, yet I cannot will a similar perspective infused with sacrality and supernaturals. I have a sense of the sacredness of the Earth and a feeling of kinship with and respect for Her creatures, and yet I cannot claim "concourse with the immortals," nor do I comprehend how nonliving entities are alive. If this were so, I probably would not tamper with Nature. To the contrary, I leave very little to fate or destiny, maintain a strong sense of purpose, and act as if, and believe that I can and should make a difference in the course of things. I care deeply, yet I lack humility.

In my struggle to come closer to the sacred, the ancient icons retrieved from those times before the Earth was overwhelmed with the burdens of ownership and war, and described so beautifully by Marija Gimbutus, carry messages and a language to me as a woman that clarify the pragmatic Earth spirituality in American Indian mythology and "cosmogyny." Continuity immanent with the Earth emerges from those forms repeated for centuries depicting life-giving, life-generating, life-taking, and life-enhancing powers.[33]

Gimbutus describes through the icon of the Great Goddess the encoding and enactment of life on Earth. The Great Goddess removes us from the romantic dreamworld, where women want to be rescued and men expect to be heroes but both often lead disillusioned lives, and also from the everyday, competitive world, where we believe we are complete unto ourselves. She places us instead on the edge of the storm—not in its tranquil eye—in the whirling energy that destroys as well as renews life. In her language we find hope for reinstating a nonviolent, Earth-centered culture.

The most compelling message from the Great Goddess is her vital force, the continuous upwelling of regenerative powers that bubble up in springs of redemption, flower into creativity, and pass on with death in a never-ending cycle of renascence. In all of her manifestations, as she inspires us with her playful, imaginative, fruitful, erotic side; as she sustains us in her attentive, nurturing, spiritual side; as she sends fear through us in her chthonic, lethal, ugly side, she relays a fundamental message of regeneration.

As Mother Goddess she is one aspect of the Great Goddess in which she is full bodied, life-generating, and life-nurturing. The diminutive Birthing Goddess with her swollen vulva bringing forth life reveals the primal beauty of woman's body. But in this explicit statement about how human life is delivered into the world, she also reminds us of the grave responsibility associated with this act and calls us to examine the environments we create, which can be receptive as well as hostile to infant growth as well as our own.

The many sides of the Goddess cannot be separated. She comes to us as the beautiful graceful egret and the fearful and disgusting vulture. Death accompanies life as it does us symbolically each day when we are reborn upon awakening. The Great Round unfolds in mythical spirals where birth and death are inseparable and insoluble and are never detached from the powers of regeneration and renewal. Life is not a spectator sport. We are all participants, and no one is excluded or privileged. The Great Genetrix invites us all to celebrate together the rituals of passage from life to death and from death to life.

The chthonic Goddess beckons us to a new kind of spirituality that is immanent rather than preeminent. We find this spirituality within ourselves, within our minds in a truly subjective sense, and above all, within the Earth. Her mountains, rocks, and springs are all the more powerful because they are the least articulate. The energy that propels birds through the skies on unfathomable migratory journeys, brings succulent fruit to our lips, and runs our automobiles derives from her. In recognizing the unity of Nature, we affirm the unity within us, men and women, people of color and "palefaces," young and old. Contrary to erasing differences, unity celebrates diversity as a fundamental sign of the health of the planet and its creatures.

The "language of the Goddess" sends us tidings of peace. In the chronology of her iconography, millennia passed without war or domination of one gender or class over another.[34] Even after agriculture flourished and populations increased, people lived together in harmony. She challenges us to reconstruct models of peaceful coexistence as we deconstruct the origins of patriarchy and violence and counter androcentric rule in our present lives wherever it is found, in families, work, and schools.

Relationships with others in solidarity and synergism that imply motives not directed at control can enter our lives. Whereas in a world that denies interdependence, neither the ground underfoot nor the helpless and homeless strewn about are visible, women and men of vision each day re-present myth, art, societal practice, and themselves. Dreams brimming with eternal images take on new meanings as we reconstitute ourselves over and over. The essence of a real "New Age" would be the upwelling of energy for the growth and welfare of all, a natural, cyclic growth, one that follows the seasons from fruition to dormancy and that is self-limiting, interdependent, biocentric, and exuberant.

We are a part of the Great Round that circles and circles but always remains mysterious and ambiguous. Each of us is an intrinsic part of the whole that is this Earth. Some of everything that has gone before courses through our veins. Not only the Pleistocene but the Earth herself from her beginning is truly in each of us, physiologically and psychologically. There really is no need to go back. She is here when we speak our minds. At first our voices may be weak and faint and unfamiliar, as if a stranger were talking. But we can become accustomed to the sound and brave enough to speak out in the Mother Tongue, in the dialect that has come down to us through the ages carved in alabaster, molded in ceramics, painted on cave walls, and echoed in our mother's wombs. We can write and speak out from the depth of unnamed truth that resonates within us with a common voice that breaks barriers and echoes from mountaintops and deep caverns.

We can speak to each other. But conversation is not enough. Nor is a critical self-consciousness that allows us to question ourselves and open ourselves to the questions of others sufficient. Our fundamental purpose in discourse must be to clarify the right of the individual to actualize her or his potential within community for the social and ecological good—without this purpose, discourse will be so much noise. We must acknowledge the tension between the rights and responsibilities of the individual and the community and the maintenance or restoration of the integrity and health of the Earth. Likewise we must face the possibility of our own dogmatism and its alarming development in all situations of life, whether in artistic expression or in the workplace. In the mindless conformity of gangs, "singles," and aging hedonists, as well as in the self-righteous testimonies of fundamentalist preachers, politicians, and academics we see the social and ecological balance ignored and undermined. We must develop a language that denotes the spirituality of matter and relationships, which is often clouded by dogmatic beliefs. Through sacrality, ritual and ceremony may someday replace procedure and war as they did in ancient cultures.[35]

The task before us in reconceptualizing culture as a biocentric community and the individual as a neoprimitive is to recover the "old ways" of bonding to Earth and to each other in interdependency. As citizens of this Earth, sharing it as we do with other sentient beings, we live in a sacred web of interrelatedness. Within this web is great diversity, but we are all children of the same Mother Earth. The common ground that unites us as equals, in a literal as well as a metaphoric sense, is the very ground under our feet. We are joined as well in a temporal plight: We are all just passing through. We humans face the additional burden of making sense of our journey. We may choose the means to our end.

That other living things as well as humans have a right to live out their lives is a notion accepted by only a few environmentalists and Native People. This is especially surprising since in purely utilitarian and homocentric terms of survival, maintaining diversity seems a very good idea. Protecting species requires preservation and restoration of habitats that have been destroyed and taken over by humans with no thought to limitations of procreation or consumption. We must support unaltered and inaccessible wildlands where nonhuman elements can progress according to the wisdom of the Earth. But just as important to humans are marginal areas around these untouched cores where the wild and the tame intermingle and stain each other slightly, and possibilities flourish. Efforts toward habitat restoration and enhancement in areas that have been devastated and depleted, coupled with a sensitivity to past cultural uses, can bring back prairie, forest, and marsh, albeit never to their original integrity.

234

As original residents are reinstated to their co-opted environs, new and appropriate stories to live by will emerge. Women in this "back to Nature" movement can write and tell these stories that carry radical knowledge of place and immanent connection to land and other life forms and that run counter to the sexist, oppressive story that has made us untamed instinct, unthinking consumers, insatiable nymphs, and victims open to exploitation. Women with a pragmatic understanding of connection—such as those involved in environmental action in the Chipko movement in the Himalayas in which they courageously oppose the destruction of their life-giving forests by physically embracing the trees—can become the transformers of the culture/Nature dichotomy and the translators of a new and unifying vision.[36]

Profoundly linked to the rituals of life in our struggle to restore wildness, our own included, we can transform boundaries that isolate and protect us into ecotone sanctuaries, sacred places where interrelationships flourish between ourselves and the natural world. We can return to the wisdom of our bodies for guidance, beginning with the semiotics of the Great Goddess, to reintegrate the primal connection to the processes of life lost to us in the last six thousand to ten thousand years. We must try to get closer to Native spirituality.

No course will suffice, however, unless we are fully present in our bodies, which explicitly reveal our essential involvement in four fundamental womanly processes on this Earth: We are bearers of life, we are bearers of food, we are bearers of sorrow, and we are bearers of the word.[37] We are, as Haraway reminds us, "(o)ntologically always pregnant."[38] But this being need not limit us or invite appropriation by men. In our own right, we are bearers of life and life-giving, energy-creating, productive, and reproductive capacities passed on to others through teaching, procreation, and creative activities. We are bearers of food. We are food. We support, nurture, and nourish with our bodies and its labors. We are the bearers of death and sorrow, which we endure through blood, birth, darkness, and doubt which in the cycle of life fuel regeneration and hope. We are bearers of the word. Contrary to what we have heard, we are not without language. We speak the "mother tongue" learned from our mothers: hums of comfort, lyrics of joy, stories, reprimands and mandates as well as hymns of brook, bird, and storm. We have a voice that resonates from the borders of the public and private realms and the natural and social domains that provides a pragmatic, moral critique of both.[39] Although often silenced, it remains alive and strong and full of understanding of the choices that remain our prerogative. To bear life and not speak up in favor of it is unthinkable. To bear life mindlessly or without the capacity to love and nurture properly is untenable. To overpopulate an Earth whose resources are limited is unconscionable.

In openly acknowledging our part in bearing life, nurturance, death, and the word, we may together elaborate a new spiritual philosophy of place and person that draws on our strengths, acknowledges our failings, and heals us of social neuroses that have made us a party to the commodification of our bodies and of the Earth—an ecosophy founded on love, love of the land and of the nonhuman, love of our species, love of ourselves. New images of women, as "deepenings," will appear that "express contradiction and opposition less than synthesis and paradox," symbols of continuity, not of reversal.[40] We stand in relation to the Earth and its creatures, including other humans. But dwelling in common in that space between us is not enough. Until each of us is accepting of our own essential differences, the territory between us becomes a deep chasm we cannot bridge. When our own identity is a mystery, we cannot relate authentically to either the more-than-human or the human. As Kristeva has reminded us, Narcissus ended up killing himself, not because of self-love, but because he did not know who he was.[41] The essential feminine is ambiguous at best; it turns on us just as we try to act it out. In litanies to our bodies, those ambiguous texts that harbor the secrets of life, we touch momentarily the shifting essence of the sublime. We come to understand and accept our embodied spirituality.

It is the task of our brothers to do likewise, to define their essential spirituality. Then perhaps, talking and listening to each other, we can envision a world where work and play are inseparable, where wealth is self-limited, where all people have access to the basic necessities and a legitimate place in the life-cycle, and where each person as an extension of Nature is kin to all and thus feels responsible to the group.

As we approach a new century, perhaps we should seek a deeper understanding of our nature, not merely as a replication of the dark side of the more-than-human outside ourselves, not solely as a mirror of monotheistic gods and goddesses placed above us, but as an entity with value in and of itself that comes from the Earth and is something more and something less than the Earth. Wherever we are, we stand in relationship to others, part of a dialogue, fibers of an intricate web that spins itself into the fabric of this present moment.

I hike on up the butte and trace the familiar horizon that encircles the meadows and foothills. The horizon is a constant reference point. It orients me to position and place. Bounded on all sides by mountains, below is a tiny bioregion, a self-contained watershed, that empties into the Hoback River, which meanders through the basin and eventually breaks through the mountain range at the Narrows, where it spills into the Snake River and then flows on to the Columbia River and finally into the Pacific Ocean.

The emerald green of the Gros Ventre Mountains to the north in summer has turned to golden brown. Eroded edges of strata curve skyward, like staircases cut off in midair. The top, at twelve thousand feet, looks out over an expanse with drainages that flow into the Snake River on the north and south slopes. I trace imaginary lines into the sky as I follow the contours and extrapolate to see how high the strata once rose before they arched downward and leveled off into the palisades that blend into the Hoback Rim, whose east-facing slopes drain into the Green River and south into the Colorado and finally into the Sea of Cortez. Over the rim I can see the Wind River Mountains, massive sisters of the Gros Ventres. Water from their north-facing slopes eventually reaches the Missouri and the Mississippi Rivers and finally spills into the Gulf of Mexico. The foothills of the Wyoming Range and Hoback Mountains dominate the southern and western horizons.

Directions are important in a world where everything shifts as I turn. Sitting in the morning sun, absorbing its warmth over a cup of coffee, facing east, I note its changing position. At night, under the dome of galaxies, our own arching milky white across the sky, I am reassured by the constancy of the North Star situated invariably over a certain point in the Gros Ventre Mountains. At the same time my certitude is disrupted by the relentlessly changing moon.

We have been here several summers, and I am just beginning to know this place. Something familiar carries over from half a lifetime spent on Wyoming rangeland, perhaps the ruggedness of people and landscape. Even so this place is a surprise: the lay of the land, the birds' comings and goings, the way the clouds form and storms move in, the animal residents, and the people, hard-working and steady, yet distant and conservative. Short on words, spoken in a Wyoming drawl, they engage in neither persuasion nor speculation. Their patois is clear-cut, nonhypothetical, and reveals their understanding of the Earth in a "local sense."[42] Conversations center on important seasonal events: the coming and going of bluebirds, the return of antelope to their wintering grounds, sightings of wolves, and fighting of fires. They report the first bugling of bull elk with reverence and the quiver of emotion in their voices. The women are straightforward and hard-working, as are the men, who sport slouchy cowboy hats and long handlebar mustaches. They are not prone to long conversations. I suspect that their wisdom, though unarticulated, runs deep enough. The long winters and ecstatic summers have taught them how to endure highs and lows. They are like the mountains, enduring. Crossing the communication barrier and becoming a good neighbor are more difficult for me than traversing the boundaries of plant communities. Local residents stand firmly behind cultural lines drawn by their homesteading ancestors, impermeable barriers to intruders like myself.

I rest on the crest in a tangled embrace of fallen aspen, the pounding in my ears and slight vertigo informing me of this aging body that I am. I lie back, relax, and look upward through the quivering, golden leaves, outward at a startling azure sky that calls up memories, inward for a sense of immanence that binds this body to this land at this moment. My breathing slows, and I feel the physiological adjustments as systems stabilize and balance returns to this organism that is matter and that matters to me. As I become fully present to it, this body that has borne me through life, is my life, is me, transports me to a place it holds in common with other women, a living and dying place where out of archaic memory comes all that any of us has known.

This body: physical, corporeal, carnal, fleshy and boney, earthy. A commensal being that hungers, tastes, savors, sucks,

*swallows, drinks, devours, gorges, binges, spits, vomits. A body that
receives food, refuses food, serves food, becomes food.*[43] *A consumer
that purges drawers, cupboards, closets, trunks, wombs, and bowels,
throwing away what cannot be stomached. A body that, fed up
with it all, fasts, starves, dries up, and withers.*

*But in living it pulsates, undulates, salivates, digests, assimi-
lates, defecates, micturates, menstruates, ovulates, copulates, ges-
tates, lactates, contracts, aborts. And births. And oozes, bleeds,
takes in, carries, gives off, attends to, delivers, brings forth, nurtures, soothes, nurses, heals, serves, punishes, rents, cuts loose,
buries, and mourns.*

*Private terrain. Public domain. Re-formed . A body that is
pumped up, cut down, tacked up, looked into, sewed up, beat
down, plugged up, thrown out. A body that dwells in the messiness
of other lives where it housecleans, cleans up, covers up, carries on,
keeps up, keeps out, keeps on—reproduces, prepares, repairs, con-
serves, stores, accumulates, hoards, sorts, gets rid of, gives away,
bequeaths, and passes on.*

*A body filled with life's force that senses, desires, delights, tin-
gles, thrills, aches, recoils. Feels . . . fall in the air, the touch of a
hand, peace at dusk, energy at dawn. Smells . . . water where it is
not flowing, the scent of a partner, clover on the breeze, the skunk's
warning in the woodpile, a rat, the sweetness of a child. Sees . . .
colors and contours, textures and motions, actions and intents, the
handwriting on the wall—through rational veneers. Sings, wails,
chants . . . and lies, in a voice that, whether strident or soft, is
never falsetto. It returns in gurgling bowels and soothing hums.
Resonates with courage and morality. Is heard and hears mother's
voice always calling, father's deep tones. Bird song. Music to our
ears. The silence that speaks loudly.*

*This body knows and can think, invent, manipulate, educate,
convert, and criticize. It plants seeds and ideas. Erotic, it under-
stands creativity, passion, rapture and ecstasy but also fear, frenzy,*

agony, and angst, loneliness, anger, and aggression. It celebrates, rejoices, opens, expands, flowers, flows, swells and creates but can also hate, seethe, foment, withdraw, contract, eject, reject, hide, avoid, hurt, and destroy. This body knows pain and has been flogged, crushed, pierced, bound, hung, stripped, singed, raped . . . and burned alive. When it thinks alone, it is seen as evil, feeble, inferior. When it moves out to and embraces others, it becomes impressionable, childlike, weak, undisciplined, seductive, sensual, fervent. Its boundaries are so thin that sometimes it knows not who it is. Yet it endures.

This flesh that is spirit. This body that is our hearts, our minds, our hands, our eyes, our ears, our breasts, our vaginas, our wombs, our bowels, our feet, our infoldings, embodied dreams, imaginings, visions, and creations. This body that swells and sub-sides with life's force and in the end returns to that somethingness that persists. This mind, this spirit that is a body and not just some body, whose nature we come to know rather than overcome. This body that cares.

I stir from this essentialist, "speculative journey," my "subjective internality,"[44] and look about me wonderingly. Never would I have imagined being here; my life has exceeded any expectations I have held. Down in the meadow is a little cabin. It is simple, compact, and functional, one room with a small guest room, study, and loft—all that is needed for habitation. The walls provide the frames for the expansive views from windows on all sides. Shadows of birds overhead fly across the wooden floors.

I rise and stride weightlessly down the ridge, through the sagebrush to the edge of the meadow where last evening I saw a red fox sleeping under a willow. She has moved from the badger dens on the knoll that she co-opted for raising her young, to the meadow where, coiled at the base of a willow in a snowbank, she will winter, wrapped in her voluptuous tail. I can relate to this corpuscular creature, living on boundaries, prowling at the interface of daylight and darkness,[46] finding the means for survival and warmth within herself and at the edges.

Back at the cabin, my sense of connection persists that goes beyond the phenomenal world, beyond me as a center, to that unnamed source. Connection to place and to the "more-than-human"[46] for me is not some sublime, undifferentiated oneness, not a merging with Nature, but rather a genuine respect for separateness, differences, and the secrets of life that surround me yet remain mysterious and ambiguous. The center, the grounding I need, is here, literally, under my feet, within reach, in that rock, on that ridge where aspen grow, up there at timberline, in the mountain bluebirds hovering preparing for migration, in the red-tailed hawk and the prey it has just consumed. It is also present in us by right of having been placed on this Earth, made from its dirt and blessed with the breath of life that has recycled through other life forms for millions of years and interfaces and is shared in common with those living with us today. Here on this Earth, which enfolds the human and nonhuman, others and ourselves, we are all joined inextricably.

This Wyoming land removes me from that "interior mumble." It draws me toward that "sacred center" where I want to be neither a cyborg nor a goddess.[47] Neither do I long for a place where all is one or where anything goes. Where I want to go is to Clark Butte, where I am always astonished. A project lies clearly before me—a natural-history study of this butte that rises like an island out of a sea of sagebrush. I want to get to know it inside and out, how it arose, how it was cut off from the rest of the mountain range, how weather and sun affect it, what plants and animals live there. I will keep a journal of my experiences as well as record everything I identify. I will count and classify, dig and probe, gather and preserve and observe—and make lists. I will gather bouquets of abundant wildflowers and branches of the ubiquitous sage for the cabin and learn, gather and use the herbs. I will write poetry and sketch and will strive for authenticity in experience and description. Perhaps in these ways the sacrality of this Earth will become more true to me. I pray that Clark Butte, no matter how thoroughly I study it, will never become a reduction, construction, or deconstruction of my perceptions of it. I want it to have its own life and integrity and essence. After all, it is *really* there. Yet as I approach its complexity, I trust its truth will constantly escape me.

In the time that is left to me I will go on learning more about this beautiful planet. There will never be time enough. It would take many more lifetimes for me to learn all I can from Clark Butte alone. I want to get started, not to conquer and control it, shatter its mystique, or fragment it with classification, but for the sheer delight of learning, the awe and beauty of hidden treasures and the complexities of interrelationships that will be revealed. I am convinced that although it sits in the midst of "multiple land use" it is nonetheless wild at its core, a place where bears might live.

Whatever I learn I will leave as a legacy to my children, my grandchildren, as well as other people's children. Like the plants in spring, my grandchildren are growing, and each new year brings added potential to their unfolding lives. I want to go on watching them as I do the birds, with appreciation and love, and with as little intrusion as possible. My children are maturing into close friends whom I can rely on in confidence and who sometimes solicit my advice and listen. My sisters and I are closer than ever before in our lives. My partner, in his enthusiasm for life and its creatures and his broad vision, continues to be one of the greatest gifts that has come my way. My many friends grow and become more dear each day. Clark Butte will ground me and offer insights into living on that ecotone where purities of mind and matter intermingle and relationships with other creatures and human friendships are founded.

Astonished as I am, I look forward: I see my children cradling their children, and I hold them close in my arms as my mother held me. I see my grandchildren facing the future, undaunted and hopeful. I see Aunt Mary riding her horse off into the sage-brush and my mother running after her, calling to her to wait. I think of our true Mother, the Earth, to whom we shall all return sooner or later. And I remember the sandhill cranes flying over, a galaxy of atoms from other dispersed beings who went before, their migrations a reality of life so profound that it far surpasses the promises of heaven. When I die, I would like whatever is left of me to join the continuing life cycles originating at this particular place, preferably in the cranes. What more could anyone ask than to fly home each spring?

NOTES

1. Griffin, *Woman and Nature*, 219.

2. A word of explanation to the reader about my use of the words *Earth* and *Nature:* By *Earth* I mean this specific planet on which we live. By *Nature* I mean the nonhuman as well as the human components of the Earth and the processes that bind organisms and nonliving environment in interrelationships. I capitalize both to emphasize the specificity and numinous quality of this dwelling place and of life processes.

3. Kristeva, "Stabat Mater," in *Tales of Love*, 254.

4. John Layard, "The Incest Taboo and the Virgin Archetype," in *Images of the Untouched*, ed. Stroud and Thomas, 172.

5. Bynum, *Holy Feast and Holy Fast*, 280.

6. Krall, "Mudhole Ecology," 351-53.

7. Pinar and Grumet, *Toward a Poor Curriculum*.

8. In my "From the Inside Out," I describe the method of writing "personal history" that I developed and used with graduate students that was originally inspired by George Steiner's "hermeneutic motion" used in translation. See Steiner, *After Babel*, 296.

9. Rorty, *Philosophy and the Mirror of Nature*.

10. In *Man in the Landscape*, Paul Shepard analyzes the movement to see landscape as scenery that came out of Western European elitist romanticism at the end of the eighteenth century.

11. Grumet, "My Face in Thine Eyes," in *Bitter Milk,* 96, referring to Douglas's *The Feminization of American Culture*. See also

Grumet, "Pedagogy for Patriarchy: The Feminization of Teaching," in *Bitter Milk,* 31-58.

12. Haraway, *Simians, Cyborgs, and Women.*

13. Cole and Wolf, *The Hidden Frontier.*

14. Dalai Lama, *My Tibet.*

15. LaChapelle, author of *Earth Wisdom* and *Sacred Land, Sacred Sex, Rapture of the Deep.*

16. James Hillman, "Salt: A Chapter in Alchemical Psychology," in *Images of the Untouched,* ed. Stroud and Thomas, 117.

2 ⚘ Flesh of the Earth

1. Merleau-Ponty, *The Visible and the Invisible,* 36.

2. Ibid.

3. An expression borrowed from Hsu Ying, a friend from the People's Republic of China.

4. Merleau-Ponty, *The Visible and the Invisible,* 78–82.

5. Ibid., 11.

6. Burgoon, "Education."

7. During the Great Depression of the Roosevelt era, being "on relief" meant that the unemployed person was enlisted in the Work Projects Administration (WPA), a federal program that provided public service employment, a small monthly wage, and some free clothing and food.

8. Merleau-Ponty, *The Visible and the Invisible,* 45.

9. Ibid., 32.

10. An eared grebe, to be more precise.

11. Merleau-Ponty, *The Visible and the Invisible,* p. 81-83.

12. Ibid., 267.

13. Ibid., 83.

14. Naess, "Self-Realization in Mixed Communities of Humans, Bears, Sheep, and Wolves," 231–41.

15. Merleau-Ponty, *The Visible and the Invisible,* 31.

16. Naess, "Self-realization in Mixed Communities," 32.

17. Merleau-Ponty, *The Visible and Invisible,* 87.

18. In reading Mike Rose's account of his Italian American, male ghetto experience, I was impressed with the differences in our experiences. To my knowledge no teacher took an active interest in my

education, a factor in breaking the cycle of despair and defeat that was important in Rose's education and to which he is deeply dedicated as a teacher.

19. Rose, *Lives on the Boundaries.*

3 ～ Navajo Tapestry

1. Schumacher, *A Guide for the Perplexed,* 1.

2. Terry Tempest Williams has since this time become a well-known nature writer and activist. Her books on region and place include *Pieces of White Shell: A Journey to Navajoland* and *Refuge: An Unnatural History of Family and Place.*

3. Spradley and McCurdy, *The Cultural Experience,* 9.

4. One of the participants facetiously suggested that perhaps the first question we should ask during interviews was "What do you think you are doing?" As the journey progressed, this became the standard joke among students.

5. Edward Abbey, recently deceased nature writer, anarchist, mythological figure of western environmental activists, and author of *Desert Solitaire* and numerous other books.

6. Krall, "Mudhole Ecology," 351–53.

7. Schoepfle, et al., "A Study of Navajo Perceptions of the Impact of Environmental Changes Relating to Energy Resource Development."

8. Reichard, *Spider Woman.*

9. Ridington and Ridington, "The Inner Eye of Shamanism and Totemism," in ed. Tedlock and Tedlock, *Teachings from the American Earth,* 191.

10. See Deyhle, "Empowerment and Cultural Conflict," for an insightful analysis of educational problems facing Navajo parents and their children. See also two helpful manuscripts concerning Navajo education by Herbert John Benally, "DINÉ BO'OHOO'AAH BINDII'A'A: Navajo Philosophy of Learning" and "Navajo Traditional Knowledge and Implications."

11. Chief Seattle quoted in *Touch the Earth,* compiled by P. C. McLuhan, 30.

12. Allen, *Grandmothers of the Light,* 205.

4 ⨯ Indwellings

1. Clement, *The Lives and Legends of Jacques Lacan,* 16–17.

2. Where excerpts from the journal of the late Carolyn Frerichs Benne, Sioux City, Iowa, are included throughout this essay, they are identified by the initials, C. F. B.

3. Paraphrase of Blatchford, "Native American Lands and Energy Development."

4. "Aleut," *Alaska's Native People,* 57.

5. Eiseley, *Notes of an Alchemist,* 17.

6. Feminists have recently pointed out that ethologists, most of whom are males, have given less attention to the behavior of female animals, who are the ones that insure the survival of offspring, than to the more dramatic breeding frenzy of males. See, for example, Sarah Blaffer Hrdy, *The Woman That Never Evolved* for an insightful critique of androcentric bias in "scientific studies" of primates. In *Primate Visions,* Donna J. Haraway points to patrilineal influences in the work of female anthropologists such as Hrdy.

7. Krall, "Behind the Chairperson's Door," in *Contemporary Curriculum Discourses,* ed., William F. Pinar, 495–513.

8. Barry Holstun Lopez in correspondence with the author, August 1980.

9. Shepard, *Thinking Animals,* 11.

10. Kramer, *Yoga Workshop* (Vancouver: Cold Mountain Center, August, 1971), quoted in LaChapelle, *Earth Wisdom,* 81.

11. Carson, *The Sense of Wonder.*

12. Named after Maxine Greene's essay "Curriculum and Consciousness" in *Curriculum Theorizing,* ed. Pinar.

13. Lawrence, *The Body of God,* 43.

14. John Layard, "The Incest Taboo and the Virgin Archetype," in *Images of the Untouched,* ed. Stroud and Thomas, 147.

15. Ibid., 165–69.

16. Harding, *Woman's Mysteries,* 117–26.

17. Edith Cobb in *The Ecology of Imagination in Childhood,* proposed that this creative core is established through early childhood experiences in the natural world.

5 ❧ The Shape of Things

1. Merleau-Ponty, *Sense and Nonsense*, 173.

2. Words of Henry Moore quoted in *Henry Moore: The Reclining Figure*, 87.

3. Walter L. Prothero, freelance writer, photographer, professional hunter, and contributing editor for *Field and Stream*. See "A Hunt in the Land Where the Sun Dies," "A Season of Grizzlies," and "Obsession."

4. de Beauvoir, *The Ethics of Ambiguity*; *Henry Moore: The Reclining Figure*; Merleau-Ponty, *Sense and Nonsense*; and Shepard and Sanders, *The Sacred Paw*.

5. For more details on stalking see Prothero, *Stalking Big Game*.

6. Shepard and Sanders, *The Sacred Paw*, xviii–xix.

7. Grumet, "Other People's Children," in *Bitter Milk*, 164–83.

8. For a view of hunting as a sacred ritual carrying over from the Paleolithic, see Shepard, *The Tender Carnivore and the Sacred Game*. Feminist critiques of hunting take serveral lines: Maria Mies posits that the patriarchal myth of man-the-hunter implies a violent relationship between man and nature (*Patriarchy and Accumulation on a World Scale*, 62). Peggy Reeves Sanday has shown that interpersonal violence is more prevalent in societies where migration and the pursuit of large animals prevail (*Female Power and Male Dominance*, 35). Vandana Shiva seems to feel that hunting as a part of subsistence is not necessarily a violent activity but that outside of tribal society it reflects violence and domination (*Staying Alive*, 50–51). Charlene Spretnak, in reviewing Sanday's work, implies that the violence exhibited in some hunters spills over into violence against women (*States of Grace*, 115–16).

9. Merleau-Ponty, *Sense and Nonsense*, 103.

10. Moore, quoted in *Henry Moore: The Reclining Figure*, 52.

11. de Beauvoir, *The Ethics of Ambiguity*, 12.

12. Illich, *H₂O and the Waters of Forgetfulness*, 11-15.

13. Moore, quoted in *Henry Moore: The Reclining Figure*, 63.

14. Shepard and Sanders, *The Sacred Paw*, xi.

15. Ibid., 102-3.

16. Ibid., 105.

17. Merleau-Ponty, *Sense and Nonsense*, 69.

18. Ibid., 37.

19. Ibid., 36.

20. de Beauvoir, *The Ethics of Ambiguity,* 41.

21. Ibid., 45.

22. Ibid., 38.

23. Ibid., 139.

24. Ibid., 129.

25. Ibid., 139.

26. Moore, quoted in *Henry Moore: The Reclining Figure,* 110.

27. Merleau-Ponty, *Sense and Nonsense,* 146.

28. Ibid., 186.

29. Flax, *Thinking Fragments,* 87.

6 ⚬ Minerva's Owl

1. Gilligan, *In a Different Voice,* 173.

2. This chapter grew from many contributing sources during the past four years. Faculty who took the time to talk to me, freely shared their views, and gave me critical feedback made a significant contribution, especially Robert Bullough, Donna Deyhle, Walter McPhie, and Andrew Gitlin. Parts of the chapter were presented on a panel at the Bergamo Conference, Dayton, Ohio, that was continued over a three-year period in (1989–91) and that was entitled "Legends of Our Own Time: Stories of Pain and Transformation in Academe." The panel was moderated by Noreen Garman and included John Albertini, William H. Baker, Edwin Cook, Bonnie Meath-Lang, Mara Sapon-Shevin, and Allan Tom.

3. James Hillman, "Salt: A Chapter in Alchemical Psychology," in *Images of the Untouched,* ed. Stroud and Thomas, 117.

4. Lawrence, *The Body of God,* 37.

5. Jung, *Civilization In Transition.*

6. Neumann, *The Great Mother.*

7. Woolf, *A Room of One's Own.*

8. Scully, *The Earth, the Temples, and the Gods.*

9. Kerenyi, *Archetypal Images of Mother and Daughter.*

10. For an interpretation of pre-Hellenic myths, see Spretnak, *Lost Goddesses of Early Greece.*

11. Krall, "The Faceless Goddess," 24–32.

12. Shiva, "Resources," in *The Development Dictionary*, ed. Sachs, 206.

13. Gimbutus, *The Goddesses and Gods of Old Europe* and *The Language of the Goddess*.

14. Lovelock, *Gaia*.

15. Bateson, *Composing a Life*.

16. de Beauvoir, *The Ethics of Ambiguity*.

17. Krall, "From the Inside Out," in *Educational Theory*, 467-78.

18. Shauna Clark, quoted by Paul Rolly in "Whistleblower Says She Wouldn't Do It Again," *Salt Lake Tribune*, Salt Lake City, 16 October 1989.

19. Lenz and Shell, eds., *The Crisis of Modernity*, vii.

20. Berger and Kellner, *Sociology Reinterpreted*, 146.

21. Grumet, "Voice," 10.

22. John P. Diggins, "The Three Faces of Authority," in *The Problem of Authority in America*, ed. Diggins and Kann, 28–30.

23. John H. Shaar, "Community or Contract? William Faulkner and the Dual Legacy," in *The Problem of Authority in America*, ed. Diggins and Kann 108.

24. Samuel Weber, "Demarcations: Deconstruction, Institutionalization, and Ambivalence," in *The Crisis of Modernity*, ed. Lenz and Shell, 303.

25. Norman Birnbaum, "Social Theory in the United States: The Legacy of the Decade 1960–1970, in *The Crisis of Modernity*, ed. Lenz and Shell, 45.

26. Flax, *Thinking Fragments*, 87.

27. Jane Flax, "Psychoanalysis as Deconstruction and Myth: On Gender, Narcissism, and Modernity's Discontents," in *The Crisis of Modernity*, ed. Lenz and Shell, 340–41.

28. Ibid., 324.

29. Ibid., 327.

30. Ibid., 328.

31. Chodorow, *Feminism and Psychoanalytic Theory*, 6.

32. Mead, *Male and Female*, 298.

33. Sprengnether, *The Spectral Mother*, 6.

34. Ibid., 195 n.11.

35. Gayatri Chakravorty Spivak, "The Politics of Interpretation," 277-79.

36. Irigaray, *This Sex Which Is Not One,* 196.

37. Jessica Benjamin, "The Oedipal Riddle: Authority, Autonomy, and the New Narcissism," in *The Problem of Authority in America* , ed. Diggins and Kann, 207–8.

38. Ibid., 215.

39. Except where specific references are noted, general references on witches used in this section, pp. 209–11, include: Adler, *Calling Down the Moon;* Daly, *Gynecology;* Griffin, *Woman and Nature;* Griffin, *Rape;* Griffin, *Pornography and Silence;* Merchant, *The Death of Nature;* Starhawk, *Dreaming the Dark;* and Starhawk, *The Spiral Dance.*

40. Bynum, *Holy Feast and Holy Fast.*

41. Griffin, *Pornography and Silence.*

42. Bynum, *Holy Feast and Holy Fast.*

43. Patricia Berry-Hillman, "Virginities of Image," in *Images of the Untouched,* 8.

44. Ibid., 28.

45. Joanne Stroud, "Introduction," in *Images of the Untouched,* ed. Stroud and Thomas, 4.

46. Berry-Hillman, "Virginities of Image," Ibid., 31.

47. Hillman, "Salt: A Chapter in Alchemical Psychology," Ibid., 131–32.

48. Peter Sellars, "Directing Mozart."

7 ⚛ Equinox

1. Dillard, *An American Childhood* , 248.

2. Merleau-Ponty, *The Visible and the Invisible,* 22.

3. Dillard, *An American Childhood,* 3.

4. Paula Gunn Allen, *The Sacred Hoop,* 149–50.

5. Flax, *Thinking Fragments,* 86.

6. Neumann, *The Archetypal World of Henry Moore,* 65.

7. Haraway, *Primate Visions,* 355.

8. Spretnak, *States of Grace,* 46.

9. Ibid., 146–47

10. Annie Kahn, Navajo medicine woman, shares her knowledge in "lifeway medicine" at her home in Lukachukai, Arizona. See Perrone, Stockel, and Krueger, "Annie Kahn."

11. Momaday, *The Way to Rainy Mountain,* 99.

12. Insights provided by Joe Aragon, Acoma, and Bernita Humeyestewa, Hopi.

13. Diamond, *In Search of the Primitive*, 170.

14. Ibid., 123.

15. Dillard, *An American Childhood*, 3.

16. Diamond, *In Search of the Primitive*, 333-34.

17. Dorothy Lee, *Freedom and Culture*.

18. Ibid., 61.

19. Ibid., 9.

20. Ibid., 57–58.

21. Bookchin, *The Ecology of Freedom*, 231–50.

22. Richard Lee, *The !Kung San*, 458.

23. Illich, *Gender*, 68.

24. Ibid., 18.

25. Diamond, *In Search of the Primitive*, 278.

26. Bookchin, *The Ecology of Freedom*, 24-31.

27. Bookchin and Foreman, in *Defending the Earth*, ed. Chase, 22.

28. Merchant, *The Death of Nature*, 42–43. See also Merchant, *Ecological Revolutions* and *Radical Ecology*.

29. Shepard, *The Tender Carnivore and the Sacred Game* , 260.

30. Snyder, *The Practice of the Wild*.

31. Shepard, "A Post-Historic Primitivism," in *The Wilderness Condition*, ed. Oelschlaeger, 40–89.

32. Allen, *Grandmothers of the Light*, 205-6.

33. Gimbutus, *The Language of the Goddess*.

34. Eisler, *The Chalice and the Blade*.

35. Bookchin, *The Rise of Urbanization and the Decline of Civilization*, 15–30.

36. Shiva, *Staying Alive*, 55–95.

37. Homans, *Bearing the Word*.

38. Haraway, *Primate Visions*, 353.

39. As an example, Linda Filippi's "Place, Feminism, and Healing" addresses the interrelatedness of the ecology of the Earth, personal well-being, and community.

40. Bynum, *Holy Feast and Holy Fast*, 289-92.

41. Kristeva, *Tales of Love*, 103–21.

42. James Hillman, "Salt: A Chapter in Alchemical Psychology," in *Images of the Untouched*, ed. Stroud and Thomas, 127.

43. Bynum, *Holy Feast and Holy Fast.*

44. Kristeva, *Tales of Love* , 123.

45. Shepard, "Savannah Dreaming—The Fox at the Fringe of the Field," in *The Others: Animals and Human Being.*

46. Abram, "The Ecology of Magic," 29–43.

47. Haraway, *Simians, Cyborgs, and Women,* 181.

BIBLIOGRAPHY

Abbey, Edward. *Desert Solitaire*. New York: Ballantine Books, 1971.

Abram, David. "The Ecology of Magic." *Orion* 10, no. 3 (1991): 28–34.

Adler, Margot. *Calling Down the Moon: Witches, Druids, Goddess-Worshippers, and Other Pagans in America Today*. New York: Viking Press, 1979.

"Aleut." In *Alaska's Native People* 6, no. 3. Anchorage: Alaska Geographic Society, 1972.

Allen, Paula Gunn. *The Sacred Hoop*. Boston: Beacon Press, 1986.

———. *Grandmothers of the Light: A Medicine Woman's Sourcebook*. Boston: Beacon Press, 1991.

Bateson, Mary Catherine. *Composing a Life*. New York: Atlantic Monthly Press, 1989.

Bell, Willis H., and Edward F. Castetter. "The Utilization of Yucca, Sotol, and Beargreass by the Aborigines in the American Southwest." Albuquerque: University of New Mexico Press, 1941. University of New Mexico Bulletin 372; Biological Series 5, no. 5.

Benally, Herbert John. "DINÉ BO'OHOO'AAH BINDII'A'A: Navajo Philosophy of Learning." *Diné Be'iiná: A Journal of Navajo Life* 1, no. 1 (Spring, 1987): 133–47. Also "Navajo Traditional Knowledge and Implications." Unpublished manuscript. Navajo Community College, Shiprock, Ariz. .

Benne, Carolyn. Journal Notes. Sioux City, Iowa. 1980.

Berger, Peter L., and Hansfried Kellner. *Sociology Reinterpreted: An*

Essay on Method and Vocation. Garden City, N.Y.: Doubleday Anchor Books, 1981.

Blatchford, Herbert. "Native American Lands and Energy Development: Southwestern Cultural and Spiritual Perspectives." Paper presented at the ninth annual conference of the National Association for Environmental Education, Albuquerque, New Mexico, 1980.

Bookchin, Murray. *The Ecology of Freedom.* Palo Alto: Cheshire Books, 1982.

————. *The Rise of Urbanization and the Decline of Civilization.* San Francisco: Sierra Club Books, 1988.

Bookchin, Murray, and Dave Foreman, *Defending the Earth: A Dialogue between Murray Bookchin and Dave Foreman.* Edited by Steve Chase. Boston: South End Press, 1991.

Burgoon, A. L. "Education." In *The Leader.* Kemmerer, Wyo.: Kemmerer Gazette, 1926.

Bynum, Carolyn Walker. *Holy Feast and Holy Fast.* Berkeley: University of California Press, 1987.

Carson, Rachel. *The Sense of Wonder.* New York: Harper & Row, 1956.

Chodorow, Nancy. *Feminism and Psychoanalytic Theory.* New Haven: Yale University Press, 1989.

Clement, Catherine. *The Lives and Legends of Jacques Lacan.* Translated by Arthur Goldhammer. New York: Columbia University Press, 1983.

Cobb, Edith. *The Ecology of Imagination in Childhood.* New York: Columbia University Press, 1977.

Cole, John W., and Eric R. Wolf. *The Hidden Frontier.* New York: Academic Press, 1974.

Dalai Lama. *My Tibet.* Introduction by Galen Rowell. Berkeley: University of California Press, 1990.

Daly, Mary. *Gynecology: The Metaethics of Radical Feminism.* Boston: Beacon Press, 1978.

de Beauvoir, Simone. *The Ethics of Ambiguity.* Secaucus, N. J.: Citadel Press, 1980.

Deyhle, Donna. "Empowerment and Cultural Conflict: Navajo

Parents and the Schooling of Their Children." *Qualitative Studies in Education* 4, no. 4 (1991): 277–97.

Diamond, Stanley. *In Search of the Primitive.* New Brunswick, N. J.: Transaction Books, 1981.

Diggins, John P., and Mark E. Kann. *The Problem of Authority in America.* Philadelphia: Temple University Press, 1981.

Dillard, Annie. *An American Childhood.* New York: Harper & Row, 1987.

Douglas, Ann. *The Feminization of American Culture.* New York: Avon Books, 1977.

Eiseley, Loren. *Notes of an Alchemist.* New York: Scribner's, 1972.

Eisler, Riane. *The Chalice and the Blade.* San Francisco: Harper, 1987.

Filippi, Linda. "Place, Feminism, and Healing: An Ecology of Pastoral Counseling." *Journal of Pastoral Care* 45, no. 3 (Fall 1991).

Flax. Jane. *Thinking Fragments: Psychoanalysis, Feminism, and Postmodernism in the Contemporary West.* Berkeley: University of California Press, 1990

Gilligan, Carol. *In a Different Voice: Psychological Theory and Women's Development.* Cambridge: Harvard University Press, 1982.

Gimbutas, Marija. *The Goddesses and Gods of Old Europe.* Berkeley: University of California Press, 1982.

———. *The Language of the Goddess.* San Francisco: Harper & Row, 1989.

Greene, Maxine. *Landscapes of Learning.* New York: Teachers College Press, 1978.

Griffin, Susan. *Women and Nature: The Roaring Inisde Her.* New York: Harper Colophon Books, 1978.

———. *Rape: the Politics of Consciousness.* San Francisco: Harper & Row, 1979.

———. *Pornography and Silence: Culture's Revenge against Nature.* New York: Harper & Row, 1981.

Grumet, Madeleine R. *Bitter Milk.* Amherst: University of Massachusetts Press, 1988.

―――. "Voice: The Search for a Feminist Rhetoric for Educational Studies." Paper presented at the annual meeting of the American Educational Research Association, Boston, April 1990.

Haraway, Donna. *Private Visions: Gender, Race, and Nature in the World of Modern Science.* London: Routledge, 1989.

―――. *Simians, Cyborgs, and Women: The Reinvention of Nature.* New York: Routledge, 1991.

Harding, M. Esther. *Women's Mysteries: Ancient and Modern.* Boston: Shambala, 1990.

Henry Moore: The Reclining Figure. Columbus, Ohio: Columbus Museum of Art, 1984.

Homans, Margaret. *Bearing the Word.* Chicago: University of Chicago Press, 1989.

Hrdy, Sarah Blaffer. *The Woman That Never Evolved.* Cambridge: Harvard University Press, 1981.

Illich, Ivan. *Gender.* New York: Pantheon, 1982.

―――. H_2O *and the Waters of Forgetfulness.* Dallas: Dallas Institute of Humanities and Culture, 1985.

Irigaray, Luce. *This Sex Which Is Not One.* Translated by Catherine Porter. Ithaca: Cornell University Press, 1985.

Jung, C. G. *Civilization in Transition.* Translated by R. F. G. Hull. London: Routledge & Kegan Paul, 1964.

Kerenyi, C. *Archetypal Images of Mother and Daughter.* Translated by Ralph Manheim. New York: Pantheon, 1967.

Kozol, Jonathan. *Savage Inequalities: Children in America's Schools.* New York: Harper Perennial, 1992.

Krall, Florence R. "Mudhole Ecology." *American Biology Teacher* 32, no. 9 (September 1970): 351–53.

―――. "From the Inside Out: Personal History as Educational Research." *Educational Theory* 38, no. 4 (Fall 1988): 467–79.

―――. "The Faceless Goddess." *Contemporary Philosophy* 13, no 1 (Summer 1990). 24–32.

Kristeva, Julia. *Tales of Love.* Translated by Leon S. Roudiez. New York: Columbia University Press, 1987.

LaChapelle, Dolores. *Earth Wisdom.* Los Angeles: Guild of Tutors Press, 1978.

————. *Sacred Land, Sacred Sex, Rapture of the Deep: Concerning Deep Ecology and Celebrating Life.* Silverton, Colo.: Finn Hill Arts, 1988.

Lawrence, D. H. *The Body of God.* Brushford Dulverton Somerset, England: Ark Press, 1970.

Lee, Dorothy. *Freedom and Culture.* Englewood Cliffs, N. J.: Prentice-Hall, 1959.

Lee, Richard. *The !Kung San.* Cambridge: Cambridge University Press, 1979.

Lenz, Gunter H., and Kurt L. Shell, eds. *The Crisis of Modernity: Recent Critical Theories of Culture and Society in the United States and West Germany.* Boulder: Westview Press, 1986.

Lopez, Barry. *Of Wolves and Men.* New York: Scribner's, 1979.

Lovelock, James. *Gaia.* Oxford: Oxford University Press, 1979.

McLuhan, P. C., ed., *Touch the Earth.* New York: Touchstone, 1971.

Mead, Margaret. *Male and Female: A Study of the Sexes in a Changing World.* New York: Dell, 1968.

Merchant, Carolyn. *The Death of Nature: Women, Ecology, and the Scientific Revolution.* San Francisco: Harper, 1980.

————. *Ecological Revolutions: Nature, Gender, and Science in New England.* Chapel Hill: University of North Carolina Press, 1989.

————. *Radical Ecology: The Search for a Livable World.* New York: Routledge, 1992.

Merleau-Ponty, Maurice. *Sense and Nonsense.* Edited by Claude Lefort and translated by Alphonso Lingis. Evanston, Ill.: Northwestern University Press, 1964.

————. *The Visible and the Invisible.* Edited by Claude Lefort and translated by Alphonso Lingis. Evanston: Northwestern University Press, 1968.

Mies, Maria. *Patriarchy and Accumulation on a World Scale.* London: Zed Books, 1986.

Momaday, N. Scott. *The Way to Rainy Mountain.* Albuquerque: University of New Mexico Press, 1969.

Naess, Arne. "Self-Realization in Mixed Communities of Humans, Bears, Sheep, and Wolves." *Inquiry* 22: 231–41.

Neumann, Erich. *The Great Mother: An Analysis of the Archetype.* Translated by Ralph Manheim. London: Routledge & Kegal Paul, 1955.

———. *The Archetypal World of Henry Moore.* Translated by R. F. C. Hull. New York: Harper Torchbooks, 1959.

Perone, Bobbette, H. Henrietta Stockel, and Victoria Krueger. "Annie Kahn: The Flower That Speaks in a Pollen Way." *Medicine Women, Curanderas, and Women Doctors.* Norman: University of Oklahoma Press, 1989.

Pinar, William F., ed., *Curriculum Theorizing: The Reconceptualists.* Berkeley: McCuchan, 1975.

———. ed., *Contemporary Curriculum Discourses.* Scottsdale: Gorsuch Scarisbrick, 1988.

Pinar, William F., and Madeleine Grumet. *Towards a Poor Curriculum.* Dubuque: Kendall/Hunt, 1976.

Prothero, Walter L. "A Hunt in the Land Where the Sun Dies." *Field & Stream,* September 1985.

———. "A Season of Grizzlies." *Outdoor Life,* Autumn 1990.

———. "Obsession." *Field & Stream,* April 1991.

———. *Stalking Big Game.* Harrisburg, Pa.: Stackpole Books, 1992.

Reichard, Gladys. *Spider Woman: A Story of Navajo Weavers and Chanters.* Glorieta, N. M.: Rio Grande Press, 1979.

Rorty, Richard. *Philosophy and the Mirror of Nature.* Princeton: Princeton University Press, 1979.

Rose, Mike. *Lives on the Boundaries.* New York: Penguin Books, 1990.

Sachs, Wolfgang, ed. *The Development Dictionary.* London: Zed Books, 1992.

Sanday, Peggy Reeves. *Female Power and Male Dominance: On the Origins of Sexual Inequality.* Cambridge: Cambridge University Press, 1981.

Schoepfle, Mark G., et al. "A Study of Navajo Perceptions of the Impact of Environmental Changes Relating to Energy Resource Development. Unpublished manuscript, Shiprock, N. M.: Navajo Community College, 23 May 1979.

Schumacher, E. F. *A Guide for the Perplexed.* New York: Harper Colophon Books, 1977.

Scully, Vincent. *The Earth, the Temples, and the Gods.* New Haven: Yale University Press, 1962.

Sellars, Peter. "Directing Mozart." Presentation at Scripps College, Claremont, California, 20 September 1990.

Shepard, Paul H. *The Tender Carnivore and the Sacred Game.* New York: Scribner's, 1973.

———. *Thinking Animals.* New York: Viking Press, 1978.

———. *Man in the Landscape: A Historic View of Esthetics of Nature.* New York: Alfred A. Knopf, 1967; College Station: Texas A&M Press, 1991.

———, and Barry Sanders. *The Sacred Paw: The Bear in Nature, Myth, and Literature.* New York: Viking, 1985; New York: Arkana, 1992.

———. "A Post-Historic Primitivism." In *The Wilderness Condition.* Edited by Max Oelschlaeger. San Francisco: Sierra Club Books, 1992.

———. *The Others: Animals and Human Being.* Forthcoming.

Shiva, Vandana. *Staying Alive: Women, Ecology, and Development.* London: Zed Books, 1986.

Snyder, Gary. *The Practice of the Wild.* San Francisco: Northpoint Press, 1990.

Spivak, Gayatri Chakravorty. "The Politics of Interpretation." *Critical Inquiry* 9, no. 1 (September 1982): 259–78.

Spradley, James P., and David W. McCurdy. *The Cultural Experience: Ethnography in Complex Society.* Chicago: Science Research Associates, 1972.

Sprengnether, Madelon. *The Spectral Mother: Freud, Feminism, and Psychoanalytic Theory.* Ithaca: Cornell University Press, 1990.

Spretnak, Charlene. *Lost Goddesses of Early Greece.* Boston: Beacon Press, 1978.

———. *States of Grace: The Recovery of Meaning in the Postmodern Age.* San Francisco: Harper, 1991.

Starhawk. *Dreaming the Dark.* Boston: Beacon Press, 1982.

BIBLIOGRAPHY

————. *The Spiral Dance: A Rebirth of the Ancient Religion of the Great Goddess.* San Francisco: Harper & Row, 1986.

Steiner, George. *After Babel: Aspects of Language and Translations.* London: Oxford University Press, 1974.

Stroud, Joanne, and Gail Thomas, eds. *Images of the Untouched: Virginity in Psyche, Myth, and Community.* Dallas: Spring, 1982.

Tedlock, Dennis, and Barbara Tedlock, eds. *Teachings from the American Earth.* New York: Liveright, 1975.

Williams, Terry Tempest. *Pieces of White Shell: A Journey to Navajoland.* New York: Scribner's, 1983

————. *Refuge: An Unnatural History of Family and Place.* New York: Pantheon, 1991.

Woolfe, Virginia. *A Room of One's Own.* San Diego: Harvest/HBJ Book, 1957.